THE DOLOROUS PASSION OF OUR LORD JESUS CHRIST

From the Meditations of
Anne Catherine Emmerich

DOVER PUBLICATIONS, INC.
Mineola, New York

Bibliographical Note

This Dover edition is an unabridged republication of *The Dolorous Passion of Our Lord Jesus Christ* from the twenty-fourth edition of *The Meditations of Anne Catherine Emmerich,* published in 1923 by Burns, Oates & Washbourne Ltd., London. It includes the preface by the Abbé de Cazalès.

International Standard Book Number: 0-486-43979-8

Manufactured in the United States of America
Dover Publications, Inc., 31 East 2nd Street, Mineola, N.Y. 11501

PREFACE TO THE FRENCH TRANSLATION.

BY THE ABBÉ DE CAZALÈS.

THE writer of this Preface was travelling in Germany, when he chanced to meet with a book, entitled, *The History of the Passion of our Lord Jesus Christ, from the Meditations of Anne Catherine Emmerich,* which appeared to him both interesting and edifying. Its style was unpretending, its ideas simple, its tone unassuming, its sentiments unexaggerated, and its every sentence expressive of the most complete and entire submission to the Church. Yet, at the same time, it would have been difficult anywhere to meet with a more touching and life-like paraphrase of the Gospel narrative. He thought that a book possessing such qualities deserved to be known on this side the Rhine, and that there could be no reason why it should not be valued for its own sake, independent of the somewhat singular source whence it emanated.

Still, the translator has by no means disguised to himself that this work is written, in the first place, for Christians ; that is to say, for men who have the right to be very diffident in giving credence to particulars concerning facts which are articles of faith ; and although he is aware that St. Bonaventure and many others, in their paraphrases of the Gospel history, have mixed up traditional details with those given in the sacred text, even these examples have not wholly reassured him. St. Bonaventure professed only to give a paraphrase, whereas these revelations appear to be something more. It is certain that the holy maiden herself gave them no higher title than that of dreams, and that the transcriber of her narratives treats as blasphemous the idea of regarding them in any degree as equivalent to a fifth Gospel; still it is evident that the confessors who exhorted Sister Emmerich to relate what she saw, the celebrated poet who passed four years near her couch, eagerly transcribing all he heard her say, and the German Bishops, who encouraged the publication of his book, considered it as something more than a paraphrase. Some explanations are needful on this head.

The writings of many Saints introduce us into a new, and, if I may be allowed the expression, a miraculous world. In all ages there have been revelations about the past, the present, the future, and even concerning things absolutely inaccessible to the human intellect. In the present day men are inclined to regard these revelations as simple hallucinations, or as caused by a sickly condition of body.

The Church, according to the testimony of her most approved writers, recognises three descriptions of ecstasy; of which the first is simply natural, and entirely brought about by certain physical tendencies and a highly imaginative mind; the second divine or angelic, arising from intercourse held with the supernatural world; and the third produced by infernal agency.* Lest we should here write a book instead of a preface, we will not enter into any development of this doctrine, which appears to us highly philosophical, and without which no satisfactory explanation can be given on the subject of the soul of man and its various states.

The Church directs certain means to be employed to ascertain by what spirit these ecstasies are produced, according to the maxim of St. John: 'Try the spirits, if they be of God.' When circumstances or events claiming to be supernatural have been properly examined according to certain rules, the Church has in all ages made a selection from them.

Many persons who have been habitually in a state of ecstasy have been canonised, and their books approved.

* See, on this head, the work of Cardinal Bona, *De Discretione Spirituum.*

But this approbation has seldom amounted to more than a declaration that these books contained nothing contrary to faith, and that they were likely to promote a spirit of piety among the faithful. For the Church is only founded on the word of Christ and on the revelations made to the Apostles. Whatever may since have been revealed to certain saints possesses purely a relative value, the reality of which may even be disputed—it being one of the admirable characteristics of the Church, that, though inflexibly one in dogma, she allows entire liberty to the human mind in all besides. Thus, we may believe private revelations, above all, when those persons to whom they were made have been raised by the Church to the rank of Saints publicly honoured, invoked, and venerated; but, even in these cases, we may, without ceasing to be perfectly orthodox, dispute their authenticity and divine origin. It is the place of reason to dispute and to select as it sees best.

With regard to the rule for discerning between the good and the evil spirit, it is no other, according to all theologians, than that of the Gospel. *A fructibus eorum cognoscetis eos. By their fruits you shall know them.* It must be examined in the first place whether the person who professes to have revelations mistrusts what passes within himself; whether he would prefer a more common path; whether far from boasting of the extraordinary graces which he receives, he seeks to hide them, and only makes them known through obedience; and, finally, whether he is continually advancing in humility, mortification, and charity. Next, the revelations themselves must be very closely examined into; it must be seen whether there is anything in them contrary to faith; whether they are conformable to Scripture and Apostolical tradition; and whether they are related in a headstrong spirit, or in a spirit of entire submission to the Church.

Whoever reads the life of Anne Catherine Emmerich, and her book, will be satisfied that no fault can be found in any of these respects either with herself or with her revelations. Her book resembles in many points the writings of a great number of saints, and her life also bears the most striking similitude to theirs. To be convinced of this fact, we need but study the writings or what is related of Saints Francis of Assissium, Bernard, Bridget, Hildegarde, Catherine of Genoa, Catherine of Sienna, Ignatius, John of the Cross, Teresa, and an immense number of other holy persons who are less known. So much being conceded, it is clear that in considering Sister Emmerich to have been inspired by God's Holy Spirit, we are not ascribing more merit to her book than is allowed by the Church to all those of the same class. They are all edifying, and may serve to promote piety, which is their sole object. We must not exaggerate their importance by holding as an absolute fact that they proceed from divine inspiration, a favour so great that its existence in any particular case should not be credited save with the utmost circumspection.

With regard, however, to our present publication, it may be urged that, considering the superior talents of the transcriber of Sister Emmerich's narrations, the language and expressions which he has made use of may not always have been identical with those which she employed. We have no hesitation whatever in allowing the force of this argument. Most fully do we believe in the entire sincerity of M. Clément Brentano, because we both know and love him, and, besides, his exemplary piety and the retired life which he leads, secluded from a world in which it would depend but on himself to hold the highest place, are guarantees amply sufficient to satisfy any impartial mind of his sincerity. A poem such as he might publish, if he only pleased, would cause him to be ranked at once among the most eminent of the German poets, whereas the office which he has taken upon himself of secretary to a poor visionary has brought him nothing but contemptuous raillery. Nevertheless, we have no intention to assert that in giving the conversations and discourses of Sister Emmerich that order and coherency in which they were greatly wanting, and writing them down in his own way, he may not unwittingly have arranged, explained, and embellished them. But this would not have the effect of destroying the originality of the recital, or impugning either the sincerity of the nun, or that of the writer.

The translator professes to be unable to understand how any man can write for mere writing's sake, and without considering the probable effects which his work will produce. This book, such as it is, appears to him to be at once unusually edifying, and highly poetical. It is perfectly clear that it has, properly speaking, no literary pretensions whatever. Neither the uneducated maiden whose visions are here related, nor the excellent Christian writer who has published them in so entire a spirit of literary disinterestedness, ever had the remotest idea of such a thing. And yet there are not, in our opinion, many highly worked-up compositions calculated to produce an effect in any degree comparable to that which will be brought about by the perusal of this unpretending little work. It is our hope that it will make a strong impression even upon worldlings, and that in many hearts it will prepare the way for better ideas,—perhaps even for a lasting change of life.

In the next place, we are not sorry to call public attention in some degree to all that class of phenomena which preceded the foundation of the Church, which has since been perpetuated uninterruptedly, and which too many Christians are disposed to reject altogether, either through ignorance and want of reflection, or purely through human respect. This is a field which has hitherto been but little explored historically, psychologically, and physiologically; and it would be well if reflecting minds were to bestow upon it a careful and attentive investigation. To our Christian readers we must remark that this work has received the approval of ecclesiastical authorities. It has been prepared for the press under the superintendence of the two late Bishops of Ratisbonne, Sailer and Wittman. These names are but little known in France; but in Germany they are identical with learning, piety, ardent charity, and a life wholly devoted to the maintenance and propagation of the Catholic faith. Many French priests have given their opinion that the translation of a book of this character could not but tend to nourish piety, without, however, countenancing that weakness of spirit which is disposed to lend more importance in some respects to private than to general revelations, and consequently to substitute matters which we are simply permitted to believe, in the place of those which are of faith.

We feel convinced that no one will take offence at certain details given on the subject of the outrages which were suffered by our divine Lord during the course of his passion. Our readers will remember the words of the psalmist: 'I am a worm and no man; the reproach of men, and the outcast of the people;' and those of the apostle: 'Tempted in all things like as we are, without sin.' Did we stand in need of a precedent, we should request our readers to remember how plainly and crudely Bossuet describes the same scenes in the most eloquent of his four sermons on the Passion of our Lord. On the other hand, there have been so many grand platonic or rhetorical sentences in the books published of late years, concerning that abstract entity, on which the writers have been pleased to bestow the Christian title of the *Word*, or *Logos*, that it may be eminently useful to show the Man-God, the Word made flesh, in all the reality of his life on earth, of his humiliation, and of his sufferings. It must be evident that the cause of truth, and still more that of edification, will not be the losers.

INTRODUCTION.

THE following meditations will probably rank high among many similar works which the contemplative love of Jesus has produced; but it is our duty here plainly to affirm that they have no pretensions whatever to be regarded as *history*. They are but intended to take one of the lowest places among those numerous representations of the Passion which have been given us by pious writers and artists, and to be considered at the very utmost as the Lenten meditations of a devout nun, related in all simplicity, and written down in the plainest and most literal language, from her own dictation. To these meditations, she herself never attached more than a mere human value, and never related them except through obedience, and upon the repeated commands of the directors of her conscience.

The writer of the following pages was introduced to this holy religious by Count Leopold de Stolberg.* Dean Bernard Overberg, her director extraordinary, and Bishop Michael Sailer,† who had often been her counsellor and consoler, urged her to relate to us in detail all that she experienced; and the latter, who survived her, took the deepest interest in the arrangement and publication of the notes taken down from her dictation. These illustrious and holy men, now dead, and whose memory is blessed, were in continual communion of prayer with Anne Cathe-

* The Count de Stolberg is one of the most eminent converts whom the Catholic Church has made from Protestantism. He died in 1819.

† The Bishop of Ratisbonne, one of the most celebrated defenders of the faith in Germany.

rine, whom they loved and respected, on account of the singular graces with which God had favoured her. The editor of this book received equal encouragement, and met with no less sympathy in his labours, from the late Bishop of Ratisbonne, Mgr. Wittman.* This holy Bishop, who was so deeply versed in the ways of Divine grace, and so well acquainted with its effects on certain souls, both from his private investigations of the subject, and his own experience, took the most lively interest in all that concerned Anne Catherine, and on hearing of the work in which the editor of this book was engaged, he strongly exhorted him to publish it. ‘These things have not been communicated to you for nothing,’ would he often say; ‘God has his views in all. Publish something at least of what you know, for you will thereby benefit many souls.’ He at the same time brought forward various instances from his own experience and that of others, showing the benefit which had been derived from the study of works of a similar character. He delighted in calling such privileged souls as Anne Catherine *the marrow of the bones of the Church,* according to the expression of St. John Chrysostom, *medulla enim hujus mundi sunt,* and he encouraged the publication of their lives and writings as far as lay in his power.

The editor of this book being taken by a kind friend to the dying bed of the holy Bishop, had no reason whatever to expect to be recognised, as he had only once in his life conversed with him for a few minutes; nevertheless the dying saint knew him again, and after a few most kind words blessed and exhorted him to continue his work for the glory of God.

Encouraged by the approbation of such men, we therefore yield to the wishes of many virtuous friends in publishing the Meditations on the Passion, of this humble religious, to whom God granted the favour of being at times simple, ingenuous, and ignorant as a child, while at others

---

* Mgr. Wittman was the worthy successor of Sailer, and a man of eminent sanctity, whose memory is held in veneration by all the Catholics of the south of Germany.

she was clear-sighted, sensible, possessed of a deep insight into the most mysterious and hidden things, and consumed with burning and heroic zeal, but ever forgetful of self, deriving her whole strength from Jesus alone, and steadfast in the most perfect humility and entire self-abnegation.

We give our readers a slight sketch of her life, intending at some future day to publish her biography more in full.

LIFE

ANNE CATHERINE EMMERICH,

RELIGIOUS OF THE ORDER OF ST. AUGUSTINE, AT THE CONVENT
OF AGNETENBERG, DULMEN, WESTPHALIA.

———◆———

ANNE CATHERINE EMMERICH was born at Flamske, a village situated about a mile and a half from Coesfeld, in the
bishopric of Munster, on the 8th of September 1774, and
was baptised in the church of St. James at Coesfeld. Her
parents, Bernard Emmerich and Anne Hiller, were poor
peasants, but distinguished for their piety and virtue.

The childhood of Anne Catherine bore a striking resemblance to that of the Venerable Anne Garzias de St.
Barthelemi, of Dominica del Paradiso, and of several other
holy persons born in the same rank of life as herself. Her
angel-guardian used to appear to her as a child; and when
she was taking care of sheep in the fields, the Good Shepherd himself, under the form of a young shepherd, would
frequently come to her assistance. From childhood she
was accustomed to have divine knowledge imparted to her
in visions of all kinds, and was often favoured by visits
from the Mother of God and Queen of Heaven, who, under the form of a sweet, lovely, and majestic lady, would
bring the Divine Child to be, as it were, her companion,
and would assure her that she loved and would ever pro-
tect her. Many of the saints would also appear to her,
and receive from her hands the garlands of flowers which
she had prepared in honour of their festivals. All these

favours and visions surprised the child less than if an earthly princess and the lords and ladies of her court had come to visit her. Nor was she, later in life, more surprised at these celestial visits, for her innocence caused her to feel far more at her ease with our Divine Lord, his Blessed Mother and the Saints, than she could ever be with even the most kind and amiable of her earthly companions. The names of Father, Mother, Brother, and Spouse, appeared to her expressive of the real connections subsisting between God and man, since the Eternal Word had been pleased to be born of a woman, and so to become our Brother, and these sacred titles were not mere words in her mouth.

While yet a child, she used to speak with innocent candour and simplicity of all that she saw, and her listeners would be filled with admiration at the histories she would relate from Holy Writ; but their questions and remarks having sometimes disturbed her peace of mind, she determined to keep silence on such subjects for the future. In her innocence of heart, she thought that it was not right to talk of things of this sort, that other persons never did so, and that her speech should be only *Yea, yea,* and *Nay, nay,* or *Praise be to Jesus Christ.* The visions with which she was favoured were so like realities, and appeared to her so sweet and delightful, that she supposed all Christian children were favoured with the same; and she concluded that those who never talked on such subjects were only more discreet and modest than herself, so she resolved to keep silence also, to be like them.

Almost from her cradle she possessed the gift of distinguishing what was good or evil, holy or profane, blessed or accursed, in material as well as in spiritual things, thus resembling St. Sibyllina of Pavia, Ida of Louvain, Ursula Benincasa, and some other holy souls. In her earliest childhood she used to bring out of the fields useful herbs, which no one had ever before discovered to be good for anything, and plant them near her father's cottage, or in some spot where she was accustomed to work and play; while on the other hand she would root up all poisonous plants, and particularly those ever used for superstitious practices or in dealings with the devil. Were she by chance in a place where some great crime had been committed, she would hastily run away, or begin to pray and do penance. She used also to perceive by intuition when she was in a consecrated spot, return thanks to God, and be filled with a sweet feeling of peace. When a priest passed by with the Blessed Sacrament, even at a great distance from her home or from the place where she was taking care of her flock, she would feel a strong attraction in the direction whence he was coming, run to meet him, and be kneeling in the road, adoring the Blessed Sacrament, long before he could reach the spot.

She knew when any object was consecrated, and experienced a feeling of disgust and repugnance when in the neighbourhood of old pagan cemeteries, whereas she was attracted to the sacred remains of the saints as steel by the magnet. When relics were shown to her, she knew what saints they had belonged to, and could give not only accounts of the minutest and hitherto unknown particulars of their lives, but also histories of the relics themselves, and of the places where they had been preserved. During her whole life she had continual intercourse with the souls in purgatory; and all her actions and prayers were offered for the relief of their sufferings. She was frequently called upon to assist them, and even reminded in some miraculous manner, if she chanced to forget them. Often, while yet very young, she used to be awakened out of her sleep by bands of suffering souls, and to follow them on cold winter's nights with bare feet, the whole length of the Way of the Cross to Coesfeld, though the ground was covered with snow.

From her infancy to the day of her death she was indefatigable in relieving the sick, and in dressing and curing wounds and ulcers, and she was accustomed to give to the poor every farthing she possessed. So tender was her conscience, that the slightest sin she fell into caused her such pain as to make her ill, and absolution then always restored her immediately to health.

The extraordinary nature of the favours bestowed on

her by Almighty God was no hindrance in the way of her devoting herself to hard labour, like any other peasant-girl; and we may also be allowed to observe that a certain degree of the spirit of prophecy is not unusually to be found among her country men and women. She was taught in the school of suffering and mortification, and there learned lessons of perfection. She allowed herself no more sleep or food than was absolutely necessary; passed whole hours in prayer every night; and in winter often knelt out of doors on the snow. She slept on the ground on planks arranged in the form of a cross. Her food and drink consisted of what was rejected by others; she always kept the best parts even of that for the poor and sick, and when she did not know of any one to give them to, she offered them to God in a spirit of child-like faith, begging him to give them to some person who was more in need than herself. When there was anything to be seen or heard which had no reference to God or religion, she found some excuse for avoiding the spot to which others were hastening, or, if there, closed her eyes and ears. She was accustomed to say that useless actions were sinful, and that when we denied our bodily senses any gratification of this kind, we were amply repaid by the progress which we made in the interior life, in the same manner as pruning renders vines and other fruit-trees more productive. From her early youth, and wherever she went, she had frequent symbolical visions, which showed her in parables, as it were, the object of her existence, the means of attaining it, and her future sufferings, together with the dangers and conflicts which she would have to go through.

She was in her sixteenth year, when one day, whilst at work in the fields with her parents and sisters, she heard the bell ringing at the Convent of the Sisters of the Annunciation, at Coesfeld. This sound so inflamed her secret desire to become a nun, and had so great an effect upon her, that she fainted away, and remained ill and weak for a long time after. When in her eighteenth year she was apprenticed at Coesfeld to a dressmaker, with whom she passed two years, and then returned to her parents. She asked to be received at the Convents of the Augustinians at Borken, of the Trappists at Darfeld, and of the Poor Clares at Munster; but her poverty, and that of these convents, always presented an insuperable obstacle to her being received. At the age of twenty, having saved twenty thalers (about 3*l.* English), which she had earned by her sewing, she went with this little sum—a perfect fortune for a poor peasant-girl—to a pious organist of Coesfeld, whose daughter she had known when she first lived in the town. Her hope was that, by learning to play on the organ, she might succeed in obtaining admittance into a convent. But her irresistible desire to serve the poor and give them everything she possessed left her no time to learn music, and before long she had so completely stripped herself of everything, that her good mother was obliged to bring her bread, milk, and eggs, for her own wants and those of the poor, with whom she shared everything. Then her mother said: 'Your desire to leave your father and myself, and enter a convent, gives us much pain; but you are still my beloved child, and when I look at your vacant seat at home, and reflect that you have given away all your savings, so as to be now in want, my heart is filled with sorrow, and I have now brought you enough to keep you for some time.' Anne Catherine replied: 'Yes, dear mother, it is true that I have nothing at all left, because it was the holy will of God that others should be assisted by me; and since I have given all to him, he will now take care of me, and bestow his divine assistance upon us all.' She remained some years at Coesfeld, employed in labour, good works, and prayer, being always guided by the same inward inspirations. She was docile and submissive as a child in the hands of her guardian-angel.

Although in this brief sketch of her life we are obliged to omit many interesting circumstances, there is one which we must not pass over in silence. When about twenty-four years of age, she received a favour from our Lord, which has been granted to many persons devoted in an especial manner to meditation on his painful Passion; namely, to experience the actual and visible sufferings of his sacred Head, when crowned with thorns. The following is the account she herself has given of the circumstances under which so mysterious a favour was bestowed upon her: 'About four years previous to my admittance into the convent, consequently in 1798, it happened that I was in the Jesuits' Church at Coesfeld, at about twelve o'clock in the day, kneeling before a crucifix and absorbed in meditation, when all on a sudden I felt a strong but pleasant heat in my head, and I saw my Divine Spouse, under the form of a young man clothed with light, come towards me from the altar, where the Blessed Sacrament was preserved in the tabernacle. In his left hand he held a crown of flowers, in his right hand a crown of thorns, and he bade me choose which I would have. I chose the crown of thorns; he placed it on my head, and I pressed it down with both hands. Then he disappeared, and I returned to myself, feeling, however, violent pain around my head. I was obliged to leave the church, which was going to be closed. One of my companions was kneeling by my side, and as I thought she might have seen what happened to me, I asked her when we got home whether there was not a wound on my forehead, and spoke to her in general terms of my vision, and of the violent pain which had followed it. She could see nothing outwardly, but was not astonished at what I told her, because she knew that I was sometimes in an extraordinary state, without her being able to understand the cause. The next day my forehead and temples were very much swelled, and I suffered terribly. This pain and swelling often returned, and sometimes lasted whole days and nights. I did not remark that there was blood on my head until my companions told me I had better put on a clean cap, because mine was covered with red spots. I let them think whatever they liked about it, only taking care to arrange my head-dress so as to hide the blood which flowed from my head, and I continued to observe the same precaution even after I entered the convent, where only one person perceived the blood, and she never betrayed my secret.'

Several other contemplative persons, especially devoted

to the passion of our Lord, have been admitted to the privilege of suffering the torture inflicted by the crown of thorns, after having seen a vision in which the two crowns were offered them to choose between, for instance, among others, St. Catherine of Sienna, and Pasithea of Crogis, a Poor Clare of the same town, who died in 1617.

The writer of these pages may here be allowed to remark that he himself has, in full daylight, several times seen blood flow down the forehead and face, and even beyond the linen wrapped round the neck of Anne Catherine. Her desire to embrace a religious life was at length gratified. The parents of a young person whom the Augustinian nuns of Dulmen wished to receive into their order, declared that they would not give their consent except on condition that Anne Catherine was taken at the same time. The nuns yielded their assent, though somewhat reluctantly, on account of their extreme poverty; and on the 13th November 1802, one week before the feast of the Presentation of the Blessed Virgin, Anne Catherine entered on her novitiate. At the present day vocations are not so severely tested as formerly; but in her case, Providence imposed special trials, for which, rigorous as they were, she felt she never could be too grateful. Sufferings or privations, which a soul, either alone or in union with others, imposes upon herself, for God's greater glory, are easy to bear; but there is one cross more nearly resembling the cross of Christ than any other, and that is, lovingly and patiently to submit to unjust punishments, rebuffs, or accusations. It was the will of God that during her year's novitiate she should, independently of the will of any creature, be tried as severely as the most strict mistress of novices could have done before any mitigations had been allowed in the rules. She learned to regard her companions as instruments in the hands of God for her sanctification; and at a later period of her life many other things appeared to her in the same light. But as it was necessary that her fervent soul should be constantly tried in the school of the Cross, God was pleased that she should remain in it all her life.

In many ways her position in the convent was excessively painful. Not one of her companions, nor even any priest or doctor, could understand her case. She had learned, when living among poor peasants, to hide the wonderful gifts which God had bestowed on her; but the case was altered now that she was in familiar intercourse with a large number of nuns, who, though certainly good and pious, were filled with ever-increasing feelings of curiosity, and even of spiritual jealousy in her regard. Then, the contracted ideas of the community, and the complete ignorance of the nuns concerning all those exterior phenomena by which the interior life manifests itself, gave her much to endure, the more so, as these phenomena displayed themselves in the most unusual and astonishing manner. She heard everything that was said against her, even when the speakers were at one end of the convent and she at the other, and her heart was most deeply wounded as if by poisoned arrows. Yet she bore all patiently and lovingly without showing that she knew what was said of her. More than once charity impelled her to cast herself at the feet of some nun who was particularly prejudiced against her, and ask her pardon with tears. Then, she was suspected of listening at the doors, for the private feelings of dislike entertained against her became known, no one knew how, and the nuns felt uncomfortable and uneasy, in spite of themselves, when in her company.

Whenever the rule (the minutest point of which was sacred in her eyes) was neglected in the slightest degree, she beheld in spirit each infringement, and at times was inspired to fly to the spot where the rule was being broken by some infringement of the vow of poverty, or disregard of the hours of silence, and she would then repeat suitable passages from the rule, without having ever learned them. She thus became an object of aversion to all those religious who broke the rule; and her sudden appearances among them had almost the effect of apparitions. God had bestowed upon her the gift of tears to so great an extent, that she often passed whole hours in the church weeping over the sins and ingratitude of men, the sufferings of the Church, the imperfections of the community, and her own faults. But these tears of sublime sorrow could be understood by none but God, before whom she shed them, and men attributed them to mere caprice, a spirit of discontent, or some other similar cause. Her confessor had enjoined that she should receive the holy communion more frequently than the other nuns, because, so ardently did she hunger after the bread of angels, that she had been more than once near dying. These heavenly sentiments awakened feelings of jealousy in her sisters, who sometimes even accused her of hypocrisy.

The favour which had been shown her in her admittance into the convent, in spite of her poverty, was also made a subject of reproach. The thought of being thus an occasion of sin to others was most painful to her, and she continually besought God to permit her to bear herself the penalty of this want of charity in her regard. About Christmas, of the year 1802, she had a very severe illness, which began by a violent pain about her heart.

This pain did not leave her even when she was cured, and she bore it in silence until the year 1812, when the mark of a cross was imprinted exteriorly in the same place, as we shall relate further on. Her weakness and delicate health caused her to be looked upon more as burdensome than useful to the community; and this, of course, told against her in all ways, yet she was never weary of working and serving the others, nor was she ever so happy as at this period of her life—spent in privations and sufferings of every description.

On the 13th of November 1803, at the age of twenty-nine, she pronounced her solemn vows, and became the spouse of Jesus Christ, in the Convent of Agnetenberg, at Dulmen. 'When I had pronounced my vows,' she says, ' my relations were again extremely kind to me. My father and my eldest brother brought me two pieces of cloth. My father, a good, but stern man, and who had been much averse to my entering the convent, had told me, when we parted, that he would willingly pay for my burial, but that he would give nothing for the convent; and he kept his word, for this piece of cloth was the winding-sheet used for my spiritual burial in the convent.'

'I was not thinking of myself,' she says again, 'I was thinking of nothing but our Lord and my holy vows. My companions could not understand me; nor could I explain my state to them. God concealed from them many of the favours which he bestowed upon me, otherwise they would have had very false ideas concerning me. Notwithstanding all my trials and sufferings, I was never more rich interiorly, and my soul was perfectly flooded with happiness. My cell only contained one chair without a seat, and another without a back; yet in my eyes, it was magnificently furnished, and when there I often thought myself in Heaven. Frequently during the night, impelled by love and by the mercy of God, I poured forth the feelings of my soul by conversing with him in loving and familiar language, as I had always done from my childhood, and then those who were watching me would accuse me of irreverence and disrespect towards God. Once, I happened to say that it appeared to me that I should be guilty of greater disrespect did I receive the Body of our Lord without having conversed familiarly with him, and I was severely reprimanded. Amid all these trials, I yet lived in peace with God and with all his creatures. When I was working in the garden, the birds would come and rest on my head and shoulders, and we would together sing the praises of God. I always beheld my angel-guardian at my side, and although the devil used frequently to assault and terrify me in various ways, he was never permitted to do me much harm. My desire for the Blessed Sacrament was so irresistible, that often at night I left my cell and went to the church, if it was open; but if not, I remained at the door or by the walls, even in winter, kneeling or prostrate, with my arms extended in ecstasy. The convent chaplain, who was so charitable as to come early to give me the Holy Communion, used to find me in this state, but as soon as he was come and had opened the church, I always recovered, and hastened to the holy table, there to receive my Lord and my God. When I was sacristan, I used all on a sudden to feel myself ravished in spirit, and ascend to the highest parts of the church, on to cornices, projecting parts of the building, and mouldings, where it seemed impossible for any being to get by human means. Then I cleaned and arranged everything, and it appeared to me that I was surrounded by blessed spirits, who transported me about and held me up in their hands. Their presence did not cause me the least uneasiness, for I had been accustomed to it from my childhood, and I used to have the most sweet and familiar intercourse with them. It was only when I was in the company of certain men that I was really alone ; and so great was then my feeling of loneliness that I could not help crying like a child that has strayed from home.'

We now proceed to her illnesses, omitting any description of some other remarkable phenomena of her ecstatic life, only recommending the reader to compare the accounts we have already given with what is related of St. Mary Magdalen of Pazzi.

Anne Catherine had always been weak and delicate, and yet had been, from her earliest childhood, in the habit of practising many mortifications, of fasting and of passing the night in watching and prayer in the open air. She had been accustomed to continual hard labour in the fields, at all seasons of the year, and her strength was also necessarily much tried by the exhausting and supernatural states through which she so frequently passed. At the convent she continued to work in the garden and in the house, whilst her spiritual labours and sufferings were ever on the increase, so that it is by no means surprising that she was frequently ill ; but her illnesses arose from yet another cause. We have learned, from careful observations made every day for the space of four years, and also from what she herself was unwillingly forced to admit, that during the whole course of her life, and especially during that part of it which she spent at the convent, when she enjoyed the highest spiritual favours, a great portion of her illnesses and sufferings came from taking upon herself the sufferings of others. Sometimes she asked for the illness of a person who did not bear it patiently, and relieved him of the whole or of a part of his sufferings, by taking them upon herself; sometimes, wishing to expiate a sin or put an end to some suffering, she gave herself up into the hands of God, and he, accepting her sacrifice, permitted her thus, in union with the merits of his passion, to expiate the sin by suffering some illness corresponding to it. She had consequently to bear, not only her own maladies, but those also of others—to suffer in expiation of the sins of her brethren, and of the faults and negligences of certain portions of the Christian community—and, finally, to endure many and various sufferings in satisfaction for the souls of purgatory. All these sufferings appeared like real illnesses, which took the most opposite and variable forms, and she was placed entirely under the care of the doctor, who endeavoured by earthly remedies to cure illnesses which in reality were the very sources of her life. She said on this subject—'Repose in suffering has always appeared to me the most desirable condition possible. The angels themselves would envy us, were envy not an imperfection. But for sufferings to be really meritorious we must patiently and gratefully accept unsuitable remedies and comforts, and all other additional trials. I did not myself fully understand my state, nor know what it was to lead to. In my soul I accepted my different sufferings, but in my body it was my duty to strive against them. I had given myself wholly and entirely to my Heavenly Spouse, and his holy will was being accomplished in me; but I was living on earth, where I was not to rebel against earthly wisdom and earthly prescriptions. Even had I fully comprehended my state, and had both time and power to explain it, there was no one near who would have been able to understand me. A doctor would simply have concluded that I was entirely mad, and would have increased his expensive and painful remedies tenfold. I have suffered much in this way during the whole of my life, and particularly when I was at the convent, from having unsuitable remedies administered to me. Often, when my doctors and nurses had reduced me to the last agony, and that I was near death, God took pity on me, and sent me some supernatural assistance, which effected an entire cure.'

Four years before the suppression of her convent she went to Flamske for two days to visit her parents. Whilst there she went once to kneel and pray for some hours before the miraculous Cross of the Church of St. Lambert, at Coesfeld. She besought the Almighty to bestow the gifts of peace and unity upon her convent, offered him the Passion of Jesus Christ for that intention, and implored him to allow her to feel a portion of the sufferings which were endured by her Divine Spouse on the Cross. From the time that she made this prayer her hands and feet became burning and painful, and she suffered constantly from fever, which she believed was the cause of the pain in her hands and feet, for she did not dare to think that her prayer had been granted. Often she was unable to walk, and the pain in her hands prevented her from working as usual in the garden. On the 3d December 1811, the convent was suppressed,* and the church closed. The nuns dispersed in all directions, but Anne Catherine remained, poor and ill. A kindhearted servant belonging to the monastery attended upon her out of charity, and an aged emigrant priest, who said Mass in the convent, remained also with her. These three individuals, being the poorest of the Community, did not leave the convent until the spring of 1812. She was still very unwell, and could not be moved without great difficulty. The priest lodged with a poor widow who lived in the neighbourhood, and Anne Catherine had in the same house a wretched little room on the ground-floor, which looked on the street. There she lived, in poverty and sickness, until the autumn of 1813. Her ecstasies in prayer, and her spiritual intercourse with the invisible world, became more and more frequent. She was about to be called to a state with which she was herself but imperfectly acquainted, and in order

* Under the Government of Jerome Bonaparte, King of Westphalia. (Abbé Cazalès.)

to enter which she did nothing but submissively abandon herself to the will of God. Our Lord was pleased about this time to imprint upon her virginal body the stigmas of his cross and of his crucifixion, which were to the Jews a stumbling-block, and to the Gentiles folly, and to many persons who call themselves Christians, both the one and the other. From her very earliest childhood she had besought our Lord to impress the marks of his cross deeply upon her heart, that so she might never forget his infinite love for men; but she had never thought of receiving any outward marks. Rejected by the world, she prayed more fervently than ever for this end. On the 28th of August, the feast of St. Augustine, the patron of her order, as she was making this prayer in bed, ravished in ecstasy and her arms stretched forth, she beheld a young man approach her surrounded with light. It was under this form that her Divine Spouse usually appeared to her, and he now made upon her body with his right hand the mark of a common cross. From this time there was a mark like a cross upon her bosom, consisting of two bands crossed, about three inches long and one wide. Later the skin often rose in blisters on this place, as if from a burn, and when these blisters burst a burning colourless liquid issued from them, sometimes in such quantities as to soak through several sheets. She was long without perceiving what the case really was, and only thought that she was in a strong perspiration. The particular meaning of this mark has never been known.

Some weeks later, when making the same prayer, she fell into an ecstasy, and beheld the same apparition, which presented her with a little cross of the shape described in her accounts of the Passion. She eagerly received and fervently pressed it to her bosom, and then returned it. She said that this cross was as soft and white as wax, but she was not at first aware that it had made an external mark upon her bosom. A short time after, having gone with her landlady's little girl to visit an old hermitage near Dulmen, she all on a sudden fell into an ecstasy, fainted away, and on her recovery was taken home by a poor peasant woman. The sharp pain which she felt in her chest continued to increase, and she saw that there was what looked like a cross, about three inches in length, pressed tightly upon her breast-bone, and looking red through the skin. As she had spoken about her vision to a nun with whom she was intimate, her extraordinary state began to be a good deal talked of. On All Souls' day, 1812, she went out for the last time, and with much difficulty succeeded in reaching the church. From that time till the end of the year she seemed to be dying, and received the last Sacraments. At Christmas a smaller cross appeared on the top of that upon her chest. It was the same shape as the larger one, so that the two together formed a double forked cross. Blood flowed from this cross every Wednesday, so as to leave the impression of its shape on paper laid over it. After a time this happened on Fridays instead. In 1814 this flow of blood took place less frequently, but the cross became as red as fire every Friday. At a later period of her life more blood flowed from this cross, especially every Good Friday; but no attention was paid to it. On the 30th March 1821, the writer of these pages saw this cross of a deep red colour, and bleeding all over. In its usual state it was colourless, and its position only marked by slight cracks in the skin. . . . Other Ecstaticas have received similar marks of the Cross; among others, Catherine of Raconis, Marina de l'Escobar, Emilia Bichieri, S. Juliani Falconieri, &c.

She received the stigmas on the last days of the year 1812. On the 29th December, about three o'clock in the afternoon, she was lying on her bed in her little room, extremely ill, but in a state of ecstasy and with her arms extended, meditating on the sufferings of her Lord, and beseeching him to allow her to suffer with him. She said five Our Fathers in honour of the Five Wounds, and felt her whole heart burning with love. She then saw a light descending towards her, and distinguished in the midst of it the resplendent form of her crucified Saviour, whose wounds shone like so many furnaces of light. Her heart was overflowing with joy and sorrow, and, at the sight of

the sacred wounds, her desire to suffer with her Lord became intensely violent. Then triple rays, pointed like
arrows, of the colour of blood, darted forth from the hands,
feet, and side of the sacred apparition, and struck her
hands, feet, and right side. The triple rays from the side
formed a point like the head of a lance. The moment
these rays touched her, drops of blood flowed from the
wounds which they made. Long did she remain in a state
of insensibility, and when she recovered her senses she did
not know who had lowered her outstretched arms. It was
with astonishment that she beheld blood flowing from the
palms of her hands, and felt violent pain in her feet and
side. It happened that her landlady's little daughter came
into her room, saw her hands bleeding, and ran to tell her
mother, who with great anxiety asked Anne Catherine
what had happened, but was begged by her not to speak
about it. She felt, after having received the stigmas, that
an entire change had taken place in her body; for the
course of her blood seemed to have changed, and to flow
rapidly towards the stigmas. She herself used to say:
'No words can describe in what manner it flows.'

We are indebted to a curious incident for our knowledge of the circumstances which we have here related. On
the 15th December 1819, she had a detailed vision of all
that had happened to herself, but so that she thought it
concerned some other nun who she imagined must be living not far off, and who she supposed had experienced the
same things as herself. She related all these details with
a very strong feeling of compassion, humbling herself,
without knowing it, before her own patience and sufferings. It was most touching to hear her say: 'I ought
never to complain any more, now that I have seen the
sufferings of that poor nun; her heart is surrounded with
a crown of thorns, but she bears it placidly and with a
smiling countenance. It is shameful indeed for me to complain, for she has a far heavier burden to bear than I have.'

These visions, which she afterwards recognised to be
her own history, were several times repeated, and it is from
them that the circumstances under which she received the

stigmas became known. Otherwise she would not have related so many particulars about what her humility never permitted her to speak of, and concerning which, when asked by her spiritual superiors whence her wounds proceeded, the utmost she said was : 'I hope that they come from the hand of God.'

The limits of this work preclude us from entering upon the subject of stigmas in general, but we may observe that the Catholic Church has produced a certain number of persons, St. Francis of Assissium being the first, who have attained to that degree of contemplative love of Jesus which is the most sublime effect of union with his sufferings, and is designated by theologians, *Vulnus divinum, Plago amoris viva*. There are known to have been at least fifty. Veronica Giuliani, a Capuchiness, who died at Città di Castello in 1727, is the last individual of the class who has been canonised (on the 26th May 1831). Her biography, published at Cologne in 1810, gives a description of the state of persons with stigmas, which in many ways is applicable to Anne Catherine. Colomba Schanolt, who died at Bamberg in 1787, Magdalen Lorger, who died at Hadamar in 1806, both Dominicanesses, and Rose Serra, a Capuchiness at Ozieri in Sardinia, who received the stigmas in 1801, are those of our own times of whom we know the most. Josephine Kumi, of the Convent of Wesen, near Lake Wallenstadt in Switzerland, who was still living in 1815, also belonged to this class of persons, but we are not entirely certain whether she had the stigmas.

Anne Catherine being, as we have said, no longer able to walk or rise from her bed, soon became unable also to eat. Before long she could take nothing but a little wine and water, and finally only pure water; sometimes, but very rarely, she managed to swallow the juice of a cherry or a plum, but she immediately vomited any solid food, taken in ever so small a quantity. This inability to take food, or rather this faculty of living for a great length of time upon nothing but water, we are assured by learned doctors is not quite unexampled in the history of the sick.

Theologians will be perfectly aware that there are many instances of contemplative ascetics, and particularly of persons frequently in a state of ecstasy and who have received the stigmas, remaining long without taking any other food than the Blessed Sacrament; for instance, B. Nicholas of Flue, St. Liduvina of Schiedam, St. Catherine of Sienna, St. Angela of Foligno, and St. Louise de l'Ascension. All the phenomena exhibited in the person of Anne Catherine remained concealed even from those who had the most intercourse with her, until the 25th February 1813, when they were discovered accidentally by one of her old convent companions. By the end of March, the whole town talked of them. On the 23d of March, the physician of the neighbourhood forced her to undergo an examination. Contrary to his expectation, he was convinced of the truth, drew up an official report of what he had seen, became her doctor and her friend, and remained such to her death. On the 28th of March, commissioners were appointed to examine into her case by the spiritual authorities of Munster. The consequence of this was that Anne Catherine was hence-forth looked upon kindly by her superiors, and acquired the friendship of the late Dean Overberg, who from that time paid her every year a visit of several days' duration, and was her consoler and spiritual director. The medical counsellor from Druffel, who was present at this examination in the capacity of doctor, never ceased to venerate her. In 1814, he published in the Medical Journal of Salzbourg a detailed account of the phenomena which he had remarked in the person of Anne Catherine, and to this we refer those of our readers who desire more particulars upon the subject. On the 4th of April, M. Garnier, the Commissary-General of the French police, came from Munster to see her; he inquired minutely into her case, and having learned that she neither prophesied nor spoke on politics, declared that there was no occasion for the police to occupy themselves about her. In 1826, he still spoke of her at Paris with respect and emotion.

On the 22d of July 1813, Overberg came to see her,

with Count de Stolberg and his family. They remained two days with her, and Stolberg, in a letter which has been several times printed, bore witness to the reality of the phenomena observed in Anne Catherine, and gave expression to his intense veneration for her. He remained her friend as long as he lived, and the members of his family never ceased recommending themselves to her prayers. On the 29th of September 1813, Overberg took the daughter of the Princess Galitzin (who died in 1806) to visit her, and they saw with their own eyes blood flow copiously from her stigmas. This distinguished lady repeated her visit, and, after becoming Princess of Salm, never varied in her sentiments, but, together with her family, remained in constant communion of prayer with Anne Catherine. Many other persons in all ranks of life were, in like manner, consoled and edified by visiting her bed of suffering. On the 23d of October 1813, she was carried to another lodging, the window of which looked out upon a garden. The condition of the saintly nun became day by day more painful. Her stigmas were a source of indescribable suffering to her, down to the moment of her death. Instead of allowing her thoughts to dwell upon those graces to the interior presence of which they bore such miraculous outward testimony, she learned from them lessons of humility, by considering them as a heavy cross laid upon her for her sins. Her suffering body itself was to preach Jesus crucified. It was difficult indeed to be an enigma to all persons, an object of suspicion to the greatest number, and of respect mingled with fear to some few, without yielding to sentiments of impatience, irritability, or pride. Willingly would she have lived in entire seclusion from the world, but obedience soon compelled her to allow herself to be examined and to have judgment passed upon her by a vast number of curious persons. Suffering, as she was, the most excruciating pains, she was not even allowed to be her own mistress, but was regarded as something which every one fancied he had a right to look at and to pass judgment upon,—often with no good results to any one, but greatly to the prejudice of her soul and body, because she was thus deprived of so much rest and recollection of spirit. There seemed to be no bounds to what was expected of her, and one fat man, who had some difficulty in ascending her narrow winding staircase, was heard to complain that a person like Anne Catherine, who ought to be exposed on the public road, where every one could see her, should remain in a lodging so difficult to reach. In former ages, persons in her state underwent in private the examination of the spiritual authorities, and carried out their painful vocation beneath the protecting shadow of hallowed walls; but our suffering heroine had been cast forth from the cloister into the world at a time when pride, coldness of heart, and incredulity were all the vogue; marked with the stigmas of the Passion of Christ, she was forced to wear her bloody robe in public, under the eyes of men who scarce believed in the Wounds of Christ, far less in those which were but their images.

Thus this holy woman, who in her youth had been in the habit of praying for long hours before pictures of all the stages of Christ's painful Passion, or before wayside crosses, was herself made like unto a cross on the public road, insulted by one passer by, bathed in warm tears of repentance by a second, regarded as a mere physical curiosity by a third, and venerated by a fourth, whose innocent hands would bring flowers to lay at her feet.

In 1817 her aged mother came from the country to die by her side. Anne Catherine showed her all the love she could by comforting and praying for her, and closing her eyes with her own hands—those hands marked with the stigmas on the 13th of March of the same year. The inheritance left to Anne Catherine by her mother was more than sufficient for one so imbued with the spirit of mortification and suffering; and in her turn she left it unimpaired to her friends. It consisted of these three sayings:—'Lord, thy will, not mine, be done;' 'Lord, give me patience, and then strike hard;' 'Those things which are not good to put in the pot are at least good to put beneath it.' The meaning of this last proverb was: If things are not fit to be eaten, they may at least be burned, in order that food may be cooked; this suffering does not nourish my heart, but by bearing it patiently, I may at least increase the fire of divine love, by which alone life can profit us anything. She often repeated these proverbs, and then thought of her mother with gratitude. Her father had died some little time before.

The writer of these pages became acquainted with her state first through reading a copy of that letter of Stolberg, to which we have already alluded, and afterwards through conversation with a friend who had passed several weeks with her. In September 1818 he was invited by Bishop Sailer to meet him at the Count de Stolberg's, in Westphalia; and he went in the first place to Sondermuhlen to see the count, who introduced him to Overberg, from whom he received a letter addressed to Anne Catherine's doctor. He paid her his first visit on the 17th of September 1818; and she allowed him to pass several hours by her side each day, until the arrival of Sailer. From the very beginning, she gave him her confidence to a remarkable extent, and this in the most touching and ingenuous manner. No doubt she was conscious that by relating without reserve the history of all the trials, joys, and sorrows of her whole life, she was bestowing a most precious spiritual alms upon him. She treated him with the most generous hospitality, and had no hesitation in doing so, because he did not oppress her and alarm her humility by excessive admiration. She laid open her interior to him in the same charitable spirit as a pious solitary would in the morning offer the flowers and fruit which had grown in his garden during the night to some wayworn traveller, who, having lost his road in the desert of the world, finds him sitting near his hermitage. Wholly devoted to her God, she spoke in this open manner as a child would have done, unsuspectingly, with no feelings of mistrust, and with no selfish end in view. May God reward her!

Her friend daily wrote down all the observations that he made concerning her, and all that she told him about her life, whether interior or exterior. Her words were

characterised alternately by the most childlike simplicity
and the most astonishing depth of thought, and they fore-
shadowed, as it were, the vast and sublime spectacle which
later was unfolded, when it became evident that the past,
the present, and the future, together with all that pertained to the sanctification, profanation, and judgment of
souls, formed before and within her an allegorical and historical drama, for which the different events of the ecclesiastical year furnished subjects, and which it divided
into scenes, so closely linked together were all the prayers
and sufferings which she offered in sacrifice for the Church
militant.

On the 22d of October 1818 Sailer came to see her,
and having remarked that she was lodging at the back of
a public-house, and that men were playing at nine-pins
under her window, said in the playful yet thoughtful manner which was peculiar to him : ' See, see ; all things are
as they should be—the invalid nun, the spouse of our
Lord, is lodging in a public-house above the ground where
men are playing at nine-pins, like the soul of man in his
body.' His interview with Anne Catherine was most
affecting ; it was indeed beautiful to behold these two
souls, who were both on fire with the love of Jesus, and
conducted by grace through such different paths, meet thus
at the foot of the Cross, the visible stamp of which was
borne by one of them. On Friday, the 23d of October,
Sailer remained alone with her during nearly the whole of
the day ; he saw blood flow from her head, her hands, and
her feet, and he was able to bestow upon her great consolation in her interior trials. He most earnestly recommended her to tell everything without reserve to the
writer of these pages, and he came to an understanding
upon the subject with her ordinary director. He heard
her confession, gave her the Holy Communion on Saturday, the 24th, and then continued his journey to the
Count de Stolberg's. On his return, at the beginning of
November, he again passed a day with her. He remained
her friend until death, prayed constantly for her, and
asked her prayers whenever he found himself in trying or

difficult positions. The writer of these pages remained until January. He returned again in May 1819, and continued to watch Anne Catherine almost uninterruptedly until her death.

The saintly maiden continually besought the Almighty to remove the exterior stigmas, on account of the trouble and fatigue which they occasioned, and her prayer was granted at the end of seven years. Towards the conclusion of the year 1819, the blood first flowed less frequently from her wounds, and then ceased altogether. On the 25th of December, scabs fell from her feet and hands, and there only remained white scars, which became red on certain days, but the pain she suffered was undiminished in the slightest degree. The mark of the cross, and the wound on her right side, were often to be seen as before, but not at any stated times. On certain days she always had the most painful sensations around her head, as though a crown of thorns were being pressed upon it. On these occasions she could not lean her head against anything, nor even rest it on her hand, but had to remain for long hours, sometimes even for whole nights, sitting up in her bed, supported by cushions, whilst her pallid face, and the irrepressible groans of pain which escaped her, made her like an awful living representation of suffering. After she had been in this state, blood invariably flowed more or less copiously from around her head. Sometimes her head-dress only was soaked with it, but sometimes the blood would flow down her face and neck. On Good Friday, April 19th, 1819, all her wounds re-opened and bled, and closed again on the following days. A most rigorous inquiry into her state was made by some doctors and naturalists. For that end she was placed alone in a strange house, where she remained from the 7th to the 29th of August; but this examination appears to have produced no particular effects in any way. She was brought back to her own dwelling on the 29th of August, and from that time until she died she was left in peace, save that she was occasionally annoyed by private disputes and public insults. On this subject Overberg wrote her the

following words : ' What have you had to suffer personally
of which you can complain? I am addressing a soul desirous of nothing so much as to become more and more
like to her divine Spouse. Have you not been treated far
more gently than was your adorable Spouse? Should it
not be a subject of rejoicing to you, according to the spirit,
to have been assisted to resemble him more closely, and
thus to be more pleasing in his eyes? You had suffered
much with Jesus, but hitherto insults had been for the
most part spared you. With the crown of thorns you had
not worn the purple mantle and the robe of scorn, much
less had you yet heard the cry, *Away with him ! Crucify
him ! Crucify him !* I cannot doubt but that these sentiments are yours. Praise be to Jesus Christ.'

On Good Friday, the 30th of March 1820, blood flowed
from her head, feet, hands, chest, and side. It happened
that when she fainted, one of the persons who were with
her, knowing that the application of relics relieved her,
placed near her feet a piece of linen in which some were
wrapped, and the blood which came from her wounds
reached this piece of linen after a time. In the evening,
when this same piece of linen with the relics was being
placed on her chest and shoulders, in which she was suffering much, she suddenly exclaimed, while in a state of
ecstasy : ' It is most wonderful, but I see my Heavenly
Spouse lying in the tomb in the earthly Jerusalem ; and
I also see him living in the heavenly Jerusalem surrounded by adoring saints, and in the midst of these saints
I see a person who is not a saint—a nun. Blood flows
from her head, her side, her hands, and her feet, and the
saints are above the bleeding parts.'

On the 9th February 1821 she fell into an ecstasy at
the time of the funeral of a very holy priest. Blood flowed
from her forehead, and the cross on her breast bled also.
Some one asked her, ' What is the matter with you ?' She
smiled, and spoke like one awakening from a dream : 'We
were by the side of the body. I have been accustomed
lately to hear sacred music, and the *De Profundis* made
a great impression upon me.' She died upon the same

day three years later. In 1821, a few weeks before Easter, she told us that it had been said to her during her prayer : ' Take notice, you will suffer on the real anniversary of the Passion, and not on the day marked this year in the Ecclesiastical Calendar.' On Friday, the 30th of March, at ten o'clock in the morning, she sank down senseless. Her face and bosom were bathed in blood, and her body appeared covered with bruises like what the blows of a whip would have inflicted. At twelve o'clock in the day, she stretched herself out in the form of a cross, and her arms were so extended as to be perfectly dislocated. A few minutes before two o'clock, drops of blood flowed from her feet and hands. On Good Friday, the 20th of April, she was simply in a state of quiet contemplation. This remarkable exception to the general rule seemed to be an effect of the providence of God, for, at the hour when her wounds usually bled, a number of curious and ill-natured individuals came to see her with the intention of causing her fresh annoyances, by publishing what they saw ; but they thus were made unintentionally to contribute to her peace, by saying that her wounds had ceased to bleed.

On the 19th of February 1822 she was again warned that she would suffer on the last Friday of March, and not on Good Friday.

On Friday the 15th, and again on Friday the 29th, the cross on her bosom and the wound of her side bled. Before the 29th, she more than once felt as though a stream of fire were flowing rapidly from her heart to her side, and down her arms and legs to the stigmas, which looked red and inflamed. On the evening of Thursday the 28th, she fell into a state of contemplation on the Passion, and remained in it until Friday evening. Her chest, head, and side bled ; all the veins of her hands were swollen, and there was a painful spot in the centre of them, which felt damp, although blood did not flow from it. No blood flowed from the stigmas excepting upon the 3d of March, the day of the finding of the Holy Cross. She had also a vision of the discovery of the true cross by St. Helena, and imagined herself to be lying in the excavation near the cross. Much blood came in the morning from her head and side, and in the afternoon from her hands and feet, and it seemed to her as though she were being made the test of whether the cross was really the Cross of Jesus Christ, and that her blood was testifying to its identity.

In the year 1823, on Holy Thursday and Good Friday, which came on the 27th and 28th of March, she had visions of the Passion, during which blood flowed from all her wounds, causing her intense pain. Amid these awful sufferings, although ravished in spirit, she was obliged to speak and give answers concerning all her little household affairs, as if she had been perfectly strong and well, and she never let fall a complaint, although nearly dying. This was the last time that her blood gave testimony to the reality of her union with the sufferings of him who has delivered himself up wholly and entirely for our salvation. Most of the phenomena of the ecstatic life which are shown us in the lives and writings of Saints Bridget, Gertrude, Mechtilde, Hildegarde, Catherine of Sienna, Catherine of Genoa, Catherine of Bologna, Colomba da Rieti, Lidwina of Schiedam, Catherine Vanini, Teresa of Jesus, Anne of St. Bartholomew, Magdalen of Pazzi, Mary Villana, Mary Buonomi, Marina d'Escobar, Crescentia de Kaufbeuern, and many other nuns of contemplative orders, are also to be found in the history of the interior life of Anne Catherine Emmerich. The same path was marked out for her by God. Did she, like these holy women, attain the end? God alone knows. Our part is only to pray that such may have been the case, and we are allowed to hope it. Those among our readers who are not acquainted with the ecstatic life from the writings of those who have lived it, will find information on this subject in the Introduction of Goërres to the writings of Henry Suso, published at Ratisbonne in 1829.

Since many pious Christians, in order to render their life one perpetual act of adoration, endeavour to see in their daily employments a symbolical representation of some manner of honouring God, and offer it to him in

union with the merits of Christ, it cannot appear extraordinary that those holy souls who pass from an active
life to one of suffering and contemplation, should sometimes see their spiritual labours under the form of those
earthly occupations which formerly filled their days. Then
their acts were prayers; now their prayers are acts; but
the form remains the same. It was thus that Anne Catherine, in her ecstatic life, beheld the series of her prayers
for the Church under the forms of parables bearing reference to agriculture, gardening, weaving, sowing, or the care
of sheep. All these different occupations were arranged,
according to their signification, in the different periods of
the common as well as the ecclesiastical year, and were
pursued under the patronage and with the assistance of the
saints of each day, the special graces of the corresponding
feasts of the Church being also applied to them. The signification of this circle of symbols had reference to all the
active part of her interior life. One example will help to
explain our meaning. When Anne Catherine, while yet
a child, was employed in weeding, she besought God to
root up the cockle from the field of the Church. If her
hands were stung by the nettles, or if she was obliged
to do afresh the work of idlers, she offered to God her
pain and her fatigue, and besought him, in the name of
Jesus Christ, that the pastor of souls might not become
weary, and that none of them might cease to labour zeal-
ously and diligently. Thus her manual labour became a
prayer.

I will now give a corresponding example of her life of
contemplation and ecstasy. She had been ill several times,
and in a state of almost continual ecstasy, during which
she often moaned, and moved her hands like a person employed in weeding. She complained one morning that her
hands and arms smarted and itched, and on examination
they were found to be covered with blisters, like what
would have been produced by the stinging of nettles. She
then begged several persons of her acquaintance to join
their prayers to hers for a certain intention. The next
day her hands were inflamed and painful, as they would

have been after hard work; and when asked the cause, she replied: 'Ah! I have had so many nettles to root up in the vineyard, because those whose duty it was to do it only pulled off the stems, and I was obliged to draw the roots with much difficulty out of a stony soil.' The person who had asked her the question began to blame these careless workmen, but he felt much confused when she replied: 'You were one of them,—those who only pull off the stems of the nettles, and leave the roots in the earth, are persons who pray carelessly.' It was afterwards discovered that she had been praying for several dioceses which were shown to her under the figure of vineyards laid waste, and in which labour was needed. The real inflammation of her hands bore testimony to this symbolical rooting up of the nettles; and we have, perhaps, reason to hope that the churches shown to her under the appearances of vineyards experienced the good effects of her prayer and spiritual labour; for since the door is opened to those who knock, it must certainly be opened above all to those who knock with such energy as to cause their fingers to be wounded.

Similar reactions of the spirit upon the body are often found in the lives of persons subject to ecstasies, and are by no means contrary to faith. St. Paula, if we may believe St. Jerome, visited the holy places in spirit just as if she had visited them bodily; and a like thing happened to St. Colomba of Rieti and St. Lidwina of Schiedam. The body of the latter bore traces of this spiritual journey, as if she had really travelled; she experienced all the fatigue that a painful journey would cause: her feet were wounded and covered with marks which looked as if they had been made by stones or thorns, and finally she had a sprain from which she long suffered.

She was led on this journey by her guardian angel, who told her that these corporeal wounds signified that she had been ravished in body and spirit.

Similar hurts were also to be seen upon the body of Anne Catherine immediately after some of her visions. Lidwina began her ecstatic journey by following her good angel to the chapel of the Blessed Virgin before Schiedam ; Anne Catherine began hers by following her angel guardian either to the chapel which was near her dwelling, or else to the Way of the Cross of Coesfeld.

Her journeys to the Holy Land were made, according to the accounts she gave of them, by the most opposite roads ; sometimes even she went all round the earth, when the task spiritually imposed upon her required it. In the course of these journeys from her home to the most distant countries, she carried assistance to many persons, exercising in their regard works of mercy, both corporal and spiritual, and this was done frequently in parables. At the end of a year she would go over the same ground again, see the same persons, and give an account of their spiritual progress or of their relapse into sin. Every part of this labour always bore some reference to the Church, and to the kingdom of God upon earth.

The end of these daily pilgrimages which she made in spirit was invariably the Promised Land, every part of which she examined in detail, and which she saw sometimes in its present state, and sometimes as it was at different periods of sacred history ; for her distinguishing characteristic and special privilege was an intuitive knowledge of the history of the Old and New Testaments, and of that of the members of the Holy Family, and of all the saints whom she was contemplating in spirit. She saw the signification of all the festival days of the ecclesiastical year under both a devotional and an historical point of view. She saw and described, day by day, with the minutest detail, and by name, places, persons, festivals, customs, and miracles, all that happened during the public life of Jesus until the Ascension, and the history of the apostles for several weeks after the Descent of the Holy Ghost. She regarded all her visions not as mere spiritual enjoyments, but as being, so to speak, fertile fields, plentifully strewn with the merits of Christ, and which had not as yet been cultivated ; she was often engaged in spirit in praying that the fruit of such and such sufferings of our Lord might be given to the Church, and she would beseech God to apply to his

Church the merits of our Saviour which were its inheritance, and of which she would, as it were, take possession,
in its name, with the most touching simplicity and in-
genuousness.

She never considered her visions to have any reference
to her exterior Christian life, nor did she regard them as
being of any historical value.   Exteriorly she knew and
believed nothing but the catechism, the common history
of the Bible, the gospels for Sundays and festivals, and
the Christian almanack, which to her far-sighted vision
was an inexhaustible mine of hidden riches, since it gave
her in a few pages a guiding thread which led her through
all time, and by means of which she passed from mystery
to mystery, and solemnised each with all the saints, in
order to reap the fruits of eternity in time, and to preserve
and distribute them in her pilgrimage around the ecclesiastical year, that so the will of God might be accomplished on earth as it is in Heaven.   She had never read
the Old or the New Testaments, and when she was tired
of relating her visions, she would sometimes say : ' Read
that in the Bible,' and then be astonished to learn that it
was not there ; ' for,' she would add, ' people are constantly
saying in these days that you need read nothing but the
Bible, which contains everything, &c. &c.'

The real task of her life was to suffer for the Church
and for some of its members, whose distress was shown
her in spirit, or who asked her prayers without knowing
that this poor sick nun had something more to do for them
than to say the *Pater noster*, but that all their spiritual
and corporal sufferings became her own, and that she had
to endure patiently the most terrible pains, without being
assisted, like the contemplatives of former days, by the
sympathising prayers of an entire community.   In the age
when she lived, she had no other assistance than that of
medicine.   While thus enduring sufferings which she had
taken upon herself for others, she often turned her thoughts
to the corresponding sufferings of the Church, and when
thus suffering for one single person, she would likewise
offer all she endured for the whole Church.

The following is a remarkable instance of the sort:—
During several weeks she had every symptom of consumption; violent irritation of the lungs, excessive perspiration, which soaked her whole bed, a racking cough, continual expectoration, and a strong continual fever. So fearful were her sufferings that her death was hourly expected and even desired. It was remarked that she had to struggle strangely against a strong temptation to irritability. Did she yield for an instant, she burst into tears, her sufferings increased tenfold, and she seemed unable to exist unless she immediately gained pardon in the sacrament of penance. She had also to combat a feeling of aversion to a certain person whom she had not seen for years. She was in despair because this person, with whom nevertheless she declared she had nothing in common, was always before her eyes in the most evil dispositions, and she wept bitterly, and with much anxiety of conscience, saying that she would not commit sin, that her grief must be evident to all, and other things which were quite unintelligible to the persons listening to her. Her illness continued to increase, and she was thought to be on the point of death. At this moment one of her friends saw her, to his great surprise, suddenly raise herself up on her bed, and say:—

'Repeat with me the prayers for those in their last agony.' He did as requested, and she answered the Litany in a firm voice. After some little time, the bell for the agonising was heard, and a person came in to ask Anne Catherine's prayers for his sister, who was just dead. Anne Catherine asked for details concerning her illness and death, as if deeply interested in the subject, and the friend above-mentioned heard the account given by the new comer of a consumption resembling in the minutest particulars the illness of Anne Catherine herself. The deceased woman had at first been in so much pain and so disturbed in mind that she had seemed quite unable to prepare herself for death; but during the last fortnight she had been better, had made her peace with God, having in the first place been reconciled to a person with whom she was at enmity, and had died in peace, fortified by the last sacraments, and attended by her former enemy. Anne Catherine gave a small sum of money for the burial and funeral-service of this person. Her sweatings, cough, and fever now left her, and she resembled a person exhausted with fatigue, whose linen has been changed, and who has been placed on a fresh bed. Her friend said to her, ' When this fearful illness came upon you, this woman grew better, and her hatred for another was the only obstacle to her making peace with God. You took upon yourself, for the time, her feelings of hatred, she died in good dispositions, and now you seem tolerably well again. Are you still suffering on her account ?' ' No, indeed !' she replied ; ' that would be most unreasonable ; but how can any person avoid suffering when even the end of his little finger is in pain ? We are all one body in Christ.' ' By the goodness of God,' said her friend, ' you are now once more somewhat at ease.' ' Not for very long, though,' she replied with a smile ; ' there are other persons who want my assistance.' Then she turned round on her bed, and rested awhile.

A very few days later, she began to feel intense pain in all her limbs, and symptoms of water on the chest manifested themselves. We discovered the sick person for whom Anne Catherine was suffering, and we saw that his sufferings suddenly diminished or immensely increased in exact inverse proportion to those of Anne Catherine.

Thus did charity compel her to take upon herself the illnesses and even the temptations of others, that they might be able in peace to prepare themselves for death. She was compelled to suffer in silence, both to conceal the weaknesses of her neighbour, and not to be regarded as mad herself ; she was obliged to receive all the aid that medicine could afford her for an illness thus taken volun- tarily for the relief of others, and to be reproached for temptations which were not her own ; finally, it was necessary that she should appear perverted in the eyes of men, that so those for whom she was suffering might be converted before God.

One day a friend in deep affliction was sitting by her bedside, when she suddenly fell into a state of ecstasy, and began to pray aloud : ' O, my sweet Jesus, permit me to carry that heavy stone !' Her friend asked her what was the matter. ' I am on my way to Jerusalem,' she replied, ' and I see a poor man walking along with the greatest difficulty, for there is a large stone upon his breast, the weight of which nearly crushes him.' Then again, after a few moments, she exclaimed : ' Give me that heavy stone, you cannot carry it any farther ; give it to me.' All on a sudden she sank down fainting, as if crushed beneath some heavy burden, and at the same moment her friend felt himself relieved from the weight of sorrow which oppressed him, and his heart overflowing with extraordinary happiness. Seeing her in such a state of suffering, he asked her what the matter was, and she looking at him with a smile, replied : ' I cannot remain here any longer. Poor man, you must take back your burden.' Instantly her friend felt all the weight of his affliction return to him, whilst she, becoming as well again as before, continued her journey in spirit to Jerusalem.

We will give one more example of her spiritual exertions. One morning she gave her friend a little bag containing some rye-flour and eggs, and pointed out to him a small house where a poor woman, who was in a consumption, was living with her husband and two little children. He was to tell her to boil and take them, as when boiled they would be good for her chest. The friend, on entering the cottage, took the bag from under his cloak, when the poor mother, who, flushed with fever, was lying on a mattress between her half-naked children, fixed her bright eyes upon him, and holding out her thin hands, exclaimed : ' O, sir, it must be God or Sister Emmerich who sends you to me ! You are bringing me some rye-flour and eggs.' Here the poor woman, overcome by her feelings, burst into tears, and then began to cough so violently that she had to make a sign to her husband to speak for her. He said that the previous night Gertrude had been much disturbed, and had talked a great

deal in her sleep, and that on awaking she had told him
her dream in these words: 'I thought that I was standing
at the door with you, when the holy nun came out of the
door of the next house, and I told you to look at her.
She stopped in front of us, and said to me : " Ah, Gertrude,
you look very ill ; I will send you some rye-flour and eggs,
which will relieve your chest." Then I awoke.' Such
was the simple tale of the poor man ; he and his wife both
eagerly expressed their gratitude, and the bearer of Anne
Catherine's alms left the house much overcome. He did
not tell her anything of this when he saw her, but a few
days after, she sent him again to the same place with a
similar present, and he then asked her how it was she
knew that poor woman ? ' You know,' she replied, ' that
I pray every evening for all those who suffer ; I should
like to go and relieve them, and I generally dream that I
am going from one abode of suffering to another, and that
I assist them to the best of my power. In this way I went
in my dream to that poor woman's house ; she was standing at the door with her husband, and I said to her : "Ah,
Gertrude, you look very ill ; I will send you some rye-
flour and eggs, which will relieve your chest." And this
I did through you, the next morning.' Both persons had
remained in their beds, and dreamed the same thing, and
the dream came true. St. Augustin, in his *City of God*,
book xviii., c. 18, relates a similar thing of two philosophers, who visited each other in a dream, and explained
some passages of Plato, both remaining asleep in their own
houses.

These sufferings, and this peculiar species of active
labour, were like a single ray of light, which enlightened
her whole life. Infinite was the number of spiritual
labours and sympathetic sufferings which came from all
parts and entered into her heart—that heart so burning
with love of Jesus Christ. Like St. Catherine of Sienna
and some other ecstatics, she often felt the most profound
feeling of conviction that our Saviour had taken her heart
out of her bosom, and placed his own there instead for
a time.

The following fragment will give some idea of the mysterious symbolism by which she was interiorly directed. During a portion of the year 1820 she performed many labours in spirit, for several different parishes; her prayers being represented under the figure of most severe labour in a vineyard. What we have above related concerning the nettles is of the same character.

On the 6th of September her heavenly guide said to her: ' " You weeded, dug around, tied, and pruned the vine; you ground down the weeds so that they could never spring up any more; and then you went away joyfully and rested from your prayers. Prepare now to labour hard from the feast of the Nativity of the Blessed Virgin to that of St. Michael; the grapes are ripening and must be well watched." Then he led me,' she continued, ' to the vineyard of St. Liboire, and showed me the vines at which I had worked. My labour had been successful, for the grapes were getting their colour and growing large, and in some parts the red juice was running down on the ground from them. My guide said to me : " When the virtues of the good begin to shine forth in public, they have to combat bravely, to be oppressed, to be tempted, and to suffer persecution. A hedge must be planted around the vineyard in order that the ripe grapes may not be destroyed by thieves and wild beasts, *i. e.* by temptation and persecution." He then showed me how to build a wall by heaping up stones, and to raise a thick hedge of thorns all around. As my hands bled from such severe labour, God, in order to give me strength, permitted me to see the mysterious signification of the vine, and of several other fruit trees. Jesus Christ is the true Vine, who is to take root and grow in us; all useless wood must be cut away, in order not to waste the sap, which is to become the wine, and in the Most Blessed Sacrament the Blood of Christ. The pruning of the vine has to be done according to certain rules which were made known to me. This pruning is, in a spiritual sense, the cutting off whatever is useless, penance and mortification, that so the true Vine may grow in us, and bring forth fruit, in the place of corrupt nature, which only bears wood and leaves. The pruning is done according to fixed rules, for it is only required that certain useless shoots should be cut off in man, and to lop off more would be to mutilate in a guilty manner. No pruning should ever be done upon the stock which has been planted in human-kind through the Blessed Virgin, and is to remain in it for ever. The true Vine unites heaven to earth, the Divinity to humanity; and it is the human part that is to be pruned, that so the divine alone may grow. I saw so many other things relating to the vine that a book as large as the Bible could not contain them. One day, when I was suffering acute pain in my chest, I besought our Lord with groans not to give me a burthen above my strength to bear; and then my Heavenly Spouse appeared, and said to me, . . . "I have laid thee on my nuptial couch, which is a couch of suffering; I have given thee suffering and expiation for thy bridal garments and jewels. Thou must suffer, but I will not forsake thee; thou art fastened to the Vine, and thou wilt not be lost." Then I was consoled for all my sufferings. It was like-wise explained to me why in my visions relating to the feasts of the family of Jesus, such, for instance, as those of St. Anne, St. Joachim, St. Joseph, &c., I always saw the Church of the festival under the figure of a shoot of the vine. The same was the case on the festivals of St. Francis of Assissium, St. Catherine of Sienna, and of all the saints who have had the stigmas.

'The signification of my sufferings in all my limbs was explained to me in the following vision : I saw a gigantic human body in a horrible state of mutilation, and raised upwards towards the sky. There were no fingers or toes on the hands and feet, the body was covered with fright-ful wounds, some of which were fresh and bleeding, others covered with dead flesh or turned into excrescences. The whole of one side was black, gangrened, and as it were half eaten away. I suffered as though it had been my own body that was in this state, and then my guide said to me, "This is the body of the Church, the body of all men and thine also." Then, pointing to each wound, he showed me at the same time some part of the world; I saw an infinite number of men and nations separated from the Church, all in their own peculiar way, and I felt pain as exquisite from this separation as if they had been torn from my body. Then my guide said to me: " Let thy sufferings teach thee a lesson, and offer them to God in union with those of Jesus for all who are separated. Should not one member call upon another, and suffer in order to cure and unite it once more to the body? When those parts which are most closely united to the body detach themselves, it is as though the flesh were torn from around the heart." In my ignorance, I thought that he was speaking of those brethren who are not in communion with us, but my guide added: " Who are our brethren? It is not our blood relations who are the nearest to our hearts, but those who are our brethren in the blood of Christ—the children of the Church who fall away." He showed me that the black and gangrened side of the body would soon be cured; that the putrified flesh which had collected around the wounds represented heretics who divide one from the other in proportion as they increase; that the dead flesh was the figure of all who are spiritually dead, and who are void of any feeling; and that the ossified parts represented obstinate and hardened heretics. I saw and felt in this manner every wound and its signification. The body reached up to heaven. It was the body of the Bride of Christ, and most painful to behold. I wept bitterly, but feeling at once deeply grieved and strengthened by sorrow and compasssion, I began again to labour with all my strength.'

Sinking beneath the weight of life and of the task imposed upon her she often besought God to deliver her, and she then would appear to be on the very brink of the grave. But each time she would say: 'Lord, not my will but thine be done! If my prayers and sufferings are useful let me live a thousand years, but grant that I may die rather than ever offend thee.' Then she would receive orders to live, and arise, taking up her cross, once more to bear it in patience and suffering after her Lord. From time to time the road of life which she was pursuing used to be shown to her, leading to the top of a mountain on which was a shining and resplendent city—the heavenly Jerusalem. Often she would think she had arrived at that blissful abode, which seemed to be quite near her, and her joy would be great. But all on a sudden she would discover that she was still separated from it by a valley, and then she would have to descend precipices. and follow indirect paths, labouring, suffering, and performing deeds of charity everywhere. She had to direct wanderers into the right road, raise up the fallen, sometimes even carry the paralytic, and drag the unwilling by force, and all these deeds of charity were as so many fresh weights fastened to her cross. Then she walked with more difficulty, bending beneath her burden and sometimes even falling to the ground.

In 1823 she repeated more frequently than usual that she could not perform her task in her present situation, that she had not strength for it, and that it was in a peaceful convent that she needed to have lived and died. She added that God would soon take her to himself, and that she had besought him to permit her to obtain by her prayers in the next world what her weakness would not permit her to accomplish in this. St. Catherine of Sienna, a short time before death, made a similar prayer.

Anne Catherine had previously had a vision concerning what her prayers might obtain after death, with regard to things that were not in existence during her life. The year 1823, the last of which she completed the whole circle, brought her immense labours. She appeared desirous to accomplish her entire task, and thus kept the promise which she had previously made of relating the history of the whole Passion. It formed the subject of her Lenten meditations during this year, and of them the present volume is composed. But she did not on this account take less part in the fundamental mystery of this penitential season, or in the different mysteries of each of the festival days of the Church, if indeed the words *to take part* be sufficient to express the wonderful manner in which she rendered visible testimony to the mystery cele‑ brated in each festival by a sudden change in her corporal and spiritual life. See on this subject the chapter entitled *Interruption of the Pictures of the Passion.*

Every one of the ceremonies and festivals of the Church was to her far more than the consecration of a remem‑ brance. She beheld in the historical foundation of each solemnity an act of the Almighty, done in time for the reparation of fallen humanity. Although these divine acts appeared to her stamped with the character of eternity, yet she was well aware that in order for man to profit by them in the bounded and narrow sphere of time, he must, as it were, take possession of them in a series of succes‑ sive moments, and that for this purpose they had to be repeated and renewed in the Church, in the order esta‑ blished by Jesus Christ and the Holy Spirit. All festivals and solemnities were in her eyes eternal graces which re‑ turned at fixed epochs in every ecclesiastical year, in the same manner as the fruits and harvests of the earth come in their seasons in the natural year.

Her zeal and gratitude in receiving and treasuring up these graces were untiring, nor was she less eager and zealous in offering them to those who neglected their value. In the same manner as her compassion for her crucified Saviour had pleased God and obtained for her the privi‑ lege of being marked with the stigmas of the Passion as with a seal of the most perfect love, so all the sufferings of the Church and of those who were in affliction were repeated in the different states of her body and soul. And all these wonders took place within her, unknown to those who were around her ; nor was she herself even more fully conscious of them than is the bee of the effects of its work, while yet she was tending and cultivating, with all the care of an industrious and faithful gardener, the fertile gar‑ den of the ecclesiastical year. She lived on its fruits, and distributed them to others ; she strengthened herself and her friends with the flowers and herbs which she culti‑ vated ; or, rather, she herself was in this garden like a sensitive plant, a sunflower, or some wonderful plant in which, independent of her own will, were reproduced all the seasons of the year, all the hours of the day, and all the changes of the atmosphere.

At the end of the ecclesiastical year of 1823, she had for the last time a vision on the subject of making up the accounts of that year. The negligences of the Church militant and of her servants were shown to Anne Catherine, under various symbols; she saw how many graces had not been coöperated with, or been rejected to a greater or less extent, and how many had been entirely thrown away. It was made known to her how our Blessed Redeemer had deposited for each year in the garden of the Church a complete treasure of his merits, sufficient for every requirement, and for the expiation of every sin. The strictest account was to be given of all graces which had been neglected, wasted, or wholly rejected, and the Church militant was punished for this negligence or infidelity of her servants by being oppressed by her enemies, or by temporal humiliations. Revelations of this description raised to excess her love for the Church, her mother. She passed days and nights in praying for her, in offering to God the merits of Christ, with continual groans, and in imploring mercy. Finally, on these occasions, she gathered together all her courage, and offered to take upon herself both the fault and the punishment, like a child presenting itself before the king's throne, in order to suffer the punishment she had incurred. It was then said to her, 'See how wretched and miserable thou art thyself; thou who art desirous to satisfy for the sins of others.' And to her great terror she beheld herself as one mournful mass of infinite imperfection. But still her love remained undaunted, and burst forth in these words, 'Yes, I am full of misery and sin; but I am thy spouse, O my Lord, and my Saviour! My faith in thee and in the redemption which thou hast brought us covers all my sins as with thy royal mantle. I will not leave thee until thou hast accepted my sacrifice, for the superabundant treasure of thy merits is closed to none of thy faithful

servants.' At length her prayer became wonderfully ener-
getic, and to human ears there was like a dispute and
combat with God, in which she was carried away and
urged on by the violence of love. If her sacrifice was
accepted, her energy seemed to abandon her, and she was
left to the repugnance of human nature for suffering.
When she had gone through this trial, by keeping her
eyes fixed on her Redeemer in the Garden of Olives, she
next had to endure indescribable sufferings of every description, bearing them all with wonderful patience and
sweetness. We used to see her remain several days together, motionless and insensible, looking like a dying
lamb. Did we ask her how she was, she would half open
her eyes, and reply with a sweet smile, ' My sufferings are
most salutary.'

At the beginning of Advent, her sufferings were a little
soothed by sweet visions of the preparations made by the
Blessed Virgin to leave her home, and then of her whole
journey with St. Joseph to Bethlehem. She accompanied
them each day to the humble inns where they rested for
the night, or went on before them to prepare their lodgings.
During this time she used to take old pieces of linen, and
at night, while sleeping, make them into baby clothes
and caps for the children of poor women, the times of
whose confinements were near at hand. The next day she
would be surprised to see all these things neatly arranged
in her drawers. This happened to her every year about
the same time, but this year she had more fatigue and
less consolation. Thus, at the hour of our Saviour's birth,
when she was usually perfectly overwhelmed with joy, she
could only crawl with the greatest difficulty to the crib
where the Child Jesus was lying, and bring him no present
but myrrh, no offering but her cross, beneath the weight
of which she sank down half dying at his feet. It seemed
as though she were for the last time making up her earthly
accounts with God, and for the last time also offering herself in the place of a countless number of men who were
spiritually and corporally afflicted. Even the little that
is known of the manner in which she took upon herself

the sufferings of others is almost incomprehensible. She very truly said: 'This year the Child Jesus has only brought me a cross and instruments of suffering.'

She became each day more and more absorbed in her sufferings, and although she continued to see Jesus travelling from city to city during his public life, the utmost she ever said on the subject was, briefly to name in which direction he was going. Once, she asked suddenly in a scarcely audible voice, 'What day is it?' When told that it was the 14th of January, she added: 'Had I but a few days more, I should have related the entire life of our Saviour, but now it is no longer possible for me to do so.' These words were the more incomprehensible as she did not appear to know even which year of the public life of Jesus she was then contemplating in spirit. In 1820 she had related the history of our Saviour down to the Ascension, beginning at the 28th of July of the third year of the public life of Jesus, after which she returned to the first year of the life of Jesus, and had continued down to the 10th of January of the third year of his public life. On the 27th of April 1823, in consequence of a journey made by the writer, an interruption of her narrative took place, and lasted down to the 21st of October. She then took up the thread of her narrative where she had left it, and continued it to the last weeks of her life. When she spoke of a few days being wanted, her friend himself did not know how far her narrative went, not having had leisure to arrange what he had written. After her death he became convinced that if she had been able to speak during the last fourteen days of her life, she would have brought it down to the 28th of July of the third year of the public life of our Lord, consequently to where she had taken it up in 1820.

Her condition daily became more frightful. She, who usually suffered in silence, uttered stifled groans, so awful was the anguish she endured. On the 15th of January she said: 'The Child Jesus brought me great sufferings at Christmas. I was once more by his manger at Bethlehem. He was burning with fever, and showed me his sufferings and those of his mother. They were so poor that they had no food but a wretched piece of bread. He bestowed still greater sufferings upon me, and said to me : " Thou art mine ; thou art my spouse ; suffer as I suffered, without asking the reason why." I do not know what my sufferings are to be, nor how long they will last. I submit blindly to my martyrdom, whether for life or for death : I only desire that the hidden designs of God may be accomplished in me. On the other hand, I am calm, and I have consolations in my sufferings. Even this morning I was very happy. Blessed be the holy Name of God !'

Her sufferings continued, if possible, to increase. Sitting up, and with her eyes closed, she fell from one side to another, while smothered groans escaped her lips. If she laid down, she was in danger of being stifled ; her breathing was hurried and oppressed, and all her nerves and muscles were shaken and trembled with anguish. After violent retching, she suffered terrible pain in her bowels, so much so that it was feared gangrene must be forming there. Her throat was parched and burning, her mouth swollen, her cheeks crimson with fever, her hands white as ivory. The scars of the stigmas shone like silver beneath her distended skin. Her pulse gave from 160 to 180 pulsations per minute. Although unable to speak from her excessive suffering, she bore every duty perfectly in mind. On the evening of the 26th, she said to her friend, ' To-day is the ninth day, you must pay for the wax taper and novena at the chapel of St. Anne.' She was alluding to a novena which she had asked to have made for her intention, and she was afraid lest her friends should forget it. On the 27th, at two o'clock in the afternoon, she received Extreme Unction, greatly to the relief both of her soul and body. In the evening her friend, the excellent curé of H———, prayed at her bedside, which was an immense comfort to her. She said to him : ' How good and beautiful all this is !' And again : ' May God be a thousand times praised and thanked !'

The approach of death did not wholly interrupt the wonderful union of her life with that of the Church. A friend having visited her on the 1st of February in the evening, had placed himself behind her bed where she could not see him, and was listening with the utmost compassion to her low moans and interrupted breathing, when suddenly all became silent, and he thought that she was dead. At this moment the evening bell ringing for the matins of the Purification was heard. It was the opening of this festival which had caused her soul to be ravished in ecstasy. Although still in a very alarming state, she let some sweet and loving words concerning the Blessed Virgin escape her lips during the night and day of the festival. Towards twelve o'clock in the day, she said in a voice already changed by the near approach of death, 'It was long since I had felt so well. I have been ill quite a week, have I not? I feel as though I knew nothing about this world of darkness! O, what light the Blessed Mother of God showed me! She took me with her, and how willingly would I have remained with her!' Here she recollected herself for a moment, and then said, placing her finger on her lip: 'But I must not speak of these things.' From that time she said that the slightest word in her praise greatly increased her sufferings.

The following days she was worse. On the 7th, in the evening, being rather more calm, she said: 'Ah, my sweet Lord Jesus, thanks be to thee again and again for every part of my life. Lord, thy will and not mine be done.' On the 8th of February, in the evening, a priest was praying near her bed, when she gratefully kissed his hand, begged him to assist at her death, and said, 'O Jesus, I live for thee, I die for thee. O Lord, praise be to thy holy name, I no longer see or hear!' Her friends wished to change her position, and thus ease her pain a little; but she said, 'I am on the Cross, it will soon all be over, leave me in peace.' She had received all the last Sacraments, but she wished to accuse herself once more in confession of a slight fault which she had already many times confessed; it was probably of the same nature as a sin which she had committed in her childhood, of which she often accused herself, and which consisted in having gone through a hedge into a neighbour's garden, and coveted some apples which had fallen on the ground. She had only *looked* at them; for, thank God, she said, she did not touch them, but she thought that was a sin against the tenth commandment. The priest gave her a general absolution; after which she stretched herself out, and those around her thought that she was dying. A person who had often given her pain now drew near her bed and asked her pardon. She looked at him in surprise, and said with the most expressive accent of truth, ' I have nothing to forgive any living creature.'

During the last days of her life, when her death was momentarily expected, several of her friends remained constantly in the room adjoining hers. They were speaking in a low tone, and so that she could not hear them, of her patience, faith, and other virtues, when all on a sudden they heard her dying voice saying: ' Ah, for the love of God, do not praise me—that keeps me here, because I then have to suffer double. O my God! how many fresh flowers are falling upon me !' She always saw flowers as the forerunners and figures of sufferings. Then she rejected all praises, with the most profound conviction of her own unworthiness, saying : 'God alone is good: everything must be paid, down to the last farthing. I am poor and loaded with sin, and I can only make up for having been praised by sufferings united to those of Jesus Christ. Do not praise me, but let me die in ignominy with Jesus on the cross.'

Boudon, in his life of Father Surin, relates a similar trait of a dying man, who had been thought to have lost the sense of hearing, but who energetically rejected a word of praise pronounced by those who were surrounding his bed.

A few hours before death, for which she was longing, saying, ' O Lord assist me ; come, O Lord Jesus !' a word of praise appeared to detain her, and she most energetically rejected it by making the following act of humility : ' I cannot die if so many good persons think well of me through a mistake ; I beg of you to tell them all that I am

a wretched sinner! Would that I could proclaim so as to
be heard by all men, how great a sinner I am! I am far
beneath the good thief who was crucified by the side of
Jesus, for he and all his contemporaries had not so terrible
an account as we shall have to render of all the graces
which have been bestowed upon the Church.' After this
declaration, she appeared to grow calm, and she said to
the priest who was comforting her : ' I feel now as peaceful and as much filled with hope and confidence as if I had
never committed a sin.' Her eyes turned lovingly towards
the cross which was placed at the foot of her bed, her
breathing became accelerated, she often drank some liquid ;
and when the little crucifix was held to her, she from humility only kissed the feet. A friend who was kneeling
by her bedside in tears, had the comfort of often holding
her the water with which to moisten her lips. As she had
laid her hand, on which the white scar of the wound was
most distinctly visible, on the counterpane, he took hold
of that hand, which was already cold, and as he inwardly
wished for some mark of farewell from her, she slightly
pressed his. Her face was calm and serene, bearing an
expression of heavenly gravity, and which can only be
compared to that of a valiant wrestler, who after making
unheard-of efforts to gain the victory, sinks back and dies
in the very act of seizing the prize. The priest again read
through the prayers for persons in their last agony, and
she then felt an inward inspiration to pray for a pious
young friend whose feast day it was. Eight o'clock struck ;
she breathed more freely for the space of a few minutes,
and then cried three times with a deep groan : ' O Lord,
assist me ; Lord, Lord, come !' The priest rang his bell,
and said, ' She is dying.' Several relations and friends
who were in the next room came in and knelt down to
pray. She was then holding in her hand a lighted taper,
which the priest was supporting. She breathed forth several
slight sighs, and then her pure soul escaped her chaste
lips, and hastened, clothed in the nuptial garment, to appear in heavenly hope before the Divine Bridegroom, and
be united for ever to that blessed company of virgins who

follow the Lamb whithersoever he goeth. Her lifeless body sank gently back on the pillows at half-past eight o'clock, P.M., on the 9th February 1824.

A person who had taken great interest in her during life wrote as follows : ' After her death, I drew near to her bed. She was supported by pillows, and lying on her left side. Some crutches, which had been prepared for her by her friends on one occasion when she had been able to take a few turns in the room, were hanging over her head, crossed, in a corner. Near them hung a little oil painting representing the death of the Blessed Virgin, which had been given her by the Princess of Salm. The expression of her countenance was perfectly sublime, and bore the traces of the spirit of self-sacrifice, the patience and resignation of her whole life ; she looked as though she had died for the love of Jesus, in the very act of performing some work of charity for others. Her right hand was resting on the counterpane—that hand on which God had bestowed the unparalleled favour of being able at once to recognise by the touch anything that was holy, or that had been consecrated by the Church—a favour which perhaps no one had ever before enjoyed to so great an extent —a favour by which the interests of religion might be inconceivably promoted, provided it was made use of with discretion, and which surely had not been bestowed upon a poor ignorant peasant girl merely for her own personal gratification. For the last time I took in mine the hand marked with a sign so worthy of our utmost veneration, the hand which was as a spiritual instrument in the instant recognition of whatever was holy, that it might be honoured even in a grain of sand—the charitable industrious hand, which had so often fed the hungry and clothed the naked—this hand was now cold and lifeless. A great favour had been withdrawn from earth, God had taken from us the hand of his spouse, who had rendered testimony to, prayed, and suffered for the truth. It appeared as though it had not been without meaning, that she had resignedly laid down upon her bed the hand which was the outward expression of a particular privilege granted by

Divine grace. Fearful of having the strong impression made upon me by the sight of her countenance diminished by the necessary but disturbing preparations which were being made around her bed, I thoughtfully left her room. If, I said to myself—if, like so many holy solitaries, she had died alone in a grave prepared by her own hands, her friends—the birds—would have covered her with flowers and leaves; if, like other religious, she had died among virgins consecrated to God, and that their tender care and respectful veneration had followed her to the grave, as was the case, for example, with St. Columba of Rieti, it would have been edifying and pleasing to those who loved her; but doubtless such honours rendered to her lifeless remains would not have been conformable to her love for Jesus, whom she so much desired to resemble in death as in life.'

The same friend later wrote as follows : 'Unfortunately there was no official post-mortem examination of her body, and none of those inquiries by which she had been so tormented during life were instituted after her death. The friends who surrounded her neglected to examine her body, probably for fear of coming upon some striking phenomenon, the discovery of which might have caused much annoyance in various ways. On Wednesday the 11th of February her body was prepared for burial. A pious female, who would not give up to any one the task of rendering her this last mark of affection, described to me as follows the condition in which she found her : " Her feet were crossed like the feet of a crucifix. The places of the stigmas were more red than usual. When we raised her head blood flowed from her nose and mouth. All her limbs remained flexible and with none of the stiffness of death even till the coffin was closed." On Friday the 13th of February she was taken to the grave, followed by the entire population of the place. She reposes in the cemetery, to the left of the cross, on the side nearest the hedge. In the grave in front of hers there rests a good old peasant of Welde, and in the grave behind a poor but virtuous female from Dernekamp.

On the evening of the day when she was buried, a

rich man went, not to Pilate, but to the curé of the place. He asked for the body of Anne Catherine, not to place it in a new sepulchre, but to buy it at a high price for a Dutch doctor. The proposal was rejected as it deserved, but it appears that the report spread in the little town that the body had been taken away, and it is said that the people went in great numbers to the cemetery to ascertain whether the grave had been robbed.'

To these details we will add the following extract from an account printed in December 1824, in the *Journal of Catholic Literature* of Kerz. This account was written by a person with whom we are unacquainted, but who appears to have been well informed : ' About six or seven weeks after the death of Anne Catherine Emmerich, a report having got about that her body had been stolen away, the grave and coffin were opened in secret, by order of the authorities, in the presence of seven witnesses. They found with surprise not unmixed with joy that corruption had not yet begun its work on the body of the pious maiden. Her features and countenance were smiling like those of a person who is dreaming sweetly. She looked as though she had but just been placed in the coffin, nor did her body exhale any corpse-like smell. *It is good to keep the secret of the king*, says Jesus the son of Sirach ; but it is also good to reveal to the world the greatness of the mercy of God.'

We have been told that a stone has been placed over her grave. We lay upon it these pages ; may they contribute to immortalise the memory of a person who has relieved so many pains of soul and body, and that of the spot where her mortal remains lie awaiting the Day of Resurrection.

TO THE READER.

WHOEVER compares the following meditations with the short history of the Last Supper given in the Gospel will discover some slight differences between them. An explanation should be given of this, although it can never be sufficiently impressed upon the reader that these writings have no pretensions whatever to add an iota to Sacred Scripture as interpreted by the Church.

Sister Emmerich saw the events of the Last Supper take place in the following order :—The Paschal Lamb was immolated and prepared in the supper-room ; our Lord held a discourse on that occasion—the guests were dressed as travellers, and ate, standing, the lamb and other food prescribed by the law—the cup of wine was twice presented to our Lord, but he did not drink of it the second time ; distributing it to his Apostles with these words : *I shall drink no more of the fruit of the vine*, &c. Then they sat down ; Jesus spoke of the traitor ; Peter feared lest it should be himself ; Judas received from our Lord the piece of bread dipped, which was the sign that it was he ; preparations were made for the washing of the feet ; Peter strove against his feet being washed ; then came the institution of the Holy Eucharist : Judas communicated, and afterwards left the apartment ; the oils were consecrated, and instructions given concerning them ; Peter and the other Apostles received ordination ; our Lord made his final discourse ; Peter protested that he would never abandon him ; and then the Supper concluded. By adopting this order, it appears, at first, as though it were in contradiction to the passages of St. Matthew (xxxi. 29), and of St. Mark (xiv. 26), in which the words : *I will drink no more of the fruit of the vine*

&c., come after the consecration, but in St. Luke, they come before. On the contrary, all that concerns the traitor Judas comes here, as in St. Matthew and St. Mark, before the consecration; whereas in St. Luke, it does not come till afterwards. St. John, who does not relate the history of the institution of the Holy Eucharist, gives us to understand that Judas went out immediately after Jesus had given him the bread; but it appears most probable, from the accounts of the other Evangelists, that Judas received the Holy Communion under both forms, and several of the fathers—St. Augustin, St. Gregory the Great, and St. Leo the Great—as well as the tradition of the Catholic Church, tell us expressly that such was the case. Besides, were the order in which St. John presents events taken literally, he would contradict, not only St. Matthew and St. Mark, but himself, for it must follow, from verse 10, chap. xiii., that Judas also had his feet washed. Now, the washing of the feet took place after the eating of the Paschal Lamb, and it was necessarily whilst it was being eaten that Jesus presented the bread to the traitor. It is plain that the Evangelists here, as in several other parts of their writings, gave their attention to the sacred narrative as a whole, and did not consider themselves bound to relate every detail in precisely the same order, which fully explains the apparent contradictions of each other, which are to be found in their Gospels. The following pages will appear to the attentive reader rather a simple and natural concordance of the Gospels than a history differing in any point of the slightest importance from that of Scripture.

MEDITATION I.

Preparations for the Pasch.

Holy Thursday, the 13*th Nisan* (29th of March).

YESTERDAY evening it was that the last great public re-past of our Lord and his friends took place in the house of Simon the Leper, at Bethania, and Mary Magdalen for the last time anointed the feet of Jesus with precious oint-ment. Judas was scandalised upon this occasion, and hastened forthwith to Jerusalem again to conspire with the high-priests for the betrayal of Jesus into their hands. After the repast, Jesus returned to the house of Lazarus, and some of the Apostles went to the inn situated beyond Bethania. During the night Nicodemus again came to Lazarus' house, had a long conversation with our Lord, and returned before daylight to Jerusalem, being accom-panied part of the way by Lazarus.

The disciples had already asked Jesus where he would eat the Pasch. To-day, before dawn, our Lord sent for Peter, James, and John, spoke to them at some length concerning all they had to prepare and order at Jerusalem, and told them that when ascending Mount Sion, they would meet the man carrying a pitcher of water. They were already well acquainted with this man, for at the last Pasch, at Bethania, it had been him who prepared the meal for Jesus, and this is why St. Matthew says : *a certain man.* They were to follow him home, and say to him : *The Master saith, My time is near at hand, with thee I make the pasch with my disciples* (Matt. xxvi. 18). They were then to be shown the supper-room, and make all necessary preparations.

I saw the two Apostles ascending towards Jerusalem, along a ravine, to the south of the Temple, and in the direction of the north side of Sion. On the southern side of the mountain on which the Temple stood, there were some rows of houses; and they walked opposite these houses, following the stream of an intervening torrent. When they had reached the summit of Mount Sion, which is higher than the mountain of the Temple, they turned their steps towards the south, and, just at the beginning of a small ascent, met the man who had been named to them; they followed and spoke to him as Jesus had commanded. He was much gratified by their words, and answered, that a supper had already been ordered to be prepared at his house (probably by Nicodemus), but that he had not been aware for whom, and was delighted to learn that it was for Jesus. This man's name was Heli, and he was the brother-in-law of Zachary of Hebron, in whose house Jesus had in the preceding year announced the death of John the Baptist. He had only one son, who was a Levite, and a friend of St. Luke, before the latter was called by our Lord, and five daughters, all of whom were unmarried. He went up every year with his servants for the festival of the Pasch, hired a room and prepared the Pasch for persons who had no friend in the town to lodge with. This year he had hired a supper-room which belonged to Nicodemus and Joseph of Arimathea. He showed the two Apostles its position and interior arrangement.

MEDITATION II.

The Supper-Room.

On the southern side of Mount Sion, not far from the ruined Castle of David, and the market held on the ascent leading to that Castle, there stood, towards the east, an ancient and solid building, between rows of thick trees, in the midst of a spacious court surrounded by strong walls. To the right and left of the entrance, other buildings were to be seen adjoining the wall, particularly to the right, where stood the dwelling of the major-domo, and close to it the house in which the Blessed Virgin and the holy women spent most of their time after the death of Jesus. The supper-room, which was originally larger, had formerly been inhabited by David's brave captains, who had there learned the use of arms.

Previous to the building of the Temple, the Ark of the Covenant had been deposited there for a considerable length of time, and traces of its presence were still to be found in an underground room. I have also seen the Prophet Malachy hidden beneath this same roof: he there wrote his prophecies concerning the Blessed Sacrament and the Sacrifice of the New Law. Solomon held this house in honour, and performed within its walls some figurative and symbolical action, which I have forgotten. When a great part of Jerusalem was destroyed by the Babylonians, this house was spared. I have seen many other things concerning this same house, but I only remember what I have now told.

This building was in a very dilapidated state when it became the property of Nicodemus and Joseph of Arimathea, who arranged the principal building in a very suitable manner, and let it as a supper-room to strangers coming to Jerusalem for the purpose of celebrating the festival of the Pasch. Thus it was that our Lord had made use of it the previous year. Moreover, the house and surrounding buildings served as warehouses for monuments and other stones, and as workshops for the labourers ; for Joseph of Arimathea possessed valuable quarries in his own country, from which he had large blocks of stone brought, that his workmen might fashion them, under his own eye, into tombs, architectural ornaments, and columns, for sale. Nicodemus had a share in this business, and used to spend many leisure hours himself in sculpturing. He worked in the room, or in a subterraneous apartment which was beneath it, excepting at the times of the festivals ; and this occupation having brought him into connection with Joseph of Arimathea, they had become friends, and often joined together in various trans-actions.

This morning, whilst Peter and John were conversing with the man who had hired the supper-room, I saw Nico-demus in the buildings to the left of the court, where a great many stones which filled up the passages leading to the supper-room had been placed. A week before, I had seen several persons engaged in putting the stones on one side, cleaning the court, and preparing the supper-room for the celebration of the Pasch; it even appears to me that there were among them some disciples of our Lord, perhaps Aram and Themein, the cousins of Joseph of Arimathea.

The supper-room, properly so called, was nearly in the centre of the court; its length was greater than its width; it was surrounded by a row of low pillars, and if the spaces between the pillars had been cleared, would have formed a part of the large inner room, for the whole edifice was, as it were, transparent; only it was usual, except on spe-cial occasions, for the passages to be closed up. The room was lighted by apertures at the top of the walls. In front, there was first a vestibule, into which three doors gave entrance; next, the large inner room, where several lamps hung from the platform; the walls were ornamented for the festival, half way up, with beautiful matting or tapestry, and an aperture had been made in the roof, and covered over with transparent blue gauze.

The back part of this room was separated from the rest by a curtain, also of blue transparent gauze. This division of the supper-room into three parts gave a resemblance to the Temple—thus forming the outer Court, the Holy, and the Holy of Holies. In the last of these divisions, on both sides, the dresses and other things necessary for the cele-bration of the feast were placed. In the centre there was a species of altar. A stone bench raised on three steps, and of a rectangular triangular shape, came out of the wall; it must have constituted the upper part of the oven used for roasting the Paschal Lamb, for to-day the steps were quite heated during the repast. I cannot describe in detail all that there was in this part of the room, but all kinds of arrangements were being made there for preparing the Paschal Supper. Above this hearth or altar, there was a species of niche in the wall, in front of which I saw an image of the Paschal Lamb, with a knife in its throat, and the blood appearing to flow drop by drop upon the altar; but I do not remember distinctly how that was done. In a niche in the wall there were three cupboards of various colours, which turned like our tabernacles, for opening or closing. A number of vessels used in the celebration of the Pasch were kept in them; later, the Blessed Sacrament was placed there.

In the rooms at the sides of the supper-room, there were some couches, on which thick coverlids rolled up were placed, and which could be used as beds. There were spacious cellars beneath the whole of this building. The Ark of the Covenant was formerly deposited under the very spot where the hearth was afterwards built. Five gutters, under the house, served to convey the refuse to the slope of the hill, on the upper part of which the house was built. I had previously seen Jesus preach and perform miraculous cures there, and the disciples frequently passed the night in the side rooms.

MEDITATION III.

Arrangements for eating the Paschal Lamb.

WHEN the disciples had spoken to Heli of Hebron, the latter went back into the house by the court, but they turned to the right, and hastened down the north side of the hill, through Sion. They passed over a bridge, and walking along a road covered with brambles, reached the other side of the ravine, which was in front of the Temple, and of the row of houses which were to the south of that building. There stood the house of the aged Simeon, who died in the Temple after the presentation of our Lord; and his sons, some of whom were disciples of Jesus in

secret, were actually living there. The Apostles spoke to
one of them, a tall dark-complexioned man, who held some
office in the Temple. They went with him to the eastern
side of the Temple, through that part of Ophel by which
Jesus made his entry into Jerusalem on Palm-Sunday, and
thence to the cattle-market, which stood in the town, to
the north of the Temple. In the southern part of this
market I saw little enclosures in which some beautiful
lambs were gambolling about. Here it was that lambs
for the Pasch were bought. I saw the son of Simeon
enter one of these enclosures; and the lambs gambolled
round him as if they knew him. He chose out four, which
were carried to the supper-room. In the afternoon I saw
him in the supper-room, engaged in preparing the Paschal
Lamb.

I saw Peter and John go to several different parts of
the town, and order various things. I saw them also
standing opposite the door of a house situated to the north
of Mount Calvary, where the disciples of Jesus lodged the
greatest part of the time, and which belonged to Seraphia
(afterwards called Veronica). Peter and John sent some
disciples from thence to the supper-room, giving them several commissions, which I have forgotten.

They also went into Seraphia's house, where they had
several arrangements to make. Her husband, who was a
member of the council, was usually absent and engaged in
business; but even when he was at home she saw little of
him. She was a woman of about the age of the Blessed
Virgin, and had long been connected with the Holy Family; for when the Child Jesus remained the three days
in Jerusalem after the feast, she it was who supplied him
with food.

The two Apostles took from thence, among other things,
the chalice of which our Lord made use in the institution
of the Holy Eucharist.

MEDITATION IV.

The Chalice used at the Last Supper.

THE chalice which the Apostles brought from Veronica's house was wonderful and mysterious in its appearance. It had been kept a long time in the Temple among other precious objects of great antiquity, the use and origin of which had been forgotten. The same has been in some degree the case in the Christian Church, where many consecrated jewels have been forgotten and fallen into disuse with time. Ancient vases and jewels, buried beneath the Temple, had often been dug up, sold, or reset. Thus it was that, by God's permission, this holy vessel, which none had ever been able to melt down on account of its being made of some unknown material, and which had been found by the priests in the treasury of the Temple among other objects no longer made use of, had been sold to some antiquaries. It was bought by Seraphia, was several times made use of by Jesus in the celebration of festivals, and, from the day of the Last Supper, became the exclusive property of the holy Christian community. This vessel was not always the same as when used by our Lord at his Last Supper, and perhaps it was upon that occasion that the various pieces which composed it were first put together. The great chalice stood upon a plate, out of which a species of tablet could also be drawn, and around it there were six little glasses. The great chalice contained another smaller vase; above it there was a small plate, and then came a round cover. A spoon was inserted in the foot of the chalice, and could be easily drawn out for use. All these different vessels were covered with fine linen, and, if I am not mistaken, were wrapped up in a case made of leather. The great chalice was composed of the cup and of the foot, which last must have been joined on to it at a later period, for it was of a different material. The cup was pear-shaped, massive, dark-coloured, and highly polished, with gold ornaments, and two small handles by which it could be lifted. The

foot was of virgin gold, elaborately worked, ornamented
with a serpent and a small bunch of grapes, and enriched
with precious stones.

The chalice was left in the Church of Jerusalem, in
the hands of St. James the Less ; and I see that it is still
preserved in that town—it will reappear some day, in the
same manner as before.   Other Churches took the little
cups which surrounded it ; one was taken to Antioch, and
another to Ephesus.   They belonged to the patriarchs,
who drank some mysterious beverage out of them when
they received or gave a Benediction, as I have seen many
times.

The great chalice had formerly been in the possession
of Abraham ; Melchisedech brought it with him from the
land of Semiramis to the land of Canaan, when he was
beginning to found some settlements on the spot where
Jerusalem was afterwards built ; he made use of it then
for offering sacrifice, when he offered bread and wine in
the presence of Abraham, and he left it in the possession
of that holy patriarch.   This same chalice had also been
preserved in Noah's Ark.

MEDITATION V.

Jesus goes up to Jerusalem.

In the morning, while the Apostles were engaged at
Jerusalem in preparing for the Pasch, Jesus, who had
remained at Bethania, took an affecting leave of the holy
women, of Lazarus, and of his Blessed Mother, and gave
them some final instructions.   I saw our Lord conversing
apart with his Mother, and he told her, among other
things, that he had sent Peter, the apostle of faith, and
John, the apostle of love, to prepare for the Pasch at Jerusalem.   He said, in speaking of Magdalen, whose grief
was excessive, that her love was great, but still somewhat
human, and that on this account her sorrow made her beside herself.   He spoke also of the schemes of the traitor

Judas, and the Blessed Virgin prayed for him. Judas had again left Bethania to go to Jerusalem, under pretence of paying some debts that were due. He spent his whole day in hurrying backwards and forwards from one Pharisee to another, and making his final agreements with them. He was shown the soldiers who had been engaged to seize the person of our Divine Saviour, and he so arranged his journeys to and fro as to be able to account for his absence. I beheld all his wicked schemes and all his thoughts. He was naturally active and obliging, but these good qualities were choked by avarice, ambition, and envy, which passions he made no effort to control. In our Lord's absence he had even performed miracles and healed the sick.

When our Lord announced to his Blessed Mother what was going to take place, she besought him, in the most touching terms, to let her die with him. But he exhorted her to show more calmness in her sorrow than the other women, told her that he should rise again, and named the very spot where he should appear to her. She did not weep much, but her grief was indescribable, and there was something almost awful in her look of deep recollection. Our Divine Lord returned thanks, as a loving Son, for all the love she had borne him, and pressed her to his heart. He also told her that he would make the Last Supper with her, spiritually, and named the hour at which she would receive his precious Body and Blood. Then once more he, in touching language, bade farewell to all, and gave them different instructions.

About twelve o'clock in the day, Jesus and the nine Apostles went from Bethania up to Jerusalem, followed by seven disciples, who, with the exception of Nathaniel and Silas, came from Jerusalem and the neighbourhood. Among these were John, Mark, and the son of the poor widow who, the Thursday previous, had offered her mite in the Temple, whilst Jesus was preaching there. Jesus had taken him into his company a few days before. The holy women set off later.

Jesus and his companions walked around Mount Olivet, about the valley of Josaphat, and even as far as Mount

Calvary. During the whole of this walk, he continued giving them instructions. He told the Apostles, among other things, that until then he had given them his bread and his wine, but that this day he was going to give them his Body and Blood, his whole self—all that he had and all that he was. The countenance of our Lord bore so touching an expression whilst he was speaking, that his whole soul seemed to breathe forth from his lips, and he appeared to be languishing with love and desire for the moment when he should give himself to man. His disciples did not understand him, but thought that he was speaking of the Paschal Lamb. No words can give an adequate idea of the love and resignation which were expressed in these last discourses of our Lord at Bethania, and on his way to Jerusalem.

The seven disciples who had followed our Lord to Jerusalem did not go there in his company, but carried the ceremonial habits for the Pasch to the supper-room, and then returned to the house of Mary, the mother of Mark. When Peter and John came to the supper-room with the chalice, all the ceremonial habits were already in the vestibule, whither they had been brought by his disciples and some companions. They had also hung the walls with drapery, cleared the higher openings in the sides, and put up three lamps. Peter and John then went to the Valley of Josaphat, and summoned our Lord and the twelve Apostles. The disciples and friends who were also to make their Pasch in the supper-room, came later.

MEDITATION VI.

The Last Pasch.

JESUS and his disciples ate the Paschal Lamb in the supper-room. They divided into three groups. Jesus ate the Paschal Lamb with the twelve Apostles in the supper-room, properly so called; Nathaniel with twelve other disciples in one of the lateral rooms, and Eliacim (the son of Cleophas and Mary, the daughter of Heli), who had been a disciple of John the Baptist, with twelve more, in another side-room.

Three lambs were immolated for them in the Temple, but there was a fourth lamb which was immolated in the supper-room, and was the one eaten by Jesus with his Apostles. Judas was not aware of this circumstance, because being engaged in plotting his betrayal of our Lord, he only returned a few moments before the repast, and after the immolation of the lamb had taken place. Most touching was the scene of the immolation of the lamb to be eaten by Jesus and his Apostles ; it took place in the vestibule of the supper-room. The Apostles and disciples were present, singing the 118th Psalm. Jesus spoke of a new period then beginning, and said that the sacrifice of Moses and the figure of the Paschal Lamb were about to receive their accomplishment, but that on this very account, the lamb was to be immolated in the same manner as formerly in Egypt, and that they were really about to go forth from the house of bondage.

The vessels and necessary instruments were prepared, and then the attendants brought a beautiful little lamb, decorated with a crown, which was sent to the Blessed Virgin in the room where she had remained with the other holy women. The lamb was fastened with its back against a board by a cord around its body, and reminded me of Jesus tied to the pillar and scourged. The son of Simeon held the lamb's head; Jesus made a slight incision in its neck with the point of a knife, which he then gave to the son of Simeon, that he might complete killing it. Jesus appeared to inflict the wound with a feeling of repugnance, and he was quick in his movements, although his countenance was grave, and his manner such as to inspire respect. The blood flowed into a basin, and the attendants brought a branch of hyssop, which Jesus dipped in it. Then he went to the door of the room, stained the side-posts and the lock with blood, and placed the branch which had been dipped in blood above the door. He then spoke to the disciples, and told them, among other things, that the exterminating angel would pass by, that they would adore in that room without fear or anxiety, when he, the true Paschal Lamb, should have been immolated —that a new epoch and a new sacrifice were about to begin, which would last to the end of the world.

They then went to the other side of the room, near the hearth where the Ark of the Covenant had formerly stood. Fire had already been lighted there, and Jesus poured some blood upon the hearth, consecrating it as an altar; and the remainder of the blood and the fat were thrown on the fire beneath the altar, after which Jesus, followed by his Apostles, walked round the supper-room, singing some psalms, and consecrating it as a new Temple. The doors were all closed during this time. Meanwhile the son of Simeon had completed the preparation of the lamb. He passed a stake through its body, fastening the front legs on a cross piece of wood, and stretching the hind ones along the stake. It bore a strong resemblance to Jesus on the cross, and was placed in the oven, to be there roasted with the three other lambs brought from the Temple.

The Paschal Lambs of the Jews were all immolated in the vestibule of the Temple, but in different parts, according as the persons who were to eat them were rich, or poor, or strangers.* The Paschal Lamb belonging to Jesus was not immolated in the Temple, but everything else was done strictly according to the law. Jesus again addressed his disciples, saying that the lamb was but a figure, that he himself would next day be the true Paschal Lamb, together with other things which I have forgotten.

When Jesus had finished his instructions concerning the Paschal Lamb and its signification, the time being come, and Judas also returned, the tables were set out. The disciples put on travelling dresses which were in the vestibule, different shoes, a white robe resembling a shirt, and a cloak, which was short in front and longer behind,

* She here again explained the manner in which the families assembled together, and in what numbers. But the writer has forgotten her words.

their sleeves were large and turned back, and they girded up their clothes around the waist. Each party went to their own table; and two sets of disciples in the side rooms, and our Lord and his Apostles in the supper-room. They held staves in their hands, and went two and two to the table, where they remained standing, each in his own place, with the stave resting on his arms, and his hands upraised.

The table was narrow, and about half a foot higher than the knees of a man; in shape it resembled a horse-shoe, and opposite Jesus, in the inner part of the half-circle, there was a space left vacant, that the attendants might be able to set down the dishes. As far as I can remember, John, James the Greater, and James the Less sat on the right-hand of Jesus; after them Bartholomew, and then, round the corner, Thomas and Judas Iscariot. Peter, Andrew, and Thaddeus sat on the left of Jesus; next came Simon, and then (round the corner) Matthew and Philip.

The Paschal Lamb was placed on a dish in the centre of the table. Its head rested on its front legs, which were fastened to a cross-stick, its hind legs being stretched out, and the dish was garnished with garlic. By the side there was a dish with the Paschal roast meat, then came a plate with green vegetables balanced against each other, and another plate with small bundles of bitter herbs, which had the appearance of aromatic herbs. Opposite Jesus there was also one dish with different herbs, and a second containing a brown-coloured sauce or beverage. The guests had before them some round loaves instead of plates, and they used ivory knives.

After the prayer, the major-domo laid the knife for cutting the lamb on the table before Jesus, who placed a cup of wine before him, and filled six other cups, each one of which stood between two Apostles. Jesus blessed the wine and drank, and the Apostles drank two together out of one cup. Then our Lord proceeded to cut up the lamb; his Apostles presented their pieces of bread in turn, and each received his share. They ate it in haste, separating the flesh from the bone, by means of their ivory knives, and the bones were afterwards burnt. They also ate the garlic and green herbs in haste, dipping them in the sauce. All this time they remained standing, only leaning slightly on the backs of their seats. Jesus broke one of the loaves of unleavened bread, covered up a part of it, and divided the remainder among his Apostles. Another cup of wine was brought, but Jesus drank not of it : 'Take this,' he said, 'and divide it among you, *for I will not drink from henceforth of the fruit of the vine, until that day when I shall drink it with you new in the kingdom of my Father*' (Matt. xxvi. 29). When they had drunk the wine, they sang a hymn ; then Jesus prayed or taught, and they again washed their hands. After this they sat down.

Our Lord cut up another lamb, which was carried to the holy women in one of the buildings of the court, where they were seated at table. The Apostles ate some more vegetables and lettuce. The countenance of our Divine Saviour bore an indescribable expression of serenity and recollection, greater than I had ever before seen. He bade the Apostles forget all their cares. The Blessed Virgin also, as she sat at table with the other women, looked most placid and calm. When the other women came up, and took hold of her veil to make her turn round and speak to them, her every movement expressed the sweetest self-control and placidity of spirit.

At first Jesus conversed lovingly and calmly with his disciples, but after a while he became grave and sad : '*Amen, Amen, I say to you, that one of you is about to betray me :*' he said, '*he that dippeth his hand with me in the dish*' (Matt. xxvi. 21, 23). Jesus was then distributing the lettuce, of which there was only one dish, to those Apostles who were by his side, and he had given Judas, who was nearly opposite to him, the office of distributing it to the others. When Jesus spoke of a traitor, an expression which filled all the Apostles with fear, he said : '*he that dippeth his hand with me in the dish,*' which means : ' one of the twelve who are eating and drinking with me—one of those with whom I am eating bread.' He did not plainly point out Judas to the others by these words; for *to dip the hand in the same dish* was an expression used to signify the most friendly and intimate intercourse. He was desirous, however, to give a warning to Judas, who was then really dipping his hand in the dish with our Saviour, to distribute the lettuce. Jesus continued to speak: '*The Son of man indeed goeth,*' he said, '*as it is written of him: but woe to that man by whom the Son of man shall be betrayed: It were better for him if that man had not been born.*'

The Apostles were very much troubled, and each one of them exclaimed: '*Lord, is it I?*' for they were all perfectly aware that they did not entirely understand his words. Peter leaned towards John, behind Jesus, and made him a sign to ask our Lord who the traitor was to be, for, having so often been reproved by our Lord, he trembled lest it should be himself who was referred to. John was seated at the right hand of Jesus, and as all were leaning on their left arms, using the right to eat, his head was close to the bosom of Jesus. He leaned then on his breast and said: '*Lord, who is it?*' I did not see Jesus say to him with his lips: '*He it is to whom I shall reach bread dipped.*' I do not know whether he whispered it to him, but John knew it, when Jesus having dipped the bread, which was covered with lettuce, gave it tenderly to Judas, who also asked: '*Is it I, Lord?*' Jesus looked at him with love, and answered him in general terms. Among the Jews, to give bread dipped was a mark of friendship and confidence; Jesus on this occasion gave Judas the morsel, in order thus to warn him, without making known his guilt to the others. But the heart of Judas burned with anger, and during the whole time of the repast, I saw a frightful little figure seated at his feet, and sometimes ascending to his heart. I did not see John repeat to Peter what he had learned from Jesus, but he set his fears at rest by a look.

MEDITATION VII.

The Washing of the Feet.

THEY arose from table, and whilst they were arranging their clothes, as they usually did before making their solemn prayer, the major-domo came in with two servants to take away the table. Jesus, standing in the midst of his Apostles, spoke to them long, in a most solemn manner. I could not repeat exactly his whole discourse, but I remember he spoke of his kingdom, of his going to his Father, of what he would leave them now 'that he was about to be taken away, &c. He also gave them some instructions concerning penance, the confession of sin, repentance, and justification.

I felt that these instructions referred to the washing of the feet, and I saw that all the Apostles acknowledged their sins and repented of them, with the exception of Judas. This discourse was long and solemn. When it was concluded, Jesus sent John and James the Less to fetch water from the vestibule, and he told the Apostles to arrange the seats in a half circle. He went himself into the vestibule, where he girded himself with a towel. During this time, the Apostles spoke among themselves, and began speculating as to which of them would be the greatest, for our Lord having expressly announced that he was about to leave them and that his kingdom was near at hand, they felt strengthened anew in their idea that he had secret plans, and that he was referring to some earthly triumph which would be theirs at the last moment.

Meanwhile Jesus, in the vestibule, told John to take a basin, and James a pitcher filled with water, with which they followed him into the room, where the major-domo had placed another empty basin.

Jesus, on returning to his disciples in so humble a manner, addressed them a few words of reproach on the subject of the dispute which had arisen between them, and said among other things, that he himself was their servant, and that they were to sit down, for him to wash their feet. They sat down, therefore, in the same order as they had sat at table. Jesus went from one to the other, poured water from the basin which John carried on the feet of each, and then, taking the end of the towel wherewith he was girded, wiped them. Most loving and tender was the manner of our Lord while thus humbling himself at the feet of his Apostles.

Peter, when his turn came, endeavoured through humility to prevent Jesus from washing his feet: '*Lord*,' he exclaimed, '*dost thou wash my feet ?*' Jesus answered: '*What I do, thou knowest not now, but thou shalt know hereafter.*' It appeared to me that he said to him privately: 'Simon, thou hast merited for my Father to reveal to thee who I am, whence I come, and whither I am going, thou alone hast expressly confessed it, therefore upon thee will I build my Church, and the gates of hell shall not prevail against it. My power will remain with thy successors to the end of the world.'

Jesus showed him to the other Apostles, and said, that when he should be no more present among them, Peter was to fill his place in their regard. Peter said: '*Thou shalt never wash my feet !*' Our Lord replied: '*If I wash thee not, thou shalt have no part with me.*' Then Peter exclaimed: '*Lord, not only my feet, but also my hands and my head.*' Jesus replied: '*He that is washed, needeth not but to wash his feet, but is clean wholly. And you are clean, but not all.*'

By these last words he referred to Judas. He had spoken of the washing of the feet as signifying purification from daily faults, because the feet, which are continually in contact with the earth, are also continually liable to be soiled, unless great care is taken.

This washing of the feet was spiritual, and served as a species of absolution. Peter, in his zeal, saw nothing in it but too great an act of abasement on the part of his Master; he knew not that to save him Jesus would the very next day humble himself even to the ignominious death of the cross.

When Jesus washed the feet of Judas, it was in the

most loving and affecting manner; he bent his sacred face even on to the feet of the traitor; and in a low voice bade him now at least enter into himself, for that he had been a faithless traitor for the last year. Judas appeared to be anxious to pay no heed whatever to his words, and spoke to John, upon which Peter became angry, and exclaimed: 'Judas, the Master speaks to thee!' Then Judas made our Lord some vague, evasive reply, such as, 'Heaven forbid, Lord!' The others had not remarked that Jesus was speaking to Judas, for his words were uttered in a low voice, in order not to be heard by them, and besides, they were all engaged in putting on their shoes. Nothing in the whole course of the Passion grieved Jesus so deeply as the treason of Judas.

Jesus finally washed the feet of John and James.

He then spoke again on the subject of humility, telling them that he that was the greatest among them was to be as their servant, and that henceforth they were to wash one another's feet. Then he put on his garments, and the Apostles let down their clothes, which they had girded up before eating the Paschal Lamb.

MEDITATION VIII.

Institution of the Holy Eucharist.

By command of our Lord, the major-domo had again laid out the table, which he had raised a little; then, having placed it once more in the middle of the room, he stood one urn filled with wine, and another with water underneath it. Peter and John went into the part of the room near the hearth, to get the chalice which they had brought from Seraphia's house, and which was still wrapped up in its covering. They carried it between them as if they had been carrying a tabernacle, and placed it on the table before Jesus. An oval plate stood there, with three fine white azymous loaves, placed on a piece of linen, by the side of the half loaf which Jesus had set aside during the Paschal meal, also a jar containing wine and water, and three boxes, one filled with thick oil, a second with liquid oil, and the third empty.

In earlier times, it had been the practice for all at table to eat of the same loaf and drink of the same cup at the end of the meal, thereby to express their friendship and brotherly love, and to welcome and bid farewell to each other. I think Scripture must contain something upon this subject.

On the day of the Last Supper, Jesus raised this custom (which had hitherto been no more than a sym- bolical and figurative rite) to the dignity of the holiest of sacraments. One of the charges brought before Caiphas, on occasion of the treason of Judas, was, that Jesus had introduced a novelty into the Paschal ceremonies, but Nicodemus proved from Scripture that it was an ancient practice.

Jesus was seated between Peter and John, the doors were closed, and everything was done in the most myste- rious and imposing manner. When the chalice was taken out of its covering, Jesus prayed, and spoke to his Apos- tles with the utmost solemnity. I saw him giving them an explanation of the Supper, and of the entire ceremony, and I was forcibly reminded of a priest teaching others to say Mass.

He then drew a species of shelf with grooves from the board on which the jars stood, and taking a piece of white linen with which the chalice was covered, spread it over the board and shelf. I then saw him lift a round plate, which he placed on this same shelf, off the top of the chalice. He next took the azymous loaves from beneath the linen with which they were covered, and placed them before him on the board ; then he took out of the chalice a smaller vase, and ranged the six little glasses on each side of it. Then he blessed the bread and also the oil, to the best of my belief, after which he lifted up the paten with the loaves upon it, in his two hands, raised his eyes, prayed offered, and replaced the paten on the table, cover- ing it up again. He then took the chalice, had some wine poured into it by Peter, and some water, which he first blessed, by John, adding to it a little more water, which he poured into a small spoon, and after this he blessed the chalice, raised it up with a prayer, made the oblation, and replaced it on the table.

John and Peter poured some water on his hands, which he held over the plate on which the azymous loaves had been placed ; then he took a little of the water which had been poured on his hands, in the spoon that he had taken out of the lower part of the chalice, and poured it on theirs. After this, the vase was passed round the table, and all the Apostles washed their hands in it. I do not remember whether this was the precise order in which these ceremonies were performed ; all I know is, that they reminded me in a striking manner of the holy sacrifice of the Mass.

Meanwhile, our Divine Lord became more and more tender and loving in his demeanour ; he told his Apostles that he was about to give them all that he had, namely, his entire self, and he looked as though perfectly transformed by love. I saw him becoming transparent, until he resembled a luminous shadow. He broke the bread into several pieces, which he laid together on the paten, and then took a corner of the first piece and dropped it into the chalice. At the moment when he was doing this, I seemed to see the Blessed Virgin receiving the Holy Sacrament in a spiritual manner, although she was not present in the supper-room. I do not know how it was done, but I thought I saw her enter without touching the ground, and come before our Lord to receive the Holy Eucharist ; after which I saw her no more. Jesus had told her in the morning, at Bethania, that he would keep the Pasch with her spiritually, and he had named the hour at which she was to betake herself to prayer, in order to receive it in spirit.

Again he prayed and taught ; his words came forth from his lips like fire and light, and entered into each of the Apostles, with the exception of Judas. He took the paten with the pieces of bread (I do not know whether he had placed it on the chalice) and said : ' *Take and eat* ;

this is my Body which is given for you.' He stretched
forth his right hand as if to bless, and, whilst he did so,
a brilliant light came from him, his words were luminous,
the bread entered the mouths of the Apostles as a brilliant substance, and light seemed to penetrate and surround them all, Judas alone remaining dark. Jesus presented the bread first to Peter, next to John* and then he
made a sign to Judas to approach. Judas was thus the
third who received the Adorable Sacrament, but the words
of our Lord appeared to turn aside from the mouth of the
traitor, and come back to their Divine Author. So perturbed was I in spirit at this sight, that my feelings cannot be described. Jesus said to him : *' That which thou
dost, do quickly.'* He then administered the Blessed Sacrament to the other Apostles, who approached two and
two.

Jesus raised the chalice by its two handles to a level
with his face, and pronounced the words of consecration
Whilst doing so, he appeared wholly transfigured, as it
were transparent, and as though entirely passing into what
he was going to give his Apostles. He made Peter and
John drink from the chalice which he held in his hand,
and then placed it again on the table. John poured the
Divine Blood from the chalice into the smaller glasses, and
Peter presented them to the Apostles, two of whom drank
together out of the same cup. I think, but am not quite
certain, that Judas also partook of the chalice ; he did not
return to his place, but immediately left the supper-room,
and the other Apostles thought that Jesus had given him
some commission to do. He left without praying or making any thanksgiving, and hence you may perceive how
sinful it is to neglect returning thanks either after receiving our daily food, or after partaking of the Life-Giving
Bread of Angels. During the entire meal, I had seen a
frightful little figure, with one foot like a dried bone, remaining close to Judas, but when he had reached the door,

---

* She was not certain that the Blessed Sacrament was administered in the order given above, for on another occasion she had
seen John the last to receive.

I beheld three devils pressing round him; one entered
into his mouth, the second urged him on, and the third
preceded him. It was night, and they seemed to be light-
ing him, whilst he hurried onward like a madman.

Our Lord poured a few drops of the Precious Blood
remaining in the chalice into the little vase of which I
have already spoken, and then placed his fingers over the
chalice, while Peter and John poured water and wine upon
them. This done, he caused them to drink again from
the chalice, and what remained of its contents was poured
into the smaller glasses, and distributed to the other
Apostles. Then Jesus wiped the chalice, put into it the
little vase containing the remainder of the Divine Blood,
and placed over it the paten with the fragments of the
consecrated bread, after which he again put on the cover,
wrapped up the chalice, and stood it in the midst of the
six small cups. I saw the Apostles receive in communion
these remains of the Adorable Sacrament, after the Resurrection.

I do not remember seeing our Lord himself eat and
drink of the consecrated elements, neither did I see Melchisedech, when offering the bread and wine, taste of them
himself. It was made known to me why priests partake
of them, although Jesus did not.

Here Sister Emmerich looked suddenly up, and appeared to be listening. Some explanation was given her
on this subject, but the following words were all that she
could repeat to us : ' If the office of distributing it had
been given to angels, they would not have partaken, but
if priests did not partake, the Blessed Eucharist would be
lost — it is through their participation that it is preserved.'

There was an indescribable solemnity and order in all
the actions of Jesus during the institution of the Holy
Eucharist, and his every movement was most majestic. I
saw the Apostles noting things down in the little rolls of
parchment which they carried on their persons. Several
times during the ceremonies I remarked that they bowed
to each other, in the same way that our priests do.

MEDITATION IX.

Private Instructions and Consecrations.

JESUS gave his Apostles some private instructions; he told them how they were to preserve the Blessed Sacrament in memory of him, even to the end of the world; he taught them the necessary forms for making use of and communicating it, and in what manner they were, by degrees, to teach and publish this mystery; finally he told them when they were to receive what remained of the consecrated Elements, when to give some to the Blessed Virgin, and how to consecrate, themselves, after he should have sent them the Divine Comforter. He then spoke concerning the priesthood, the sacred unction, and the preparation of the Chrism and Holy Oils.* He had there three boxes, two of which contained a mixture of oil and balm. He taught them how to make this mixture, what parts of the body were to be anointed with them, and upon what occasions. I remember, among other things, that he mentioned a case in which the Holy Eucharist could not be administered; perhaps what he said had reference to Extreme Unction, for my recollections on this point are not very clear. He spoke of different kinds of anointing, and in particular of that of kings, and he said that even wicked kings who were anointed, derived from it especial powers. He put ointment and oil in the empty box, and mixed them together, but I cannot say for cer-

---

* It was not without surprise that the editor, some years after these things had been related by Sister Emmerich, read, in the Latin edition of the Roman Catechism (Mayence, Muller), in reference to the Sacrament of Confirmation, that, according to the tradition of the holy Pope Fabian, Jesus taught his Apostles in what manner they were to prepare the Holy Chrism, after the institution of the Blessed Sacrament. The Pope says expressly, in the 54th paragraph of his Second Epistle to the Bishops of the East: ' Our predecessors received from the Apostles and delivered to us that our Saviour Jesus Christ, after having made the Last Supper with his Apostles and washed their feet, taught them how to prepare the Holy Chrism.'

tain whether it was at this moment, or at the time of the
consecration of the bread, that he blessed the oil.

I then saw Jesus anoint Peter and John, on whose
hands he had already poured the water which had flowed
on his own, and two whom he had given to drink out of
the chalice.   Then he laid his hands on their shoulders
and heads, while they, on their part, joined their hands
and crossed their thumbs, bowing down profoundly before
him—I am not sure whether they did not even kneel. He
anointed the thumb and fore-finger of each of their hands,
and marked a cross on their heads with Chrism. He said
also that this would remain with them unto the end of
the world.

James the Less, Andrew, James the Greater, and Bartholomew, were also consecrated. I saw likewise that on
Peter's bosom he crossed a sort of stole worn round the
neck, whilst on the others he simply placed it crosswise,
from the right shoulder to the left side. I do not know
whether this was done at the time of the institution of
the Blessed Sacrament, or only for the anointing.

I understood that Jesus communicated to them by this
unction something essential and supernatural, beyond my
power to describe. He told them that when they should
have received the Holy Spirit they were to consecrate the
bread and wine, and anoint the other Apostles. It was
made known to me then that, on the day of Pentecost,
Peter and John imposed their hands upon the other Apostles, and a week later upon several of the disciples. After
the Resurrection, John gave the Adorable Sacrament for
the first time to the Blessed Virgin. This event was
solemnised as a festival among the Apostles. It is a festival no longer kept in the Church on earth, but I see it
celebrated in the Church triumphant. For the first few
days after Pentecost I saw only Peter and John consecrate
the Blessed Eucharist, but after that the others also consecrated.

Our Lord next proceeded to bless fire in a brass vessel,
and care was taken that it should not go out, but it was
kept near the spot where the Blessed Sacrament had been

deposited, in one division of the ancient Paschal hearth, and fire was always taken from it when needed for spiritual purposes.

All that Jesus did upon this occasion was done in private, and taught equally in private. The Church has retained all that was essential of these secret instructions, and, under the inspiration of the Holy Ghost, developed and adapted them to all her requirements.

Whether Peter and John were both consecrated bishops, or Peter alone as bishop and John as priest, or to what dignity the other four Apostles were raised, I cannot pretend to say. But the different ways in which our Lord arranged the Apostles' stoles appear to indicate different degrees of consecration.

When these holy ceremonies were concluded, the chalice (near which the blessed Chrism also stood) was re-covered, and the Adorable Sacrament carried by Peter and John into the back part of the room, which was divided off by a curtain, and from thenceforth became the Sanctuary. The spot where the Blessed Sacrament was deposited was not very far above the Paschal stove. Joseph of Arimathea and Nicodemus took care of the Sanctuary and of the supper-room during the absence of the Apostles.

Jesus again instructed his Apostles for a considerable length of time, and also prayed several times. He frequently appeared to be conversing with his Heavenly Father, and to be overflowing with enthusiasm and love. The Apostles also were full of joy and zeal, and asked him various questions which he forthwith answered. The scriptures must contain much of this last discourse and conversation. He told Peter and John different things to be made known later to the other Apostles, who in their turn were to communicate them to the disciples and holy women, according to the capacity of each for such knowledge. He had a private conversation with John, whom he told that his life would be longer than the lives of the others. He spoke to him also concerning seven Churches, some crowns and angels, and instructed him in the meaning of certain mysterious figures, which signified, to the best of my belief, different epochs. The other Apostles were slightly jealous of this confidential communication being made to John.

Jesus spoke also of the traitor. ' Now he is doing this or that,' he said, and I, in fact, saw Judas doing exactly as he said of him. As Peter was vehemently protesting that he would always remain faithful, our Lord said to him : ' *Simon, Simon, behold Satan hath desired to have you that he may sift you as wheat. But I have prayed for thee that thy faith fail not: and thou being once converted, confirm thy brethren.*'

Again, our Lord said, that whither he was going they could not follow him, when Peter exclaimed: '*Lord, I am ready to go with thee both into prison and to death.*' And Jesus replied : ' *Amen, amen, I say to thee, Before the cock crow twice, thou shalt deny me thrice.*'

Jesus, while making known to his Apostles that trying times were at hand for them, said: ' *When I sent you without purse, or scrip, or shoes, did you want anything ?*' They answered : ' *Nothing.*' ' *But now,*' he continued, ' *he that hath a purse let him take it, and likewise a scrip, and he that hath not, let him sell his coat and buy a sword. For I say to you, that this that is written must yet be ful-filled in me :* AND WITH THE WICKED WAS HE RECKONED. *For the things concerning me have an end.*' The Apostles only understood his words in a carnal sense, and Peter showed him two swords, which were short and thick, like cleavers. Jesus said: ' *It is enough:* let us go hence.' Then they sang the thanksgiving hymn, put the table on one side, and went into the vestibule.

There, Jesus found his Mother, Mary of Cleophas, and Magdalen, who earnestly besought him not to go to Mount Olivet, for a report had spread that his enemies were seeking to lay hands on him. But Jesus comforted them in few words, and hastened onward—it being then about nine o'clock. They went down the road by which Peter and John had come to the supper-room, and directed their steps towards Mount Olivet.

I have always seen the Pasch and the institution of

the Blessed Sacrament take place in the order related above. But my feelings were each time so strongly excited and my emotion so great, that I could not give much attention to all the details, but now I have seen them more distinctly. No words can describe how painful and exhausting is such a sight as that of beholding the hidden recesses of hearts, the love and constancy of our Saviour, and to know at the same time all that is going to befall him. How would it be possible to observe all that is merely external! the heart is overflowing with admiration, gratitude, and love—the blindness of men seems perfectly incomprehensible—and the soul is overwhelmed with sorrow at the thought of the ingratitude of the whole world, and of her own sins!

The eating of the Paschal Lamb was performed by Jesus rapidly, and in entire conformity with all the legal ordinances. The Pharisees were in the habit of adding some minute and superstitious ceremonies.

THE PASSION.

'If thou knowest not how to meditate on high and heavenly things, rest on the Passion of Christ, and willingly dwell in his sacred wounds. For, if thou fly devoutly to the wounds and precious stigmas of Jesus, thou shalt feel great comfort in tribulation.' *Imit. of Christ*, book ii. chap. i.

INTRODUCTION.

On the evening of the 18th of February, 1823, a friend of Sister Emmerich went up to the bed, where she was lying apparently asleep; and being much struck by the beautiful and mournful expression of her countenance, felt himself inwardly inspired to raise his heart fervently to God, and offer the Passion of Christ to the Eternal Father, in union with the sufferings of all those who have carried their cross after him. While making this short prayer, he chanced to fix his eyes for a moment upon the stigmatised hands of Sister Emmerich. She immediately hid them under the counterpane, starting as if some one had given her a blow. He felt surprised at this, and asked her, 'What has happened to you?' 'Many things,' she answered, in an expressive tone. Whilst he was considering what her meaning could be, she appeared to be asleep. At the end of about a quarter of an hour, she suddenly started up with all the eagerness of a person having a violent struggle with another, stretched out both her arms, clenching her hand, as if to repel an enemy standing on the left side of her bed, and exclaimed in an indignant voice: 'What do you mean by this contract of Magdalum?' Then

she continued to speak with the warmth of a person who
is being questioned during a quarrel—'Yes, it is that accursed spirit—the liar from the beginning—Satan, who is
reproaching him about the Magdalum contract, and other
things of the same nature, and says that he spent all that
money upon himself.' When asked, 'Who has spent
money? Who is being spoken to in that way?' she replied,
'Jesus, my adorable Spouse, on Mount Olivet.' Then she
again turned to the left, with menacing gestures, and exclaimed, 'What meanest thou, O father of lies, with thy
Magdalum contract? Did he not deliver twenty-seven poor
prisoners at Thirza, with the money derived from the sale
of Magdalum? I saw him, and thou darest to say that he
has brought confusion into the whole estate, driven out its
inhabitants, and squandered the money for which it was
sold? But thy time is come, accursed spirit! thou wilt be
chained, and his heel will crush thy head.'

Here she was interrupted by the entrance of another
person ; her friends thought that she was in delirium, and
pitied her. The following morning she owned that the
previous night she had imagined herself to be following
our Saviour to the Garden of Olives, after the institution
of the Blessed Eucharist, but that just at that moment
some one having looked at the stigmas on her hands
with a degree of veneration, she felt so horrified at this
being done in the presence of our Lord, that she hastily
hid them, with a feeling of pain. She then related her
vision of what took place in the Garden of Olives, and as
she continued her narrations the following days, the friend
who was listening to her was enabled to connect the different scenes of the Passion together. But as, during
Lent, she was also celebrating the combats of our Lord
with Satan in the desert, she had to endure in her own
person many sufferings and temptations. Hence there were
a few pauses in the history of the Passion, which were,
however, easily filled up by means of some later communications.

She usually spoke in common German, but when in a
state of ecstasy, her language became much purer, and

her narrations partook at once of child-like simplicity and dignified inspiration. Her friend wrote down all that she had said, directly he returned to his own apartments; for it was seldom that he could so much as even take notes in her presence. The Giver of all good gifts bestowed upon him memory, zeal, and strength to bear much trouble and fatigue, so that he has been enabled to bring this work to a conclusion. His conscience tells him that he has done his best, and he humbly begs the reader, if satisfied with the result of his labours, to bestow upon him the alms of an occasional prayer.

CHAPTER I.

Jesus in the Garden of Olives.

WHEN Jesus left the supper-room with the eleven Apostles, after the institution of the Adorable Sacrament of the Altar, his soul was deeply oppressed and his sorrow on the increase. He led the eleven, by an unfrequented path, to the Valley of Josaphat. As they left the house, I saw the moon, which was not yet quite at the full, rising in front of the mountain.

Our Divine Lord, as he wandered with his Apostles about the valley, told them that here he should one day return to judge the world, but not in a state of poverty and humiliation, as he then was, and that men would tremble with fear, and cry: '*Mountains, fall upon us!*' His disciples did not understand him, and thought, by no means for the first time that night, that weakness and exhaustion had affected his brain. He said to them again: '*All you shall be scandalised in me this night. For it is written:* I WILL STRIKE THE SHEPHERD, AND THE SHEEP OF THE FLOCK SHALL BE DISPERSED. *But after I shall be risen again, I will go before you into Galilee.*'

The Apostles were still in some degree animated by

the spirit of enthusiasm and devotion with which their reception of the Blessed Sacrament and the solemn and affecting words of Jesus had inspired them. They eagerly crowded round him, and expressed their love in a thousand different ways, earnestly protesting that they would never abandon him. But as Jesus continued to talk in the same strain, Peter exclaimed: ' *Although all shall be scandalised in thee, I will never be scandalised !'* and our Lord answered him: ' *Amen, I say to thee, that in this night, before the cock crow, thou wilt deny me thrice.'* But Peter still insisted, saying: ' *Yea, though I should die with thee, I will not deny thee.'* And the others all said the same. They walked onward and stopped, by turns, for the sadness of our Divine Lord continued to increase. The Apostles tried to comfort him by human arguments, assuring him that what he foresaw would not come to pass. They tired themselves in these vain efforts, began to doubt, and were assailed by temptation.

They crossed the brook Cedron, not by the bridge where, a few hours later, Jesus was taken prisoner, but by another, for they had left the direct road. Gethsemani, whither they were going, was about a mile and a half distant from the supper-hall, for it was three quarters of a mile from the supper-hall to the Valley of Josaphat, and about as far from thence to Gethsemani. The place called Gethsemani (where latterly Jesus had several times passed the night with his disciples) was a large garden, surrounded by a hedge, and containing only some fruit trees and flowers, while outside there stood a few deserted unclosed buildings.

The Apostles and several other persons had keys of this garden, which was used sometimes as a pleasure ground, and sometimes as a place of retirement for prayer. Some arbours made of leaves and branches had been raised there, and eight of the Apostles remained in them, and were later joined by others of the disciples. The Garden of Olives was separated by a road from that of Gethsemani, and was open. surrounded only by an

earthern wall, and smaller than the Garden of Gethsemani.
There were caverns, terraces, and many olive-trees to be
seen in this garden, and it was easy to find there a suitable spot for prayer and meditation. It was to the wildest
part that Jesus went to pray.

It was about nine o'clock when Jesus reached Gethsemani with his disciples. The moon had risen, and
already gave light in the sky, although the earth was still
dark. Jesus was most sorrowful, and told his Apostles
that danger was at hand. The disciples felt uneasy, and
he told eight of those who were following him, to remain
in the Garden of Gethsemani whilst he went on to pray.
He took with him Peter, James, and John, and going on
a little further, entered into the Garden of Olives. No
words can describe the sorrow which then oppressed his
soul, for the time of trial was near. John asked him how
it was that he, who had hitherto always consoled them,
could now be so dejected? '_My soul is sorrowful even
unto death_,' was his reply. And he beheld sufferings and
temptations surrounding him on all sides, and drawing
nearer and nearer, under the forms of frightful figures
borne on clouds. Then it was that he said to the three
Apostles : '_Stay you here and watch with me. Pray, lest
ye enter into temptation._' Jesus went a few steps to the
left, down a hill, and concealed himself beneath a rock, in
a grotto about six feet deep, while the Apostles remained
in a species of hollow above. The earth sank gradually
the further you entered this grotto, and the plants which
were hanging from the rock screened its interior like a
curtain from persons outside.

When Jesus left his disciples, I saw a number of
frightful figures surrounding him in an ever-narrowing
circle.

His sorrow and anguish of soul continued to increase,
and he was trembling all over when he entered the grotto
to pray, like a wayworn traveller hurriedly seeking shelter
from a sudden storm, but the awful visions pursued him
even there, and became more and more clear and distinct.
Alas ! this small cavern appeared to contain the awful

picture of all the sins which had been or were to be committed from the fall of Adam to the end of the world, and
of the punishment which they deserved. It was here, on
Mount Olivet, that Adam and Eve took refuge when
driven out of Paradise to wander homeless on earth,
and they had wept and bewailed themselves in this very
grotto.

I felt that Jesus, in delivering himself up to Divine
Justice in satisfaction for the sins of the world, caused
his divinity to return, in some sort, into the bosom of the
Holy Trinity, concentrated himself, so to speak, in his
pure, loving and innocent humanity, and strong only in
his ineffable love, gave it up to anguish and suffering.

He fell on his face, overwhelmed with unspeakable
sorrow, and all the sins of the world displayed themselves
before him, under countless forms and in all their real de-
formity. He took them all upon himself, and in his prayer
offered his own adorable Person to the justice of his Heavenly Father, in payment for so awful a debt. But Satan,
who was enthroned amid all these horrors, and even filled
with diabolical joy at the sight of them, let loose his fury
against Jesus, and displayed before the eyes of his soul
increasingly awful visions, at the same time addressing his
adorable humanity in words such as these : ' Takest thou
even this sin upon thyself? Art thou willing to bear its
penalty? Art thou prepared to satisfy for all these sins ?'

And now a long ray of light, like a luminous path in
the air, descended from Heaven ; it was a procession of
angels who came up to Jesus and strengthened and re-
invigorated him. The remainder of the grotto was filled
with frightful visions of our crimes ; Jesus took them all
upon himself, but that adorable Heart, which was so filled
with the most perfect love for God and man, was flooded
with anguish, and overwhelmed beneath the weight of so
many abominable crimes. When this huge mass of iniquities, like the waves of a fathomless ocean, had passed
over his soul, Satan brought forward innumerable temptations, as he had formerly done in the desert, even daring
to adduce various accusations against him. ' And takest

thou all these things upon thyself,' he exclaimed, ' thou
who art not unspotted thyself?' Then he laid to the
charge of our Lord, with infernal impudence, a host of
imaginary crimes. He reproached him with the faults of
his disciples, the scandals which they had caused, and the
disturbances which he had occasioned in the world by
giving up ancient customs. No Pharisee, however wily
and severe, could have surpassed Satan on this occasion ;
he reproached Jesus with having been the cause of the
massacre of the Innocents, as well as of the sufferings of
his parents in Egypt, with not having saved John the
Baptist from death, with having brought disunion into
families, protected men of despicable character, refused to
cure various sick persons, injured the inhabitants of Gergesa by permitting men possessed by the devil to overturn
their vats,* and demons to make swine cast themselves
into the sea ; with having deserted his family, and squandered the property of others ; in one word Satan, in the
hopes of causing Jesus to waver, suggested to him every
thought by which he would have tempted at the hour of
death an ordinary mortal who might have performed all
these actions without a superhuman intention ; for it was
hidden from him that Jesus was the Son of God, and he
tempted him only as the most just of men. Our Divine
Saviour permitted his humanity thus to preponderate over
his divinity, for he was pleased to endure even those
temptations with which holy souls are assailed at the
hour of death concerning the merit of their good works.
That he might drink the chalice of suffering even to the
dregs, he permitted the evil spirit to tempt his sacred
humanity, as he would have tempted a man who should
wish to attribute to his good works some special value in
themselves, over and above what they might have by
their union with the merits of our Saviour. There was

* On the 11th of December 1812, in her visions of the public
life of Jesus, she saw our Lord permit the devils whom he had
expelled from the men of Gergesa to enter into a herd of swine.
She also saw, on this particular occasion, that the possessed men
first overturned a large vat filled with some fermented liquid.

not an action out of which he did not contrive to frame
some accusation, and he reproached Jesus, among other
things, with having spent the price of the property of
Mary Magdalen at Magdalum, which he had received
from Lazarus.

Among the sins of the world which Jesus took upon
himself, I saw also my own; and a stream, in which I
distinctly beheld each of my faults, appeared to flow towards me from out of the temptations with which he was
encircled. During this time my eyes were fixed upon my
Heavenly Spouse; with him I wept and prayed, and with
him I turned towards the consoling angels. Ah, truly did
our dear Lord writhe like a worm beneath the weight of
his anguish and sufferings!

Whilst Satan was pouring forth his accusations against
Jesus, it was with difficulty that I could restrain my indignation, but when he spoke of the sale of Magdalen's
property, I could no longer keep silence, and exclaimed:
‘How canst thou reproach him with the sale of this property as with a crime? Did I not myself see our Lord
spend the sum which was given him by Lazarus in works
of mercy, and deliver twenty-eight debtors imprisoned at
Thirza?’

At first Jesus looked calm, as he kneeled down and
prayed, but after a time his soul became terrified at the
sight of the innumerable crimes of men, and of their ingratitude towards God, and his anguish was so great that
he trembled and shuddered as he exclaimed: ‘ *Father, if
it is possible, let this chalice pass from me! Father, all
things are possible to thee, remove this chalice from me!*’
But the next moment he added: ‘ *Nevertheless, not my will
but thine be done.*’ His will and that of his Father were
one, but now that his love had ordained that he should be
left to all the weakness of his human nature, he trembled
at the prospect of death.

I saw the cavern in which he was kneeling filled with
frightful figures; I saw all the sins, wickedness, vices,
and ingratitude of mankind torturing and crushing him to
the earth; the horror of death and terror which he felt

as man at the sight of the expiatory sufferings about to
come upon him, surrounded and assailed his Divine Person under the forms of hideous spectres. He fell from
side to side, clasping his hands; his body was covered
with a cold sweat, and he trembled and shuddered. He
then arose, but his knees were shaking and apparently
scarcely able to support him; his countenance was pale,
and quite altered in appearance, his lips white, and his
hair standing on end. It was about half-past ten o'clock
when he arose from his knees, and, bathed in a cold sweat,
directed his trembling, weak footsteps towards his three
Apostles. With difficulty did he ascend the left side of
the cavern, and reach a spot where the ground was level,
and where they were sleeping, exhausted with fatigue,
sorrow and anxiety. He came to them, like a man overwhelmed with bitter sorrow, whom terror urges to seek
his friends, but like also to a good shepherd, who, when
warned of the approach of danger, hastens to visit his
flock, the safety of which is threatened; for he well knew
that they also were being tried by suffering and temptation. The terrible visions never left him, even while he
was thus seeking his disciples. When he found that they
were asleep, he clasped his hands and fell down on his
knees beside them, overcome with sorrow and anxiety,
and said : ' *Simon, sleepest thou ?*' They awoke, and raised
him up, and he, in his desolation of spirit, said to them :
' *What ? Could you not watch one hour with me ?*' When
they looked at him, and saw him pale and exhausted,
scarcely able to support himself, bathed in sweat, trembling and shuddering,—when they heard how changed
and almost inaudible his voice had become, they did not
know what to think, and had he not been still surrounded
by a well-known halo of light, they would never have
recognised him as Jesus. John said to him : ' Master, what
has befallen thee ? Must I call the other disciples ? Ought
we to take to flight?' Jesus answered him : ' Were I to
live, teach, and perform miracles for thirty-three years
longer, that would not suffice for the accomplishment of
what must be fulfilled before this time to-morrow. Call

not the eight; I did not bring them hither, because they
could not see me thus agonising without being scandalised; they would yield to temptation, forget much of the
past, and lose their confidence in me. But you, who have
seen the Son of Man transfigured, may also see him under
a cloud, and in dereliction of spirit; nevertheless, *watch
and pray, lest ye fall into temptation, for the spirit indeed
is willing, but the flesh is weak.*'

By these words he sought at once to encourage them
to persevere, and to make known to them the combat
which his human nature was sustaining against death, together with the cause of his weakness. In his overwhelming sorrow, he remained with them nearly a quarter of an
hour, and spoke to them again. He then returned to the
grotto, his mental sufferings being still on the increase,
while his disciples, on their part, stretched forth their
hands towards him, wept, and embraced each other, asking, 'What can it be? What is happening to him? He
appears to be in a state of complete desolation.' After this,
they covered their heads, and began to pray, sorrowfully
and anxiously.

About an hour and a half had passed since Jesus entered the Garden of Olives. It is true that Scripture tells
us he said, ' *Could you not watch one hour with me ?*' but
his words should not be taken literally, nor according to
our way of counting time. The three Apostles who were
with Jesus had prayed at first, but then they had fallen
asleep, for temptation had come upon them by reason of
their want of trust in God. The other eight, who had remained outside the garden, did not sleep, for our Lord's
last words, so expressive of suffering and sadness, had filled
their hearts with sinister forebodings, and they wandered
about Mount Olivet, trying to find some place of refuge in
case of danger.

The town of Jerusalem was very quiet; the Jews were
in their houses, engaged in preparing for the feast, but I
saw, here and there, some of the friends and disciples of
Jesus walking to and fro, with anxious countenances, conversing earnestly together, and evidently expecting some

great event. The Mother of our Lord, Magdalen, Martha, Mary of Cleophas, Mary Salome, and Salome had gone from the supper-hall to the house of Mary, the mother of Mark. Mary was alarmed at the reports which were spreading, and wished to return to the town with her friends, in order to hear something of Jesus. Lazarus, Nicodemus, Joseph of Arimathea, and some relations from Hebron, came to see and endeavour to tranquillise her, for, as they were aware, either from their own knowledge or from what the disciples had told them, of the mournful predictions which Jesus had made in the supper-room, they had made inquiries of some Pharisees of their acquaintance, and had not been able to hear that any conspiracy was on foot for the time against our Lord. Being utterly ignorant of the treason of Judas, they assured Mary that the danger could not yet be very great, and that the enemies of Jesus would not make any attempts upon his person, at least until the festival was over. Mary told them how restless and disturbed in mind Judas had latterly appeared, and how abruptly he had left the supper-room. She felt no doubt of his having gone to betray our Lord, for she had often warned him that he was a son of perdition. The holy women then returned to the house of Mary, the mother of Mark.

When Jesus, unrelieved of all the weight of his sufferings, returned to the grotto, he fell prostrate, with his face on the ground and his arms extended, and prayed to his Eternal Father; but his soul had to sustain a second interior combat, which lasted three-quarters of an hour. Angels came and showed him, in a series of visions, all the sufferings that he was to endure in order to expiate sin; how great was the beauty of man, the image of God, before the fall, and how that beauty was changed and obliterated when sin entered the world. He beheld how all sins originated in that of Adam, the signification and essence of concupiscence, its terrible effects on the powers of the soul, and likewise the signification and essence of all the sufferings entailed by concupiscence. They showed him the satisfaction which he would have to offer to Divine Justice, and how it would consist of a degree of suffering in his soul and body which would comprehend all the sufferings due to the concupiscence of all mankind, since the debt of the whole human race had to be paid by that humanity which alone was sinless—the humanity of the Son of God. The angels showed him all these things under different forms, and I felt what they were saying, although I heard no voice. No tongue can describe what anguish and what horror overwhelmed the soul of Jesus at the sight of so terrible an expiation—his sufferings were so great, indeed, that a bloody sweat issued forth from all the pores of his sacred body.

Whilst the adorable humanity of Christ was thus crushed to the earth beneath this awful weight of suffering, the angels appeared filled with compassion; there was a pause, and I perceived that they were earnestly desiring to console him, and praying to that effect before the throne of God. For one instant there appeared to be, as it were, a struggle between the mercy and justice of God and that love which was sacrificing itself. I was permitted to see an image of God, not, as before, seated on a throne, but under a luminous form. I beheld the divine nature of the Son in the Person of the Father, and, as it were, withdrawn into his bosom; the Person of the Holy Ghost proceeded from the Father and the Son, it was, so to speak, between them, and yet the whole formed only one God—but these things are indescribable.

All this was more an inward perception than a vision under distinct forms, and it appeared to me that the Divine Will of our Lord withdrew in some sort into the Eternal Father, in order to permit all those sufferings which his human will besought his Father to spare him, to weigh upon his humanity alone. I saw this at the time when the angels, filled with compassion, were desiring to console Jesus, who, in fact, was slightly relieved at that moment. Then all disappeared, and the angels retired from our Lord, whose soul was about to sustain fresh assaults.

When our Redeemer, on Mount Olivet, was pleased to

experience and overcome that violent repugnance of human nature to suffering and death which constitutes a portion of all sufferings, the tempter was permitted to do to him what he does to all men who desire to sacrifice themselves in a holy cause. In the first portion of the agony, Satan displayed before the eyes of our Lord the enormity of that debt of sin which he was going to pay, and was even bold and malicious enough to seek faults in the very works of our Saviour himself. In the second agony, Jesus beheld, to its fullest extent and in all its bitterness, the expiatory suffering which would be required to satisfy Divine Justice. This was displayed to him by angels; for it belongs not to Satan to show that expiation is possible, and the father of lies and despair never exhibits the works of Divine Mercy before men. Jesus having victoriously resisted all these assaults by his entire and absolute submission to the will of his Heavenly Father, a succession of new and terrifying visions were presented before his eyes, and that feeling of doubt and anxiety which a man on the point of making some great sacrifice always experiences, arose in the soul of our Lord, as he asked himself the tremendous question: ' And what good will result from this sacrifice?' Then a most awful picture of the future was displayed before his eyes and overwhelmed his tender heart with anguish.

When God had created the first Adam, he cast a deep sleep upon him, opened his side, and took one of his ribs, of which he made Eve, his wife and the mother of all the living. Then he brought her to Adam, who exclaimed: ' *This now is bone of my bones, and flesh of my flesh. . . . Wherefore a man shall leave father and mother, and shall cleave to his wife, and they shall be two in one flesh.*' That was the marriage of which it is written: ' *This is a great Sacrament, I speak in Christ and in the Church.*' Jesus Christ, the second Adam, was pleased also to let sleep come upon him—the sleep of death on the cross, and he was also pleased to let his side be opened, in order that the second Eve, his virgin Spouse, the Church, the mother of all the living, might be formed from it. It was his will

to give her the blood of redemption, the water of purification, and his spirit—the three which render testimony
on earth—and to bestow upon her also the holy Sacraments, in order that she might be pure, holy, and unde-
filed; he was to be her head, and we were to be her members, under submission to the head, the bone of his bones,
and the flesh of his flesh.   In taking human nature, that
he might suffer death for us, he had also left his Eternal
Father, to cleave to his Spouse, the Church, and he became one flesh with her, by feeding her with the Adorable
Sacrament of the Altar, in which he unites himself unceasingly with us.   He has been pleased to remain on
earth with his Church, until we shall all be united together by him within her fold, and he has said : '*The gates
of hell shall never prevail against her.*'   To satisfy his unspeakable love for sinners, our Lord had become man and
a brother of these same sinners, that so he might take upon
himself the punishment due to all their crimes.   He had
contemplated with deep sorrow the greatness of this debt
and the unspeakable sufferings by which it was to be ac-
quitted.   Yet he had most joyfully given himself up to
the will of his Heavenly Father as a victim of expiation.
Now, however, he beheld all the future sufferings, combats, and wounds of his heavenly Spouse ; in one word, he
beheld the ingratitude of men.

The soul of Jesus beheld all the future sufferings of
his Apostles, disciples, and friends ; after which he saw
the primitive Church, numbering but few souls in her fold
at first, and then in proportion as her numbers increased,
disturbed by heresies and schisms breaking out among her
children, who repeated the sin of Adam by pride and dis-
obedience.   He saw the tepidity, malice, and corruption of
an infinite number of Christians, the lies and deceptions
of proud teachers, all the sacrileges of wicked priests, the
fatal consequences of each sin, and the abomination of
desolation in the kingdom of God, in the sanctuary of those
ungrateful human beings whom he was about to redeem
with his blood at the cost of unspeakable sufferings.

The scandals of all ages, down to the present day and

even to the end of the world—every species of error, deception, mad fanaticism, obstinacy, and malice—were displayed before his eyes, and he beheld, as it were floating before him, all the apostates, heresiarchs, and pretended reformers, who deceive men by an appearance of sanctity. The corrupters and the corrupted of all ages outraged and tormented him for not having been crucified after their fashion, or for not having suffered precisely as they settled or imagined he should have done. They vied with each other in tearing the seamless robe of his Church; many ill-treated, insulted, and denied him, and many turned contemptuously away, shaking their heads at him, avoiding his compassionate embrace, and hurrying on to the abyss where they were finally swallowed up. He saw countless numbers of other men who did not dare openly to deny him, but who passed on in disgust at the sight of the wounds of his Church, as the Levite passed by the poor man who had fallen among robbers. Like unto cowardly and faithless children, who desert their mother in the middle of the night, at the sight of the thieves and robbers to whom their negligence or their malice has opened the door, they fled from his wounded Spouse. He beheld all these men, sometimes separated from the True Vine, and taking their rest amid the wild fruit trees, sometimes like lost sheep, left to the mercy of the wolves, led by base hirelings into bad pasturages, and refusing to enter the fold of the Good Shepherd who gave his life for his sheep. They were wandering homeless in the desert in the midst of the sand blown about by the wind, and were obstinately determined not to see his City placed upon a hill, which could not be hidden, the House of his Spouse, his Church built upon a rock, and with which he had promised to remain to the end of ages. They built upon the sand wretched tenements, which they were continually pulling down and rebuilding, but in which there was neither altar nor sacrifice; they had weathercocks on their roofs, and their doctrines changed with the wind, consequently they were for ever in opposition one with the other. They never could come to a mutual understanding, and were for ever unsettled, often destroying their own dwellings and hurling the fragments against the Corner-Stone of the Church, which always remained unshaken.

As there was nothing but darkness in the dwellings of these men, many among them, instead of directing their steps towards the Candle placed on the Candlestick in the House of the Spouse of Christ, wandered with closed eyes around the gardens of the Church, sustaining life only by inhaling the sweet odours which were diffused from them far and near, stretching forth their hands towards shadowy idols, and following wandering stars which led them to wells where there was no water. Even when on the very brink of the precipice, they refused to listen to the voice of the Spouse calling them, and, though dying with hunger, derided, insulted, and mocked at those servants and messengers who were sent to invite them to the Nuptial Feast. They obstinately refused to enter the garden, because they feared the thorns of the hedge, although they had neither wheat with which to satisfy their hunger nor wine to quench their thirst, but were simply intoxicated with pride and self-esteem, and being blinded by their own false lights, persisted in asserting that the Church of the Word made flesh was invisible. Jesus beheld them all, he wept over them, and was pleased to suffer for all those who do not see him and who will not carry their crosses after him in his City built upon a hill—his Church founded upon a rock, to which he has given himself in the Holy Eucharist, and against which the gates of Hell will never prevail.

Bearing a prominent place in these mournful visions which were beheld by the soul of Jesus, I saw Satan, who dragged away and strangled a multitude of men redeemed by the blood of Christ and sanctified by the unction of his Sacrament. Our Divine Saviour beheld with bitterest anguish the ingratitude and corruption of the Christians of the first and of all succeeding ages, even to the end of the world, and during the whole of this time the voice of the tempter was incessantly repeating : ‘Canst thou resolve to suffer for such ungrateful reprobates?’ while the various apparitions succeeded each other with intense rapidity, and so violently weighed down and crushed the soul of Jesus, that his sacred humanity was overwhelmed with unspeakable anguish. Jesus—the Anointed of the Lord—the Son of Man—struggled and writhed as he fell on his knees, with clasped hands, as it were annihilated beneath the weight of his suffering. So violent was the struggle which then took place between his human will and his repugnance to suffer so much for such an ungrateful race, that from every pore of his sacred body there burst forth large drops of blood, which fell trickling on to the ground. In his bitter agony, he looked around, as though seeking help, and appeared to take Heaven, earth, and the stars of the firmament to witness of his sufferings.

Jesus, in his anguish of spirit, raised his voice, and gave utterance to several cries of pain. The three Apostles awoke, listened, and were desirous of approaching him, but Peter detained James and John, saying: 'Stay you here; I will join him.' Then I saw Peter hastily run forward and enter the grotto. 'Master,' he exclaimed, 'what has befallen thee?' But at the sight of Jesus, thus bathed in his own blood, and sinking to the ground beneath the weight of mortal fear and anguish, he drew back, and paused for a moment, overcome with terror. Jesus made him no answer, and appeared unconscious of his presence. Peter returned to the other two, and told them that the Lord had not answered him except by groans and sighs. They became more and more sorrowful after this, covered their heads, and sat down to weep and pray.

I then returned to my Heavenly Spouse in his most bitter agony. The frightful visions of the future ingratitude of the men whose debt to Divine Justice he was taking upon himself, continued to become more and more vivid and tremendous. Several times I heard him exclaim: 'O my Father, can I possibly suffer for so ungrateful a race? *O my Father, if this chalice may not pass from me, but I must drink it, thy will be done!*'

Amid all these apparitions, Satan held a conspicuous

place, under various forms, which represented different
species of sins. Sometimes he appeared under the form of
a gigantic black figure, sometimes under those of a tiger,
a fox, a wolf, a dragon, or a serpent. Not, however, that
he really took any of these shapes, but merely some one
of their characteristics, joined with other hideous forms.
None of these frightful apparitions entirely resembled any
creature, but were symbols of abomination, discord, contradiction, and sin—in one word, were demoniacal to the
fullest extent. These diabolical figures urged on, dragged,
and tore to pieces, before the very eyes of Jesus, countless
numbers of those men for whose redemption he was entering upon the painful way of the Cross. At first I but
seldom saw the serpent; soon, however, it made its appearance, with a crown upon its head. This odious reptile was of gigantic size, apparently possessed of unbounded
strength, and led forward countless legions of the enemies
of Jesus in every age and of every nation. Being armed
with all kinds of destructive weapons, they sometimes tore
one another in pieces, and then renewed their attacks upon
our Saviour with redoubled rage. It was indeed an awful
sight; for they heaped upon him the most fearful outrages,
cursing, striking, wounding, and tearing him in pieces.
Their weapons, swords, and spears flew about in the air,
crossing and recrossing continually in all directions, like
the flails of threshers in an immense barn; and the rage
of each of these fiends seemed exclusively directed against
Jesus—that grain of heavenly wheat descended to the
earth to die there, in order to feed men eternally with the
Bread of Life.

Thus exposed to the fury of these hellish bands, some
of which appeared to me wholly composed of blind men,
Jesus was as much wounded and bruised as if their blows
had been real. I saw him stagger from side to side, sometimes raising himself up, and sometimes falling again,
while the serpent, in the midst of the crowds whom it
was unceasingly leading forward against Jesus, struck the
ground with its tail, and tore to pieces or swallowed all
whom it thus knocked to the ground

It was made known to me that these apparitions were all those persons who in divers ways insult and outrage Jesus, really and truly present in the Holy Sacrament. I recognised among them all those who in any way profane the Blessed Eucharist. I beheld with horror all the outrages thus offered to our Lord, whether by neglect, irreverence, and omission of what was due to him; by open contempt, abuse, and the most awful sacrileges; by the worship of worldly idols; by spiritual darkness and false knowledge; or, finally, by error, incredulity, fanaticism, hatred, and open persecution. Among these men I saw many who were blind, paralysed, deaf, and dumb, and even children;—blind men who would not see the truth; paralytic men who would not advance, according to its directions, on the road leading to eternal life; deaf men who refused to listen to its warnings and threats; dumb men who would never use their voices in its defence; and, finally, children who were led astray by following parents and teachers filled with the love of the world and forgetfulness of God, who were fed on earthly luxuries, drunk with false wisdom, and loathing all that pertained to religion. Among the latter, the sight of whom grieved me especially, because Jesus so loved children, I saw many irreverent, ill-behaved acolytes, who did not honour our Lord in the holy ceremonies in which they took a part. I beheld with terror that many priests, some of whom even fancied themselves full of faith and piety, also outraged Jesus in the Adorable Sacrament. I saw many who believed and taught the doctrine of the Real Presence, but did not sufficiently take it to heart, for they forgot and neglected the palace, throne, and seat of the Living God; that is to say, the church, the altar, the tabernacle, the chalice, the monstrance, the vases and ornaments; in one word, all that is used in his worship, or to adorn his house.

Entire neglect reigned everywhere, all things were left to moulder away in dust and filth, and the worship of God was, if not inwardly profaned, at least outwardly dishonoured. Nor did this arise from real poverty, but from indifference, sloth, preoccupation of mind about vain earthly concerns, and often also from egotism and spiritual death; for I saw neglect of this kind in churches the pastors and congregations of which were rich, or at least tolerably well off. I saw many others in which worldly, tasteless, unsuitable ornaments had replaced the magnificent adornments of a more pious age.

I saw that often the poorest of men were better lodged in their cottages than the Master of heaven and earth in his churches. Ah, how deeply did the inhospitality of men grieve Jesus, who had given himself to them to be their Food! Truly, there is no need to be rich in order to receive him who rewards a hundredfold the glass of cold water given to the thirsty; but how shameful is not our conduct when in giving drink to the Divine Lord, who thirsts for our souls, we give him corrupted water in a filthy glass! In consequence of all this neglect, I saw the weak scandalised, the Adorable Sacrament profaned, the churches deserted, and the priests despised. This state of impurity and negligence extended even to the souls of the faithful, who left the tabernacle of their hearts unprepared and uncleansed when Jesus was about to enter them, exactly the same as they left his tabernacle on the altar.

Were I to speak for an entire year, I could never detail all the insults offered to Jesus in the Adorable Sacrament which were made known to me in this way. I saw their authors assault Jesus in bands, and strike him with different arms, corresponding to their various offences. I saw irreverent Christians of all ages, careless or sacrilegious priests, crowds of tepid and unworthy communicants, wicked soldiers profaning the sacred vessels, and servants of the devil making use of the Holy Eucharist in the frightful mysteries of hellish worship. Among these bands I saw a great number of theologians, who had been drawn into heresy by their sins, attacking Jesus in the Holy Sacrament of his Church, and snatching out of his Heart, by their seductive words and promises, a number of souls for whom he had shed his blood. Ah! it was indeed an awful sight, for I saw the Church as the body of Christ; and all these bands of men, who were separating themselves from the Church, mangled and tore off whole pieces of his living flesh.   Alas ! he looked at them in the most touching manner, and lamented that they should thus cause their own eternal loss.   He had given his own divine Self to us for our Food in the Holy Sacrament, in order to unite in one body—that of the Church, his Spouse— men who were to an infinite extent divided and separated from each other; and now he beheld himself torn and rent in twain in that very body ; for his principal work of love, the Holy Communion, in which men should have been made wholly one, was become, by the malice of false teachers, the subject of separation.   I beheld whole nations thus snatched out of his bosom, and deprived of any participation in the treasure of graces left to the Church. Finally, I saw all who were separated from the Church plunged into the depths of infidelity, superstition, heresy, and false worldly philosophy; and they gave vent to their fierce rage by joining together in large bodies to attack the Church, being urged on by the serpent which was disporting itself in the midst of them.   Alas ! it was as though Jesus himself had been torn in a thousand pieces !

So great was my horror and terror, that my Heavenly Spouse appeared to me, and mercifully placed his hand upon my heart, saying : ' No one has yet seen all these things, and thy heart would burst with sorrow if I did not give thee strength.'

I saw the blood flowing in large drops down the pale face of our Saviour, his hair matted together, and his beard bloody and entangled.   After the vision which I have last described, he fled, so to speak, out of the cave, and returned to his disciples.   But he tottered as he walked ; his appearance was that of a man covered with wounds and bending beneath a heavy burden, and he stumbled at every step.

When he came up to the three Apostles, they were not lying down asleep as they had been the first time, but

their heads were covered, and they had sunk down on
their knees, in an attitude often assumed by the people
of that country when in sorrow or desiring to pray. They
had fallen asleep, overpowered by grief and fatigue.
Jesus, trembling and groaning, drew nigh to them, and
they awoke.

But when, by the light of the moon, they saw him
standing before them, his face pale and bloody, and his
hair in disorder, their weary eyes did not at the first
moment recognise him, for he was indescribably changed.
He clasped his hands together, upon which they arose
and lovingly supported him in their arms, and he told
them in sorrowful accents that the next day he should be
put to death,—that in one hour's time he should be
seized, led before a tribunal, maltreated, outraged, scourged,
and finally put to a most cruel death. He besought them
to console his Mother, and also Magdalen. They made
no reply, for they knew not what to say, so greatly had
his appearance and language alarmed them, and they even
thought his mind must be wandering. When he desired
to return to the grotto, he had not strength to walk. I
saw John and James lead him back, and return when he
had entered the grotto. It was then about a quarter-past
eleven.

During this agony of Jesus, I saw the Blessed Virgin
also overwhelmed with sorrow and anguish of soul, in the
house of Mary, the mother of Mark. She was with
Magdalen and Mary in the garden belonging to the house,
and almost prostrate from grief, with her whole body
bowed down as she knelt. She fainted several times, for
she beheld in spirit different portions of the agony of
Jesus. She had sent some messengers to make inquiries
concerning him, but her deep anxiety would not suffer
her to await their return, and she went with Magdalen
and Salome as far as the Valley of Josaphat. She walked
along with her head veiled, and her arms frequently
stretched forth towards Mount Olivet; for she beheld in
spirit Jesus bathed in a bloody sweat, and her gestures
were as though she wished with her extended hands to

wipe the face of her Son. I saw these interior movements of her soul towards Jesus, who thought of her, and turned his eyes in her direction, as if to seek her assistance. I beheld the spiritual communication which they had with each other, under the form of rays passing to and fro between them. Our Divine Lord thought also of Magdalen, was touched by her distress, and therefore recommended his Apostles to console her; for he knew that her love for his adorable Person was greater than that felt for him by any one save his Blessed Mother, and he foresaw that she would suffer much for his sake, and never offend him more.

About this time, the eight Apostles returned to the arbour of Gethsemani, and after talking together for some time, ended by going to sleep. They were wavering, discouraged, and sorely tempted. They had each been seeking for a place of refuge in case of danger, and they anxiously asked one another, 'What shall we do when they have put him to death? We have left all to follow him; we are poor and the offscouring of the world; we gave ourselves up entirely to his service, and now he is so sorrowful and so dejected himself, that he can afford us no consolation.' The other disciples had at first wandered about in various directions, but then, having heard something concerning the awful prophecies which Jesus had made, they had nearly all retired to Bethphage.

I saw Jesus still praying in the grotto, struggling against the repugnance to suffering which belonged to human nature, and abandoning himself wholly to the will of his Eternal Father. Here the abyss opened before him, and he had a vision of the first part of Limbo. He saw Adam and Eve, the patriarchs, prophets, and just men, the parents of his Mother, and John the Baptist, awaiting his arrival in the lower world with such intense longing, that the sight strengthened and gave fresh courage to his loving heart. His death was to open Heaven to these captives, — his death was to deliver them out of that prison in which they were languishing in eager hope! When Jesus had, with deep emotion, looked upon these

saints of antiquity, angels presented to him all the bands
of saints of future ages, who, joining their labours to the
merits of his Passion, were, through him, to be united to
his Heavenly Father. Most beautiful and consoling was
this vision, in which he beheld salvation and sanctification
flowing forth in ceaseless streams from the fountain of redemption opened by his death.

The apostles, disciples, virgins, and holy women, the
martyrs, confessors, hermits, popes, and bishops, and large
bands of religious of both sexes—in one word, the entire
army of the blessed—appeared before him. All bore on
their heads triumphal crowns, and the flowers of their
crowns differed in form, in colour, in odour, and in perfection, according to the difference of the sufferings, labours and victories which had procured them eternal
glory. Their whole life, and all their actions, merits, and
power, as well as all the glory of their triumph, came
solely from their union with the merits of Jesus Christ.

The reciprocal influence exercised by these saints upon
each other, and the manner in which they all drank from
one sole Fountain — the Adorable Sacrament and the
Passion of our Lord—formed a most touching and wonderful spectacle. Nothing about them was devoid of deep
meaning,—their works, martyrdom, victories, appearance,
and dress,—all, though indescribably varied, was confused
together in infinite harmony and unity; and this unity in
diversity was produced by the rays of one single Sun, by
the Passion of the Lord, of the Word made flesh, in whom
was life, the light of men, which shined in darkness, and
the darkness did not comprehend it.

The army of the future saints passed before the soul
of our Lord, which was thus placed between the desiring
patriarchs, and the triumphant band of the future blessed,
and these two armies joining together, and completing one
another, so to speak, surrounded the loving Heart of our
Saviour as with a crown of victory. This most affecting
and consoling spectacle bestowed a degree of strength and
comfort upon the soul of Jesus. Ah! he so loved his brethren and creatures that, to accomplish the redemption of

one single soul, he would have accepted with joy all the sufferings to which he was now devoting himself. As these visions referred to the future, they were diffused to a certain height in the air.

But these consoling visions faded away, and the angels displayed before him the scenes of his Passion quite close to the earth, because it was near at hand. I beheld every scene distinctly portrayed, from the kiss of Judas to the last words of Jesus on the cross, and I saw in this single vision all that I see in my meditations on the Passion. The treason of Judas, the flight of the disciples, the insults which were offered our Lord before Annas and Caiphas, Peter's denial, the tribunal of Pilate, Herod's mockery, the scourging and crowning with thorns, the condemnation to death, the carrying of the cross, the linen cloth presented by Veronica, the crucifixion, the insults of the Pharisees, the sorrows of Mary, of Magdalen, and of John, the wound of the lance in his side, after death;— in one word, every part of the Passion was shown to him in the minutest detail. He accepted all voluntarily, submitting to everything for the love of man. He saw also and felt the sufferings endured at that moment by his Mother, whose interior union with his agony was so entire that she had fainted in the arms of her two friends.

When the visions of the Passion were concluded, Jesus fell on his face like one at the point of death ; the angels disappeared, and the bloody sweat became more copious, so that I saw it had soaked his garment. Entire darkness reigned in the cavern, when I beheld an angel descend to Jesus. This angel was of higher stature than any whom I had before beheld, and his form was also more distinct and more resembling that of a man. He was clothed like a priest in a long floating garment, and bore before him, in his hands, a small vase, in shape resembling the chalice used at the Last Supper. At the top of this chalice, there was a small oval body, about the size of a bean, and which diffused a reddish light. The angel, without touching the earth with his feet, stretched forth his right hand to Jesus, who arose, when he placed the mysterious food in his mouth, and gave him to drink from the luminous chalice. Then he disappeared.

Jesus having freely accepted the chalice of his sufferings, and received new strength, remained some minutes longer in the grotto, absorbed in calm meditation, and returning thanks to his Heavenly Father. He was still in deep affliction of spirit, but supernaturally comforted to such a degree as to be able to go to his disciples without tottering as he walked, or bending beneath the weight of his sufferings. His countenance was still pale and altered, but his step was firm and determined. He had wiped his face with a linen cloth, and re-arranged his hair, which hung about his shoulders, matted together and damp with blood.

When Jesus came to his disciples, they were lying, as before, against the wall of the terrace, asleep, and with their heads covered. Our Lord told them that then was not the time for sleep, but that they should arise and pray : ' *Behold the hour is at hand, and the Son of Man shall be betrayed into the hands of sinners,*' he said : '*Arise, let us go, behold he is at hand that will betray me. It were better for him, if that man had not been born.*' The Apostles arose in much alarm, and looked round with anxiety. When they had somewhat recovered themselves, Peter said warmly : ' Lord, I will call the others, that so we may defend thee.' But Jesus pointed out to them at some distance in the valley, on the other side of the Brook of Cedron, a band of armed men, who were advancing with torches, and he said that one of their number had betrayed him. He spoke calmly, exhorted them to console his Mother, and said : ' Let us go to meet them—I shall deliver myself up without resistance into the hands of my enemies.' He then left the Garden of Olives with the three Apostles, and went to meet the archers on the road which led from that garden to Gethsemani.

When the Blessed Virgin, under the care of Magdalen and Salome, recovered her senses, some disciples, who had seen the soldiers approaching, conducted her back to the house of Mary, the mother of Mark. The archers took a shorter road than that which Jesus followed when he left the supper-room.

The grotto in which Jesus had this day prayed was not the one where he usually prayed on Mount Olivet. He commonly went to a cabin at a greater distance off, where, one day, after having cursed the barren fig-tree, he had prayed in great affliction of spirit, with his arms stretched out, and leaning against a rock.

The traces of his body and hands remained impressed on the stone, and were honoured later, but it was not known on what occasion the miracle had taken place. I have several times seen similar impressions left upon the stone, either by the Prophets of the Old Testament, or by Jesus, Mary, or some of the Apostles, and I have also seen those made by the body of St. Catherine on Mount Sinai. These impressions do not seem deep, but resemble what would be made upon a thick piece of dough, if a person leaned his hand upon it.

CHAPTER II.

Judas and his Band.

JUDAS had not expected that his treason would have produced such fatal results. He had been anxious to obtain the promised reward, and to please the Pharisees by delivering up Jesus into their hands, but he had never calculated on things going so far, or thought that the enemies of his Master would actually bring him to judgment and crucify him; his mind was engrossed with the love of gain alone, and some astute Pharisees and Sadducees, with whom he had established an intercourse, had constantly urged him on to treason by flattering him. He was sick of the fatiguing, wandering, and persecuted life which the Apostles led. For several months past he had continually stolen from the alms which were consigned to his care, and his avarice, grudging the expenses incurred by Magdalen when she poured the precious ointment on the feet of our Lord, incited him to the commission of the greatest of crimes. He had always hoped that Jesus would establish a temporal kingdom, and bestow upon him some brilliant and lucrative post in it, but finding himself disappointed, he turned his thoughts to amassing a fortune. He saw that sufferings and persecutions were on the increase for our Lord and his followers, and he sought to make friends with the powerful enemies of our Saviour before the time of danger, for he saw that Jesus did not become a king, whereas the actual dignity and power of the High Priest, and of all who were attached to his service, made a very strong impression upon his mind.

He began to enter by degrees into a close connection with their agents, who were constantly flattering him, and assuring him in strong terms that, in any case, an end would speedily be put to the career of our Divine Lord. He listened more and more eagerly to the criminal suggestions of his corrupt heart, and he had done nothing during the last few days but go backwards and forwards in order to induce the chief priests to come to some agreement. But they were unwilling to act at once, and treated him with contempt. They said that sufficient time would not intervene before the festival day, and that there would be a tumult among the people. The Sanhedrin alone listened to his proposals with some degree of attention. After Judas had sacrilegiously received the Blessed Sacrament, Satan took entire possession of him, and he went off at once to complete his crime. He in the first place sought those persons who had hitherto flattered and entered into agreements with him, and who still received him with pretended friendship. Some others joined the party, and among the number Annas and Caiphas, but the latter treated him with considerable pride and scorn. All these enemies of Christ were extremely undecided and far from feeling any confidence of success, because they mistrusted Judas.

I saw the empire of Hell divided against itself; Satan desired the crime of the Jews, and earnestly longed for the death of Jesus, the Converter of souls, the holy Teacher, the Just Man, who was so abhorrent to him; but at the same time he felt an extraordinary interior fear of the death of the innocent Victim, who would not conceal himself from his persecutors. I saw him then, on the one hand, stimulate the hatred and fury of the enemies of Jesus, and on the other, insinuate to some of their number that Judas was a wicked, despicable character, and that the sentence could not be pronounced before the festival, or a sufficient number of witnesses against Jesus be gathered together.

Every one proposed something different, and some questioned Judas, saying : ' Shall we be able to take him? Has he not armed men with him?' And the traitor replied : ' No, he is alone with eleven disciples ; he is greatly depressed, and the eleven are timid men.' He told them that now or never was the time to get possession of the person of Jesus, that later he might no longer have it in his power to give our Lord up into their hands, and that perhaps he should never return to him again, because for several days past it had been very clear that the other disciples and Jesus himself suspected and would certainly kill him if he returned to them. He told them likewise that if they did not at once seize the person of Jesus, he would make his escape, and return with an army of his partisans, to have himself proclaimed king. These threats of Judas produced some effect, his proposals were acceded to, and he received the price of his treason—thirty pieces of silver. These pieces were oblong, with holes in their sides, strung together by means of rings in a kind of chain, and bearing certain impressions.

Judas could not help being conscious that they regarded him with contempt and distrust, for their language and gestures betrayed their feelings, and pride suggested to him to give back the money as an offering for the Temple, in order to make them suppose his intentions to have been just and disinterested. But they rejected his proposal, because the price of blood could not be offered in the Temple. Judas saw how much they despised him, and his rage was excessive. He had not expected to reap the bitter fruits of his treason even before it was accomplished, but he had gone so far with these men that he was in their power, and escape was no longer possible. They watched him carefully, and would not let him leave their presence, until he had shown them exactly what steps were to be taken in order to secure the person of Jesus. Three Pharisees accompanied him when he went down into a room where the soldiers of the Temple (some only of whom were Jews, and the rest of various nations) were assembled. When everything was settled, and the necessary number of soldiers gathered together, Judas hastened first to the supper-room, accompanied by a servant of the Pharisees, for the purpose of ascertaining whether Jesus had left, as they would have seized his person there without difficulty, if once they had secured the doors. He agreed to send them a messenger with the required information.

A short time before when Judas had received the price of his treason, a Pharisee had gone out, and sent seven slaves to fetch wood with which to prepare the Cross for our Saviour, in case he should be judged, because the next day there would not be sufficient time on account of the commencement of the Paschal festivity. They procured this wood from a spot about three-quarters of a mile distant, near a high wall, where there was a great quantity of other wood belonging to the Temple, and dragged it to a square situated behind the tribunal of Caiphas. The principal piece of the Cross came from a tree formerly growing in the Valley of Josaphat, near the torrent of Cedron, and which, having fallen across the stream, had been used as a sort of bridge. When Nehemias hid the sacred fire and the holy vessels in the pool of Bethsaida, it had been thrown over the spot, together with other pieces of wood,—then later taken away, and left on one side. The Cross was prepared in a very peculiar manner, either with the object of deriding the royalty of Jesus, or from what men might term chance. It was composed of five pieces of wood, exclusive of the inscription. I saw many other things concerning the Cross, and the meaning of different circumstances was also made known to me, but I have forgotten all that.

Judas returned, and said that Jesus was no longer in the supper-room, but that he must certainly be on Mount Olivet, in the spot where he was accustomed to pray. He requested that only a small number of men might be sent with him, lest the disciples who were on the watch should perceive anything and raise a sedition. Three hundred men were to be stationed at the gates and in the streets of Ophel, a part of the town situated to the south of the Temple, and along the valley of Millo as far as the house of Annas, on the top of Mount Sion, in order to be ready to send reinforcements if necessary, for, he said, all the people of the lower class of Ophel were partisans of Jesus. The traitor likewise bade them be careful, lest he should escape them—since he, by mysterious means, had so often hidden himself in the mountain, and made himself suddenly invisible to those around. He recommended them, besides, to fasten him with a chain, and make use of certain magical forms to prevent his breaking it. The Jews listened to all these pieces of advice with scornful indifference, and replied, ' If we once have him in our hands, we will take care not to let him go.'

Judas next began to make his arrangements with those who were to accompany him. He wished to enter the garden before them, and embrace and salute Jesus as if he were returning to him as his friend and disciple, and then for the soldiers to run forward and seize the person of Jesus. He was anxious that it should be thought they had come there by chance, that so, when they had made their appearance, he might run away like the other disciples and be no more heard of. He likewise thought that, perhaps, a tumult would ensue, that the Apostles might defend themselves, and Jesus pass through the midst of his enemies, as he had so often done before. He dwelt upon these thoughts especially, when his pride was hurt by the disdainful manner of the Jews in his regard ; but he did not repent, for he had wholly given himself up to Satan. It was his desire also that the soldiers following him should not carry chains and cords, and his accomplices pretended to accede to all his wishes, although in reality they acted with him as with a traitor who was not to be trusted, but to be cast off as soon as he had done what was wanted. The soldiers received orders to keep close to Judas, watch him carefully, and not let him escape until Jesus was seized, for he had received his reward, and it was feared that he might run off with the money, and Jesus not be taken after all, or another be taken in his place. The band of men chosen to accompany Judas was composed of twenty soldiers, selected from the temple guard and from others of the military who were under the orders of Annas and Caiphas. They were dressed very much like the Roman soldiers, had morions like them, and wore hanging straps round their thighs, but their beards were long, whereas the Roman soldiers at Jerusalem had whiskers only, and shaved their chins and upper lips. They all had swords, some of them being also armed with spears, and they carried sticks with lanterns and torches; but when they set off they only lighted one. It had at first been intended that Judas should be accompanied by a more numerous escort, but he drew their attention to the fact that so large a number of men would be too easily seen, because Mount Olivet commanded a view of the whole valley. Most of the soldiers remained, therefore, at Ophel, and sentinels were stationed on all sides to put down any attempt which might be made to release Jesus. Judas set off with the twenty soldiers, but he was followed at some distance by four archers, who were only common bailiffs, carrying cords and chains, and after them came the six agents with whom Judas had been in communication for some time. One of these was a priest and a confidant of Annas, a second was devoted to Caiphas, the third and fourth were Pharisees, and the other two Sadduceans and Herodians. These six men were courtiers of Annas and Caiphas, acting in the capacity of spies, and most bitter enemies of Jesus.

The soldiers remained on friendly terms with Judas until they reached the spot where the road divides the Garden of Olives from the Garden of Gethsemani, but there they refused to allow him to advance alone, and entirely changed their manner, treating him with much insolence and harshness.

CHAPTER III.

Jesus is arrested.

JESUS was standing with his three Apostles on the road between Gethsemani, and the Garden of Olives, when Judas and the band who accompanied him made their appearance. A warm dispute arose between Judas and the soldiers, because he wished to approach first and speak to Jesus quietly as if nothing was the matter, and then for them to come up and seize our Saviour, thus letting him suppose that he had no connection with the affair. But the men answered rudely, 'Not so, friend, thou shalt not escape from our hands until we have the Galilean safely bound,' and seeing the eight Apostles who hastened to rejoin Jesus when they heard the dispute which was going on, they (notwithstanding the opposition of Judas) called up four archers, whom they had left at a little distance, to assist. When by the light of the moon Jesus and the three Apostles first saw the band of armed men, Peter wished to repel them by force of arms, and said : ' Lord, the other eight are close at hand, let us attack the archers,' but Jesus bade him hold his peace, and then turned and walked back a few steps. At this moment four disciples came out of the garden, and asked what was taking place. Judas was about to reply, but the soldiers interrupted, and would not let him speak. These four disciples were James the Less, Philip, Thomas, and Nathaniel ; the last named, who was a son of the aged Simeon, had with a few others joined the eight Apostles at Gethsemani, being perhaps sent by the friends of Jesus to know what was going on, or possibly simply incited by curiosity and anxiety. The other disciples were wandering to and fro, on the look out, and ready to fly at a moment's notice.

Jesus walked up to the soldiers and said in a firm and
clear voice, ' *Whom seek ye?*' The leaders answered, ' *Jesus
of Nazareth.*' Jesus said to them, ' *I am he.*' Scarcely
had he pronounced these words than they all fell to the
ground, as if struck with apoplexy. Judas, who stood by
them, was much alarmed, and as he appeared desirous of
approaching, Jesus held out his hand and said : ' *Friend,
whereto art thou come?*' Judas stammered forth something about business which had brought him. Jesus
answered in few words, the sense of which was : ' *It
were better for thee that thou hadst never been born ;*' however, I cannot remember the words exactly. In the mean
time, the soldiers had risen, and again approached Jesus,
but they waited for the sign of the kiss, with which Judas
had promised to salute his Master that they might recognise him. Peter and the other disciples surrounded Judas,
and reviled him in unmeasured terms, calling him thief
and traitor ; he tried to mollify their wrath by all kinds
of lies, but his efforts were vain, for the soldiers came up
and offered to defend him, which proceeding manifested
the truth at once.

Jesus again asked, ' *Whom seek ye?*' They replied:
' *Jesus of Nazareth.*' Jesus made answer, ' *I have told
you that I am he,*' ' *if therefore you seek me, let these go
their way.*' At these words the soldiers fell for the
second time to the ground, in convulsions similar to those
of epilepsy, and the Apostles again surrounded Judas and
expressed their indignation at his shameful treachery.
Jesus said to the soldiers, '*Arise,*' and they arose, but at
first quite speechless from terror. They then told Judas
to give them the signal agreed upon instantly, as their
orders were to seize upon no one but him whom Judas
kissed. Judas therefore approached Jesus, and gave him
a kiss, saying, ' *Hail Rabbi.*' Jesus replied, ' *What,
Judas, dost thou betray the Son of Man with a kiss?*' The
soldiers immediately surrounded Jesus, and the archers
laid hands upon him. Judas wished to fly, but the
Apostles would not allow it ; they rushed at the soldiers
and cried out, ' *Master, shall we strike with the sword?*'

Peter, who was more impetuous than the rest, seized the sword, and struck Malchus, the servant of the high priest, who wished to drive away the Apostles, and cut off his right ear ; Malchus fell to the ground, and a great tumult ensued.

The archers had seized upon Jesus, and wished to bind him ; while Malchus and the rest of the soldiers stood around. When Peter struck the former, the rest were occupied in repulsing those among the disciples who approached too near, and in pursuing those who ran away. Four disciples made their appearance in the distance, and looked fearfully at the scene before them; but the soldiers were still too much alarmed at their late fall to trouble themselves much about them, and besides they did not wish to leave our Saviour without a certain number of men to guard him. Judas fled as soon as he had given the traitorous kiss, but was met by some of the disciples, who overwhelmed him with reproaches. Six Pharisees, however, came to his rescue, **and he** escaped whilst the archers were busily occupied in pinioning Jesus.

When Peter struck Malchus, Jesus said to him, '*Put up again thy sword into its place ; for all that take the sword shall perish with the sword. Thinkest thou that I cannot ask my Father, and he will give me presently more than twelve legions of angels ? How then shall the Scriptures be fulfilled, that so it must be done ?*' Then he said, 'Let me cure this man;' and approaching Malchus, he touched his ear, prayed, and it was healed. The soldiers who were standing near, as well as the archers and the six Pharisees, far from being moved by this miracle, continued to insult our Lord, and said to the bystanders, ' It is a trick of the devil, the powers of witchcraft made the ear appear to be cut off, and now the same power gives it the appearance of being healed.'

Then Jesus again addressed them, ' *You are come out as it were to a robber, with swords and clubs, to apprehend me. I sat daily with you teaching in the Temple, and you laid not hands upon me, but this is your hour and the power of darkness.*' The Pharisees ordered him to be bound still more strongly, and made answer in a contemptuous tone, 'Ah! thou couldst not overthrow us by thy witchcraft.' Jesus replied, but I do not remember his words, and all the disciples fled. The four archers and the six Pharisees did not fall to the ground at the words of Jesus, because, as was afterwards revealed to me, they as well as Judas, who likewise did not fall, were entirely in the power of Satan, whereas all those who fell and rose again were afterwards converted, and became Christians; they had only surrounded Jesus, and not laid hands upon him. Malchus was instantly converted by the cure wrought upon him, and during the time of the Passion his employment was to carry messages backwards and forwards to Mary and the other friends of our Lord.

The archers, who now proceeded to pinion Jesus with the greatest brutality, were pagans of the lowest extraction, short, stout, and active, with sandy complexions, resembling those of Egyptian slaves, and bare legs, arms, and neck.

They tied his hands as tightly as possible with hard new cords, fastening the right-hand wrist under the left elbow, and the left-hand wrist under the right elbow. They encircled his waist with a species of belt studded with iron points, and bound his hands to it with osier bands, while on his neck they put a collar covered with iron points, and to this collar were appended two leathern straps, which were crossed over his chest like a stole and fastened to the belt. They then fastened four ropes to different parts of the belt, and by means of these ropes dragged our Blessed Lord from side to side in the most cruel manner. The ropes were new; I think they were purchased when the Pharisees first determined to arrest Jesus. The Pharisees lighted fresh torches, and the procession started. Ten soldiers walked in front, the archers who held the ropes and dragged Jesus along, followed, and the Pharisees and ten other soldiers brought up the rear. The disciples wandered about at a distance, and wept and moaned as if beside themselves from grief. John alone followed, and walked at no great distance from the soldiers, until the Pharisees, seeing him, ordered the guards to arrest him. They endeavoured to obey, but he ran away, leaving in their hands a cloth with which he was covered, and of which they had taken hold when they endeavoured to seize him. He had slipped off his coat, that he might escape more easily from the hands of his enemies, and kept nothing on but a short under garment without sleeves, and the long band which the Jews usually wore, and which was wrapped round his neck, head, and arms. The archers behaved in the most cruel manner to Jesus as they led him along ; this they did to curry favour with the six Pharisees, who they well knew perfectly hated and detested our Lord. They led him along the roughest road they could select, over the sharpest stones, and through the thickest mire ; they pulled the cords as tightly as possible ; they struck him with knotted cords, as a butcher would strike the beast he is about to slaughter ; and they accompanied this cruel treatment with such ignoble and indecent insults that I cannot recount them. The feet of Jesus were bare ; he wore, besides the ordinary dress, a seamless woollen garment, and a cloak which was thrown over all. I have forgotten to state that when Jesus was arrested, it was done without any order being presented or legal ceremony taking place ; he was treated as a person without the pale of the law.

The procession proceeded at a good pace ; when they left the road which runs between the Garden of Olives and that of Gethsemani, they turned to the right, and soon reached a bridge which was thrown over the Torrent of Cedron. When Jesus went to the Garden of Olives with the Apostles, he did not cross this bridge, but went by a private path which ran through the Valley of Josaphat, and led to another bridge more to the south. The bridge over which the soldiers led Jesus was long, being thrown over not only the torrent, which was very large in this part, but likewise over the valley, which extends a considerable distance to the right and to the left, and is much lower than the bed of the river. I saw our Lord fall twice before he reached the bridge, and these falls were caused entirely by the barbarous manner in which the soldiers dragged him ; but when they were half over the bridge they gave full vent to their brutal inclinations, and struck Jesus with such violence that they threw him off the bridge into the water, and scornfully recommended him to quench his thirst there.   If God had not preserved him, he must have been killed by this fall ; he fell first on his knee, and then on his face, but saved himself a little by stretching out his hands, which, although so tightly bound before, were loosened, I know not whether by miracle, or whether the soldiers had cut the cords before they threw him into the water.   The marks of his feet, his elbows, and his fingers were miraculously impressed on the rock on which he fell, and these impressions were afterwards shown for the veneration of Christians.   These stones were less hard than the unbelieving hearts of the wicked men who surrounded Jesus, and bore witness at this terrible moment to the Divine Power which had touched them.

I had not seen Jesus take anything to quench the thirst which had consumed him ever since his agony in the garden, but he drank when he fell into the Cedron, and I heard him repeat these words from the prophetic Psalm, ' *In his thirst he will drink water from the torrent*' (Psalm cviii.).

The archers still held the ends of the ropes with which Jesus was bound, but it would have been difficult to drag him out of the water on that side, on account of a wall which was built on the shore ; they turned back and dragged him quite through the Cedron to the shore, and then made him cross the bridge a second time, accompanying their every action with insults, blasphemies, and blows. His long woollen garment, which was quite soaked through, adhered to his legs, impeded every movement, and rendered it almost impossible for him to walk, and when he reached the end of the bridge he fell quite down.   They pulled him up again in the most cruel manner, struck him with cords, and fastened the ends of his wet garment to the belt, abusing him at the same time in the most cowardly manner.   It was not quite midnight when I saw the four archers inhumanly dragging Jesus over a narrow path, which was choked up with stones, fragments of rock, thistles, and thorns, on the opposite shore of the Cedron. The six brutal Pharisees walked as close to our Lord as they could, struck him constantly with thick pointed sticks, and seeing that his bare and bleeding feet were torn by the stones and briars, exclaimed scornfully : 'His precursor, John the Baptist, has certainly not prepared a good path for him here;' or, 'The words of Malachy, "*Behold, I send my angel before thy face, to prepare the way before thee,*" do not exactly apply now.' Every jest uttered by these men incited the archers to greater cruelty.

The enemies of Jesus remarked that several persons made their appearance in the distance; they were only disciples who had assembled when they heard that their Master was arrested, and who were anxious to discover what the end would be ; but the sight of them rendered the Pharisees uneasy, lest any attempt should be made to rescue Jesus, and they therefore sent for a reinforcement of soldiers. At a very short distance from an entrance opposite to the south side of the Temple, which leads through a little village called Ophel to Mount Sion, where the residences of Annas and Caiphas were situated, I saw a band of about fifty soldiers, who carried torches, and appeared ready for anything ; the demeanour of these men was outrageous, and they gave loud shouts, both to announce their arrival, and to congratulate their comrades upon the success of the expedition. This caused a slight confusion among the soldiers who were leading Jesus, and Malchus and a few others took advantage of it to depart, and fly towards Mount Olivet.

When the fresh band of soldiers left Ophel, I saw those disciples who had gathered together disperse ; some went one way, and some another. The Blessed Virgin and about nine of the holy women, being filled with anxiety, directed their steps towards the Valley of Josaphat, accompanied by Lazarus, John the son of Mark, the son of Veronica, and the son of Simon. The last-named was at Gethsemani with Nathaniel and the eight Apostles, and had fled when the soldiers appeared. He was giving the Blessed Virgin the account of all that had been done, when the fresh band of soldiers joined those who were leading Jesus, and she then heard their tumultuous vociferations, and saw the light of the torches they carried. This sight quite over-came her; she became insensible, and John took her into the house of Mary, the mother of Mark.

The fifty soldiers who were sent to join those who had taken Jesus, were a detachment from a company of three hundred men posted to guard the gates and environs of Ophel; for the traitor Judas had reminded the High Priests that the inhabitants of Ophel (who were princi-pally of the labouring class, and whose chief employment was to bring water and wood to the Temple) were the most attached partisans of Jesus, and might perhaps make some attempts to rescue him. The traitor was aware that Jesus had both consoled, instructed, assisted, and cured the diseases of many of these poor workmen, and that Ophel was the place where he halted during his journey from Bethania to Hebron, when John the Baptist had just been executed. Judas also knew that Jesus had cured many of the masons who were injured by the fall of the Tower of Siloe. The greatest part of the inhabitants of Ophel were converted after the death of our Lord, and joined the first Christian community that was formed after Pentecost, and when the Christians separated from the Jews and erected new dwellings, they placed their huts and tents in the valley which is situated between Mount Olivet and Ophel, and there St. Stephen lived. Ophel was on a hill to the south of the Temple, surrounded by walls, and its inhabitants were very poor. I think it was smaller than Dulmer.*

The slumbers of the good inhabitants of Ophel were disturbed by the noise of the soldiers; they came out of their houses and ran to the entrance of the village to ask the cause of the uproar; but the soldiers received them roughly, ordered them to return home, and in reply to

* Dulmen is a small town in Westphalia, where Sister Emme-rich lived at this time.

their numerous questions, said, 'We have just arrested
Jesus, your false prophet—he who has deceived you so
grossly; the High Priests are about to judge him, and he
will be crucified.' Cries and lamentations arose on all
sides; the poor women and children ran backwards and
forwards, weeping and wringing their hands; and calling
to mind all the benefits they had received from our Lord,
they cast themselves on their knees to implore the protec-
tion of Heaven. But the soldiers pushed them on one side,
struck them, obliged them to return to their houses, and
exclaimed, 'What farther proof is required? Does not
the conduct of these persons show plainly that the Galilæan incites rebellion?'

They were, however, a little cautious in their expressions and demeanour for fear of causing an insurrection in
Ophel, and therefore only endeavoured to drive the inhabitants away from those parts of the village which Jesus was
obliged to cross.

When the cruel soldiers who led our Lord were near
the gates of Ophel he again fell, and appeared unable to
proceed a step farther, upon which one among them, being
moved to compassion, said to another, 'You see the poor
man is perfectly exhausted, he cannot support himself with
the weight of his chains; if we wish to get him to the
High Priest alive we must loosen the cords with which his
hands are bound, that he may be able to save himself a
little when he falls.' The band stopped for a moment,
the fetters were loosened, and another kind-hearted soldier
brought some water to Jesus from a neighbouring fountain. Jesus thanked him, and spoke of the 'fountains of
living water,' of which those who believed in him should
drink; but his words enraged the Pharisees still more, and
they overwhelmed him with insults and contumelious language. I saw the heart of the soldier who had caused
Jesus to be unbound, as also that of the one who brought
him water, suddenly illuminated by grace; they were both
converted before the death of Jesus, and immediately
joined his disciples.

The procession started again, and reached the gate of

Ophel. Here Jesus was again saluted by the cries of grief and sympathy of those who owed him so much gratitude, and the soldiers had considerable difficulty in keeping back the men and women who crowded round from all parts. They clasped their hands, fell on their knees, lamented, and exclaimed, 'Release this man unto us, release him! Who will assist, who will console us, who will cure our diseases? Release him unto us!' It was indeed heart-rending to look upon Jesus; his face was white, disfigured, and wounded, his hair dishevelled, his dress wet and soiled, and his savage and drunken guards were dragging him about and striking him with sticks like a poor dumb animal led to the slaughter. Thus was he conducted through the midst of the afflicted inhabitants of Ophel, and the paralytic whom he had cured, the dumb to whom he had restored speech, and the blind whose eyes he had opened, united, but in vain, in offering supplications for his release.

Many persons from among the lowest and most degraded classes had been sent by Annas, Caiphas, and the other enemies of Jesus, to join the procession, and assist the soldiers both in ill-treating Jesus, and in driving away the inhabitants of Ophel. The village of Ophel was seated upon a hill, and I saw a great deal of timber placed there ready for building. The procession had to proceed down a hill, and then pass through a door made in the wall. On one side of this door stood a large building erected originally by Solomon, and on the other the pool of Bethsaida. After passing this, they followed a westerly direction down a steep street called Millo, at the end of which a turn to the south brought them to the house of Annas. The guards never ceased their cruel treatment of our Divine Saviour, and excused such conduct by saying that the crowds who gathered together in front of the procession compelled them to severity. Jesus fell seven times between Mount Olivet and the house of Annas.

The inhabitants of Ophel were still in a state of consternation and grief, when the sight of the Blessed Virgin, who passed through the village accompanied by the holy

women and some other friends on her way from the Valley
of Cedron to the house of Mary the mother of Mark, excited them still more, and they made the place reëcho
with sobs and lamentations, while they surrounded and
almost carried her in their arms. Mary was speechless
from grief, and did not open her lips after she reached the
house of Mary the mother of Mark, until the arrival of
John, who related all he had seen since Jesus left the
supper-room; and a little later she was taken to the house
of Martha, which was near that of Lazarus. Peter and
John, who had followed Jesus at a distance, went in haste
to some servants of the High Priest with whom the latter
was acquainted, in order to endeavour by their means to
obtain admittance into the tribunal where their Master
was to be tried. These servants acted as messengers, and
had just been ordered to go to the houses of the ancients,
and other members of the Council, to summon them to
attend the meeting which was convoked. As they were
anxious to oblige the Apostles, but foresaw much difficulty
in obtaining their admittance into the tribunal, they gave
them cloaks similar to those they themselves wore, and
made them assist in carrying messages to the members in
order that afterwards they might enter the tribunal of Caiphas, and mingle, without being recognised, among the soldiers and false witnesses, as all other persons were to be
expelled. As Nicodemus, Joseph of Arimathea, and other
well-intentioned persons were members of this Council,
the Apostles undertook to let them know what was going
to be done in the Council, thus securing the presence of
those friends of Jesus whom the Pharisees had purposely
omitted to invite. In the mean time Judas wandered up
and down the steep and wild precipices at the south of
Jerusalem, despair marked on his every feature, and the
devil pursuing him to and fro, filling his imagination with
still darker visions, and not allowing him a moment's
respite.

CHAPTER IV.

Means employed by the enemies of Jesus for carrying out their designs against him.

No sooner was Jesus arrested than Annas and Caiphas were informed, and instantly began to arrange their plans with regard to the course to be pursued. Confusion speedily reigned everywhere—the rooms were lighted up in haste, guards placed at the entrances, and messengers dispatched to different parts of the town to convoke the members of the Council, the Scribes, and all who were to take a part in the trial. Many among them had, however, assembled at the house of Caiphas as soon as the treacherous compact with Judas was completed, and had remained there to await the course of events. The different classes of ancients were likewise assembled, and as the Pharisees, Sadducees, and Herodians were congregated in Jerusalem from all parts of the country for the celebration of the festival, and had long been concerting measures with the Council for the arrest of our Lord, the High Priests now sent for those whom they knew to be the most bitterly opposed to Jesus, and desired them to assemble the witnesses, gather together every possible proof, and bring all before the Council. The proud Sadducees of Nazareth, of Capharnaum, of Thirza, of Gabara, of Jotapata, and of Silo, whom Jesus had so often reproved before the people, were actually dying for revenge. They hastened to all the inns to seek out those persons whom they knew to be enemies of our Lord, and offered them bribes in order to secure their appearance. But, with the exception of a few ridiculous calumnies, which were certain to be disproved as soon as investigated, nothing tangible could be brought forward against Jesus, excepting, indeed, those foolish accusations which he had so often refuted in the synagogue.

The enemies of Jesus hastened, however, to the tribunal of Caiphas, escorted by the Scribes and Pharisees of Jerusalem, and accompanied by many of those merchants whom our Lord drove out of the Temple when

they were holding market there; as also by the proud
doctors whom he had silenced before all the people, and
even by some who could not forgive the humiliation of
being convicted of error when he disputed with them in
the Temple at the age of twelve. There was likewise a
large body of impenitent sinners whom he had refused to
cure, relapsed sinners whose diseases had returned, worldly
young men whom he would not receive as disciples, ava-
ricious persons whom he had enraged by causing the money
which they had been in hopes of possessing to be distributed in alms. Others there were whose friends he had
cured, and who had thus been disappointed in their ex-
pectations of inheriting property; debauchees whose vic-
tims he had converted; and many despicable characters
who made their fortunes by flattering and fostering the
vices of the great.

All these emissaries of Satan were overflowing with
rage against everything holy, and consequently with an
indescribable hatred of the Holy of the Holies. They were
farther incited by the enemies of our Lord, and therefore
assembled in crowds round the palace of Caiphas, to bring
forward all their false accusations and to endeavour to
cover with infamy that spotless Lamb, who took upon
himself the sins of the world, and accepted the burden in
order to reconcile man with God.

Whilst all these wicked beings were busily consulting
as to what was best to be done, anguish and anxiety filled
the hearts of the friends of Jesus, for they were ignorant
of the mystery which was about to be accomplished, and
they wandered about, sighing, and listening to every different opinion. Each word they uttered gave rise to feelings of suspicion on the part of those whom they addressed,
and if they were silent, their silence was set down as
wrong. Many well-meaning but weak and undecided characters yielded to temptation, were scandalised, and lost
their faith; indeed, the number of those who persevered
was very small indeed. Things were the same then as
they oftentimes are now, persons were willing to serve
God if they met with no opposition from their fellow-

creatures, but were ashamed of the Cross if held in contempt by others. The hearts of some were, however, touched by the patience displayed by our Lord in the midst of his sufferings, and they walked away silent and sad.

CHAPTER V.

A Glance at Jerusalem.

THE customary prayers and preparations for the celebration of the festival being completed, the greatest part of the inhabitants of the densely-populated city of Jerusalem, as also the strangers congregated there, were plunged in sleep after the fatigues of the day, when, all at once, the arrest of Jesus was announced, and every one was aroused, both his friends and foes, and numbers immediately responded to the summons of the High Priest, and left their dwellings to assemble at his court. In some parts the light of the moon enabled them to grope their way in safety along the dark and gloomy streets, but in other parts they were obliged to make use of torches. Very few of the houses were built with their windows looking on the street, and, generally speaking, their doors were in inner courts, which gave the streets a still more gloomy appearance than is usual at this hour. The steps of all were directed towards Sion, and an attentive listener might have heard persons stop at the doors of their friends, and knock, in order to awaken them—then hurry on, then again stop to question others, and, finally, set off anew in haste towards Sion. Newsmongers and servants were hurrying forward to ascertain what was going on, in order that they might return and give the account to those who remained at home; and the bolting and barricading of doors might be plainly heard, as many persons were much alarmed and feared an insurrection, while a thousand different propositions were made and opinions given, such as the following:—'Lazarus and his sisters will soon know who is this man in whom they have placed such firm re-

liance. Joanna, Chusa, Susannah, Mary the mother of
Mark, and Salome will repent, but too late, the impru-
dence of their conduct; Seraphia, the wife of Sirach, will
be compelled to make an apology to her husband now, for
he has so often reproached her with her partiality for the
Galilæan. The partisans of this fanatical man, this inciter
of rebellion, pretended to be filled with compassion for all
who looked upon things in a different light from themselves, and now they will not know where to hide their
heads. He will find no one now to cast garments and
strew olive-branches at his feet. Those hypocrites who
pretended to be so much better than other persons will
receive their deserts, for they are all implicated with the
Galilæan. It is a much more serious business than was at
first thought. I should like to know how Nicodemus and
Joseph of Arimathea will get out of it; the High Priests
have mistrusted them for some time; they made common
cause with Lazarus: but they are extremely cunning. All
will now, however, be brought to light.'

Speeches such as these were uttered by persons who
were exasperated, not only against the disciples of Jesus,
but likewise with the holy women who had supplied his
temporal wants, and had publicly and fearlessly expressed
their veneration for his doctrines, and their belief in his
Divine mission.

But although many persons spoke of Jesus and his
followers in this contemptuous manner, yet there were
others who held very different opinions, and of these some
were frightened, and others, being overcome with sorrow,
sought friends to whom they might unburden their hearts,
and before whom they could, without fear, give vent to
their feelings; but the number of those sufficiently daring
openly to avow their admiration for Jesus was but small.

Nevertheless, it was in parts only of Jerusalem that
these disturbances took place—in those parts where the
messengers had been sent by the High Priests and the
Pharisees, to convoke the members of the Council and to
call together the witnesses. It appeared to me that I saw
feelings of hatred and fury burst forth in different parts

of the city, under the form of flames, which flames traversed the streets, united with others which they met, and proceeded in the direction of Sion, increasing every moment, and at last came to a stop beneath the tribunal of Caiphas, where they remained, forming together a perfect whirlwind of fire.

The Roman soldiers took no part in what was going on; they did not understand the excited feelings of the people, but their sentinels were doubled, their cohorts drawn up, and they kept a strict look out; this, indeed, was customary at the time of the Paschal solemnity, on account of the vast number of strangers who were then assembled together. The Pharisees endeavoured to avoid the neighbourhood of the sentinels, for fear of being questioned by them, and of contracting defilement by answering their questions. The High Priests had sent a message to Pilate intimating their reasons for stationing soldiers round Ophel and Sion; but he mistrusted their intentions, as much ill-feeling existed between the Romans and the Jews. He could not sleep, but walked about during the greatest part of the night, hearkening to the different reports and issuing orders consequent on what he heard; his wife slept, but her sleep was disturbed by frightful dreams, and she groaned and wept alternately.

In no part of Jerusalem did the arrest of Jesus produce more touching demonstrations of grief than among the poor inhabitants of Ophel, the greatest part of whom were day-labourers, and the rest principally employed in menial offices in the service of the Temple. The news came unexpectedly upon them; for some time they doubted the truth of the report, and wavered between hope and fear; but the sight of their Master, their Benefactor, their Consoler, dragged through the streets, torn, bruised, and illtreated in every imaginable way, filled them with horror; and their grief was still farther increased by beholding his afflicted Mother wandering about from street to street, accompanied by the holy women, and endeavouring to obtain some intelligence concerning her Divine Son. These holy women were often obliged to hide in corners and

under door-ways for fear of being seen by the enemies of
Jesus; but even with these precautions they were oftentimes insulted, and taken for women of bad character—
their feelings were frequently harrowed by hearing the
malignant words and triumphant expressions of the cruel
Jews, and seldom, very seldom, did a word of kindness or
pity strike their ears. They were completely exhausted
before reaching their place of refuge, but they endeavoured
to console and support one another, and wrapped thick
veils over their heads. When at last seated, they heard a
sudden knock at the door, and listened breathlessly—the
knock was repeated, but softly, therefore they made certain
that it was no enemy, and yet they opened the door cau-
tiously, fearing a stratagem. It was indeed a friend, and
they eagerly questioned him, but derived no consolation
from his words; therefore, unable to rest quiet any longer,
they issued forth and walked about for a time, and then
again returned to their place of refuge—still more heartbroken than before.

The majority of the Apostles, overcome with terror,
were wandering about among the valleys which surround
Jerusalem, and at times took refuge in the caverns beneath
Mount Olivet. They started if they came in contact with
one another, spoke in trembling tones, and separated on
the least noise being heard. First they concealed themselves in one cave and then in another, next they endeavoured to return to the town, while some of their number
climbed to the top of Mount Olivet and cast anxious
glances at the torches, the light of which they could see
glimmering at and about Sion; they listened to every distant sound, made a thousand different conjectures, and
then returned to the valley, in hopes of getting some certain intelligence.

The streets in the vicinity of Caiphas's tribunal were
brightly illuminated with lamps and torches, but, as the
crowds gathered around it, the noise and confusion continued to increase. Mingling with these discordant sounds
might be heard the bellowing of the beasts which were
tethered on the outside of the walls of Jerusalem, and the

plaintive bleating of the lambs. There was something most touching in the bleating of these lambs, which were to be sacrificed on the following day in the Temple,—the *one* Lamb alone who was about to be offered a willing sacrifice opened not his mouth, like a sheep in the hands of the butcher, which resists not, or the lamb which is silent before the shearer ; and that Lamb was the Lamb of God—the Lamb without spot—the true Paschal Lamb —Jesus Christ himself.

The sky looked dark, gloomy, and threatening—the moon was red, and covered with livid spots ; it appeared as if dreading to reach its full, because its Creator was then to die.

Next I cast a glance outside the town, and, near the south gate, I beheld the traitor, Judas Iscariot, wandering about, alone, and a prey to the tortures of his guilty conscience ; he feared even his own shadow, and was followed by many devils, who endeavoured to turn his feelings of remorse into black despair. Thousands of evil spirits were busying themselves in all parts, tempting men first to one sin and then to another. It appeared as if the gates of hell were flung open, and Satan madly striving and exerting his whole energies to increase the heavy load of iniquities which the Lamb without spot had taken upon himself. The angels wavered between joy and grief; they desired ardently to fall prostrate before the throne of God, and to obtain permission to assist Jesus ; but at the same time they were filled with astonishment, and could only adore that miracle of Divine justice and mercy which had existed in Heaven for all eternity, and was now about to be accomplished ; for the angels believe, like us, in God, the Father Almighty, Creator of Heaven and Earth, and in Jesus Christ, his only Son, our Lord, who was conceived by the Holy Ghost, born of the Virgin Mary, who began on this night to suffer under Pontius Pilate, and the next day was to be crucified, to die, and be buried ; descend into hell, rise again on the third day, ascend into Heaven, be seated at the right hand of God the Father Almighty, and from thence come to judge the

living and the dead; they likewise believe in the Holy
Ghost, the Holy Catholic Church, the communion of
Saints, the forgiveness of sins, the resurrection of the
body, and life everlasting.

CHAPTER VI.

Jesus before Annas.

IT was towards midnight when Jesus reached the palace
of Annas, and his guards immediately conducted him into
a very large hall, where Annas, surrounded by twenty-
eight councillors, was seated on a species of platform,
raised a little above the level of the floor, and placed
opposite to the entrance. The soldiers who first arrested
Jesus now dragged him roughly to the foot of the tribunal. The room was quite full, between soldiers, the
servants of Annas, a number of the mob who had been
admitted, and the false witnesses who afterwards adjourned
to Caiphas's hall.

Annas was delighted at the thought of our Lord being
brought before him, and was looking out for his arrival
with the greatest impatience. The expression of his countenance was most repulsive, as it showed in every linea-
ment not only the infernal joy with which he was filled,
but likewise all the cunning and duplicity of his heart.
He was the president of a species of tribunal instituted for
the purpose of examining persons accused of teaching false
doctrines; and if convicted there, they were then taken
before the High Priest.

Jesus stood before Annas. He looked exhausted and
haggard; his garments were covered with mud, his hands
manacled, his head bowed down, and he spoke not a
word. Annas was a thin ill-humoured-looking old man,
with a scraggy beard. His pride and arrogance were
great; and as he seated himself he smiled ironically,
pretending that he knew nothing at all, and that he was
perfectly astonished at finding that the prisoner, whom

he had just been informed was to be brought before him, was no other than Jesus of Nazareth. ' Is it possible,' said he, ' is it possible that thou art Jesus of Nazareth ? Where are thy disciples, thy numerous followers ? Where is thy kingdom ? I fear affairs have not turned out as thou didst expect. The authorities, I presume, discovered that it was quite time to put a stop to thy conduct, disrespectful as it was towards God and his priests, and to such violations of the Sabbath. What disciples hast thou now ? Where are they all gone ? Thou art silent ! Speak out, seducer ! speak out, thou inciter of rebellion ! Didst thou not eat the Paschal lamb in an unlawful manner, at an improper time, and in an improper place ? Dost thou not desire to introduce new doctrines ? Who gave thee the right of preaching ? Where didst thou study ? Speak, what are the tenets of thy religion ?'

Jesus then raised his weary head, looked at Annas, and said, ' *I have spoken openly to the world ; I have always taught in the synagogue, and in the Temple, whither all the Jews resort ; and in secret I have spoken nothing. Why askest thou me ? Ask them who have heard what I have spoken unto them ; behold, they know what things I have said.*'

At this answer of Jesus the countenance of Annas flushed with fury and indignation. A base menial who was standing near perceived this, and he immediately struck our Lord on the face with his iron gauntlet, exclaiming at the same moment, ' *Answerest thou the High Priest so ?*' Jesus was so nearly prostrated by the violence of the blow, that when the guards likewise reviled and struck him, he fell quite down, and blood trickled from his face on to the floor. Laughter, insults, and bitter words resounded through the hall. The archers dragged him roughly up again, and he mildly answered, ' *If I have spoken evil, give testimony of the evil ; but if well, why strikest thou me ?*'

Annas became still more enraged when he saw the calm demeanour of Jesus, and, turning to the witnesses, he desired them to bring forward their accusations. They all began to speak at once :—' He has called himself king; he says that God is his Father; that the Pharisees are an adulterous generation. He causes insurrection among the people; he cures the sick by the help of the devil on the Sabbath-day. The inhabitants of Ophel assembled round him a short time ago, and addressed him by the titles of Saviour and Prophet. He lets himself be called the Son of God; he says that he is sent by God; he predicts the destruction of Jerusalem. He does not fast; he eats with sinners, with pagans, and with publicans, and associates with women of evil repute. A short time ago he said to a man who gave him some water to drink at the gates of Ophel, "that he would give unto him the waters of eternal life, after drinking which he would thirst no more." He seduces the people by words of double meaning,' &c., &c.

These accusations were all vociferated at once; some of the witnesses stood before Jesus and insulted him while they spoke by derisive gestures, and the archers went so far as even to strike him, saying at the same time, 'Speak; why dost thou not answer?' Annas and his adherents added mockery to insult, exclaiming at every pause in the accusations, 'This is thy doctrine, then, is it? What canst thou answer to this? Issue thy orders, great King; man sent by God, give proofs of thy mission.' 'Who art thou?' continued Annas, in a tone of cutting contempt; 'by whom art thou sent? Art thou the son of an obscure carpenter, or art thou Elias, who was carried up to heaven in a fiery chariot? He is said to be still living, and I have been told that thou canst make thyself invisible when thou pleasest. Perhaps thou art the prophet Malachy, whose words thou dost so frequently quote. Some say that an angel was his father, and that he likewise is still alive. An impostor as thou art could not have a finer opportunity of taking persons in than by passing thyself off as this prophet. Tell me, without farther preamble, to what order of kings thou dost belong? Thou art greater than Solomon,—at least thou pretendest so to be, and dost even expect to be believed. Be easy, I

will no longer refuse the title and the sceptre which are
so justly thy due.'

Annas then called for the sheet of parchment, about a
yard in length, and six inches in width ; on this he wrote
a series of words in large letters, and each word expressed
some different accusation which had been brought against
our Lord. He then rolled it up, placed it in a little hollow
tube, fastened it carefully on the top of · a reed, and presented this reed to Jesus, saying at the same time, with a
contemptuous sneer, ' Behold the sceptre of thy kingdom;
it contains thy titles, as also the account of the honours
to which thou art entitled, and of thy right to the throne.
Take them to the High Priest, in order that he may acknowledge thy regal dignity, and treat thee according to
thy deserts. Tie the hands of this king, and take him
before the High Priest.'

The hands of Jesus, which had been loosened, were
then tied across his breast in such a manner as to make
him hold the pretended sceptre, which contained the
accusations of Annas, and he was led to the Court of
Caiphas, amidst the hisses, shouts, and blows lavished
upon him by the brutal mob.

The house of Annas was not more than three hundred
steps from that of Caiphas ; there were high walls and
common-looking houses on each side of the road, which
was lighted up by torches and lanterns placed on poles,
and there were numbers of Jews standing about talking
in an angry excited manner. The soldiers could scarcely
make their way through the crowd, and those who had
behaved so shamefully to Jesus at the Court of Annas
continued their insults and base usage during the whole
of the time spent in walking to the house of Caiphas. I
saw money given to those who behaved the worst to Jesus
by armed men belonging to the tribunal, and I saw them
push out of the way all who looked compassionately at
him. The former were allowed to enter the Court of
Caiphas.

CHAPTER VII.

The Tribunal of Caiphas.

To enter Caiphas's tribunal persons had to pass through a large court, which may be called the exterior court; from thence they entered into an inner court, which extended all round the building. The building itself was of far greater length than breadth, and in the front there was a kind of open vestibule surrounded on three sides by columns of no great height. On the fourth side the columns were higher, and behind them was a room almost as large as the vestibule itself, where the seats of the members of the Council were placed on a species of round platform raised above the level of the floor. That assigned to the High Priest was elevated above the others; the criminal to be tried stood in the centre of the half-circle formed by the seats. The witnesses and accusers stood either by the side or behind the prisoner. There were three doors at the back of the judges' seats which led into another apartment, filled likewise with seats. This room was used for secret consultation. Entrances placed on the right and left hand sides of this room opened into the interior court, which was round, like the back of the building. Those who left the room by the door on the right-hand side saw on the left-hand side of the court the gate which led to a subterranean prison excavated under the room. There were many underground prisons there, and it was in one of these that Peter and John were confined a whole night, when they had cured the lame man in the Temple after Pentecost. Both the house and the courts were filled with torches and lamps, which made them as light as day. There was a large fire lighted in the middle of the porch, on each side of which were hollow pipes to serve as chimneys for the smoke, and round this fire were standing soldiers, menial servants, and witnesses of the lowest class who had received bribes for giving their false testimony. A few women were there likewise, whose employment was to pour out a species of red beverage for the soldiers, and to bake cakes, for which services they received a small compensation. The majority of the judges were already seated around Caiphas, the others came in shortly afterwards, and the porch was almost filled, between true and false witnesses, while many other persons likewise endeavoured to come in to gratify their curiosity, but were prevented. Peter and John entered the outer court, in the dress of travellers, a short time before Jesus was led through, and John succeeded in penetrating into the inner court, by means of a servant with whom he was acquainted. The door was instantly closed after him, therefore Peter, who was a little behind, was shut out. He begged the maid-servant to open the door for him, but she refused both his entreaties and those of John, and he must have remained on the outside had not Nicodemus and Joseph of Arimathea, who came up at this moment, taken him with them. The two Apostles then returned the cloaks which they had borrowed, and stationed themselves in a place from whence they could see the judges, and hear everything that was going on. Caiphas was seated in the centre of the raised platform, and seventy of the members of the Sanhedrim were placed around him, while the public officers, the Scribes, and the ancients were standing on either side, and the false witnesses behind them. Soldiers were posted from the base of the platform to the door of the vestibule through which Jesus was to enter. The countenance of Caiphas was solemn in the extreme, but the gravity was accompanied by unmistakable signs of suppressed rage and sinister intentions. He wore a long mantle of a dull red colour, embroidered in flowers and trimmed with golden fringe; it was fastened at the shoulders and on the chest, besides being ornamented in the front with gold clasps. His head-attire was high, and adorned with hanging ribbons, the sides were open, and it rather resembled a bishop's mitre. Caiphas had been waiting with his adherents belonging to the Great Council for some time, and so impatient was he that he arose several times, went into the outer court in his magnificent dress, and asked angrily whether Jesus of Nazareth was come. When

he saw the procession drawing near he returned to his
seat.

CHAPTER VIII.

Jesus before Caiphas.

JESUS was led across the court, and the mob received
him with groans and hisses. As he passed by Peter and
John, he looked at them, but without turning his head,
for fear of betraying them. Scarcely had he reached the
council-chamber, than Caiphas exclaimed in a loud tone,
'Thou art come, then, at last, thou enemy of God, thou
blasphemer, who dost disturb the peace of this holy night!'
The tube which contained the accusations of Annas, and
was fastened to the pretended sceptre in the hands of
Jesus, was instantly opened and read.

Caiphas made use of the most insulting language, and
the archers again struck and abused our Lord, vociferating
at the same time, 'Answer at once! Speak out! Art thou
dumb?' Caiphas, whose temper was indescribably proud
and arrogant, became even more enraged than Annas had
been, and asked a thousand questions one after the other,
but Jesus stood before him in silence, and with his eyes
cast down. The archers endeavoured to force him to speak
by repeated blows, and a malicious child pressed his thumb
into his lips, tauntingly bidding him to bite. The witnesses were then called for. The first were persons of the
lowest class, whose accusations were as incoherent and in-
consistent as those brought forward at the court of Annas,
and nothing could be made out of them; Caiphas therefore turned to the principal witnesses, the Pharisees and
the Sadducees, who had assembled from all parts of the
country. They endeavoured to speak calmly, but their
faces and manner betrayed the virulent envy and hatred
with which their hearts were overflowing, and they repeated over and over again the same accusations, to which
he had already replied so many times : 'That he cured the
sick, and cast out devils, by the help of devils—that he

profaned the Sabbath—incited the people to rebel—called
the Pharisees a race of vipers and adulterers—predicted
the destruction of Jerusalem—frequented the society of
publicans and sinners—assembled the people and gave
himself out as a king, a prophet, and the Son of God.'
They deposed 'that he was constantly speaking of his
kingdom,—that he forbade divorce,—called himself the
Bread of Life, and said that whoever did not eat his flesh
and drink his blood would not have eternal life.'

Thus did they distort and misinterpret the words he
had uttered, the instructions he had given, and the parables by which he had illustrated his instructions, giving
them the semblance of crimes.   But these witnesses could
not agree in their depositions, for one said, ' He calls himself king ;' and a second instantly contradicted, saying,
' No, he allows persons to call him so ; but directly they
attempted to proclaim him, he fled.' Another said, ' He
calls himself the Son of God,' but he was interrupted by a
fourth, who exclaimed, ' No, he only styles himself the
Son of God because he does the will of his Heavenly
Father.' Some of the witnesses stated that he had cured
them, but that their diseases had returned, and that his
pretended cures were only performed by magic. They
spoke likewise of the cure of the paralytic man at the
pool of Bethsaida, but they distorted the facts so as to
give them the semblance of crimes, and even in these accusations they could not agree, contradicting one another.
The Pharisees of Sephoris, with whom he had once had a
discussion on the subject of divorces, accused him of teaching false doctrines, and a young man of Nazareth, whom
he had refused to allow to become one of his disciples, was
likewise base enough to bear witness against him.

It was found to be utterly impossible to prove a single
fact, and the witnesses appeared to come forward for the
sole purpose of insulting Jesus, rather than to demonstrate
the truth of their statements. Whilst they were disputing
with one another, Caiphas and some of the other members
of the Council employed themselves in questioning Jesus,
and turning his answers into derision.   ' What species of

king art thou? Give proofs of thy power! Call the legions
of angels of whom thou didst speak in the Garden of
Olives! What hast thou done with the money given unto
thee by the widows, and other simpletons whom thou didst
seduce by thy false doctrines? Answer at once : speak
out,—art thou dumb? Thou wouldst have been far wiser
to have kept silence when in the midst of the foolish mob :
there thou didst speak far too much.'

All these questions were accompanied by blows from
the under-servants of the members of the tribunal, and
had our Lord not been supported from above, he could
not have survived this treatment. Some of the base witnesses endeavoured to prove that he was an illegitimate
son ; but others declared that his mother was a pious Virgin, belonging to the Temple, and that they afterwards
saw her betrothed to a man who feared God. The witnesses
upbraided Jesus and his disciples with not having offered
sacrifice in the Temple. It is true that I never did see
either Jesus or his disciples offer any sacrifice in the
Temple, excepting the Paschal lamb; but Joseph and
Anna used frequently during their lifetime to offer sacrifice for the Child Jesus. However, even this accusation
was puerile, for the Essenians never offered sacrifice, and
no one thought the less well of them for not doing so.
The enemies of Jesus still continued to accuse him of being
a sorcerer, and Caiphas affirmed several times that the confusion in the statements of the witnesses was caused solely
by witchcraft.

Some said that he had eaten the Paschal lamb on the
previous day, which was contrary to the law, and that the
year before he had made different alterations in the manner
of celebrating this ceremony. But the witnesses contradicted one another to such a degree that Caiphas and his
adherents found, to their very great annoyance and anger,
that not one accusation could be really proved. Nicodemus
and Joseph of Arimathea were called up, and being commanded to say how it happened that they had allowed
him to eat the Pasch on the wrong day in a room which
belonged to them, they proved from ancient documents

that from time immemorial the Galilæans had been allowed
to eat the Pasch a day earlier than the rest of the Jews.
They added that every other part of the ceremony had
been performed according to the directions given in the
law, and that persons belonging to the Temple were present at the supper. This quite puzzled the witnesses, and
Nicodemus increased the rage of the enemies of Jesus by
pointing out the passages in the archives which proved the
right of the Galilæans, and gave the reason for which this
privilege was granted. The reason was this : the sacrifices
would not have been finished by the Sabbath if the immense multitudes who congregated together for that purpose had all been obliged to perform the ceremony on the
same day ; and although the Galilæans had not always
profited by this right, yet its existence was incontestably
proved by Nicodemus ; and the anger of the Pharisees was
heightened by his remarking that the members of the
Council had cause to be greatly offended at the gross contradictions in the statements of the witnesses, and that the
extraordinary and hurried manner in which the whole
affair had been conducted showed that malice and envy
were the sole motives which induced the accusers, and
made them bring the case forward at a moment when all
were busied in the preparations for the most solemn feast
of the year. They looked at Nicodemus furiously, and
could not reply, but continued to question the witnesses
in a still more precipitate and imprudent manner. Two
witnesses at last came forward, who said, ' This man said,
" *I will destroy this Temple made with hands, and within
three days I will build another not made with hands.*" '
However, even these witnesses did not agree in their statements, for one said that the accused wished to build a new
Temple, and that he had eaten the Pasch in an unusual
place, because he desired the destruction of the ancient
Temple ; but the other said, ' Not so : the edifice where he
ate the Pasch was built by human hands, therefore he
could not have referred to that.'

The wrath of Caiphas was indescribable ; for the cruel
treatment which Jesus had suffered, his Divine patience,

and the contradictions of the witnesses, were beginning to make a great impression on many persons present, a few hisses were heard, and the hearts of some were so touched that they could not silence the voice of their consciences. Ten soldiers left the court under pretext of indisposition, but in reality overcome by their feelings. As they passed by the place where Peter and John were standing, they exclaimed, 'The silence of Jesus of Nazareth, in the midst of such cruel treatment, is superhuman: it would melt a heart of iron: the wonder is, that the earth does not open and swallow such reprobates as his accusers must be. But tell us, where must we go?' The two Apostles either mistrusted the soldiers, and thought they were only seeking to betray them, or they were fearful of being recognised by those around and denounced as disciples of Jesus, for they only made answer in a melancholy tone: 'If truth calls you, follow it, and all will come right of itself.' The soldiers instantly went out of the room, and left Jerusalem soon after. They met persons on the outskirts of the town, who directed them to the caverns which lay to the south of Jerusalem, on the other side of Mount Sion, where many of the Apostles had taken refuge. These latter were at first alarmed at seeing strangers enter their hiding-place; but the soldiers soon dispelled all fear, and gave them an account of the sufferings of Jesus.

The temper of Caiphas, which was already perturbed, became quite infuriated by the contradictory statements of the two last witnesses, and rising from his seat he approached Jesus, and said: '*Answerest thou nothing to the things which these witness against thee?*'

Jesus neither raised his head nor looked at the High Priest, which increased the anger of the latter to the greatest degree; and the archers perceiving this seized our Lord by the hair, pulled his head back, and gave him blows under the chin; but he still kept his eyes cast down. Caiphas raised his hands, and exclaimed in an enraged tone: '*I adjure thee by the living God that thou tell us if thou be Christ* the Messiah, *the son of* the living God?'

A momentary and solemn pause ensued. Then Jesus

in a majestic and superhuman voice replied, ' *Thou hast
said it. Nevertheless I say to you, Hereafter you shall see
the Son of Man sitting on the right hand of the power of
God, and coming in the clouds of Heaven.*' Whilst Jesus
was pronouncing these words, a bright light appeared to
me to surround him ; Heaven was opened above his head ;
I saw the Eternal Father ; but no words from a human pen
can describe the intuitive view that was then vouchsafed
me of him.   I likewise saw the angels, and the prayers of
the just ascending to the throne of God.

At the same moment I perceived the yawning abyss
of hell like a fiery meteor at the feet of Caiphas ; it was
filled with horrible devils ; a slight gauze alone appeared
to separate him from its dark flames.   I could see the demoniacal fury with which his heart was overflowing, and
the whole house looked to me like hell.   At the moment
that our Lord pronounced the solemn words, ' *I am the
Christ, the Son of the living God,*' hell appeared to be
shaken from one extremity to the other, and then, as it
were, to burst forth and inundate every person in the
house of Caiphas with feelings of redoubled hatred towards
our Lord. These things are always shown to me under the
appearance of some material object, which renders them
less difficult of comprehension, and impresses them in a
more clear and forcible manner on the mind, because we
ourselves being material beings, facts are more easily illustrated in our regard if manifested through the medium of
the senses.   The despair and fury which these words produced in hell were shown to me under the appearance of
a thousand terrific figures in different places.   I remember
seeing, among other frightful things, a number of little
black objects, like dogs with claws, which walked on their
hind legs ; I knew at the time what kind of wickedness
was indicated by this apparition, but I cannot remember
now.   I saw these horrible phantoms enter into the bodies
of the greatest part of the bystanders, or else place themselves on their head or shoulders.   I likewise at this moment saw frightful spectres come out of the sepulchres on
the other side of Sion ; I believe they were evil spirits. I

saw in the neighbourhood of the Temple many other apparitions, which resembled prisoners loaded with chains : I do not know whether they were demons, or souls condemned to remain in some particular part of the earth, and who were then going to Limbo, which our Lord's condemnation to death had opened to them.

It is extremely difficult to explain these facts, for fear of scandalising those who have no knowledge of such things; but persons who see feel them, and they often cause the very hair to stand on end on the head. I think that John saw some of these apparitions, for I heard him speak about them afterwards. All whose hearts were not radically corrupted felt excessively terrified at these events, but the hardened were sensible of nothing but an increase of hatred and anger against our Lord.

Caiphas then arose, and, urged on by Satan, took up the end of his mantle, pierced it with his knife, and rent it from one end to the other, exclaiming at the same time, in a loud voice, ' *He hath blasphemed, what further need have we of witnesses ? Behold, now you have heard the blasphemy : what think you ?*' All who were then present arose, and exclaimed with astounding malignancy, ' *He is guilty of death !*'

During the whole of this frightful scene, the devils were in the most tremendous state of excitement ; they appeared to have complete possession not only of the enemies of Jesus, but likewise of their partisans and cowardly followers. The powers of darkness seemed to me to proclaim a triumph over the light, and the few among the spectators whose hearts still retained a glimmering of light were filled with such consternation that, covering their heads, they instantly departed. The witnesses who belonged to the upper classes were less hardened than the others ; their consciences were racked with remorse, and they followed the example given by the persons mentioned above, and left the room as quickly as possible, while the rest crowded round the fire in the vestibule, and ate and drank after receiving full pay for their services. The High Priest then addressed the archers, and said, ' I deliver

this king up into your hands; render the blasphemer the
honours which are his due.'   After these words he retired
with the members of his Council into the round room behind the tribunal, which could not be seen from the vestibule.

In the midst of the bitter affliction which inundated
the heart of John, his thoughts were with the Mother of
Jesus; he feared that the dreadful news of the condemnation of her Son might be communicated to her suddenly,
or that perhaps some enemy might give the information in
a heartless manner.   He therefore looked at Jesus, and
saying in a low voice, 'Lord, thou knowest why I leave
thee,' went away quickly to seek the Blessed Virgin, as if
he had been sent by Jesus himself.   Peter was quite overcome between anxiety and sorrow, which, joined to fatigue,
made him chilly; therefore, as the morning was cold, he
went up to the fire where many of the common people
were warming themselves.   He did his best to hide his
grief in their presence, as he could not make up his mind
to go home and leave his beloved Master.

CHAPTER IX.

The Insults received by Jesus in the Court of Caiphas.

No sooner did Caiphas, with the other members of the
Council, leave the tribunal than a crowd of miscreants—
the very scum of the people — surrounded Jesus like a
swarm of infuriated wasps, and began to heap every imaginable insult upon him.   Even during the trial, whilst
the witnesses were speaking, the archers and some others
could not restrain their cruel inclinations, but pulled out
handfuls of his hair and beard, spat upon him, struck him
with their fists, wounded him with sharp-pointed sticks,
and even ran needles into his body; but when Caiphas
left the hall they set no bounds to their barbarity.   They
first placed a crown, made of straw and the bark of trees,
upon his head, and then took it off, saluting him at the

same time with insulting expressions, like the following : ' Behold the Son of David wearing the crown of his father.' ' A greater than Solomon is here ; this is the king who is preparing a wedding feast for his son.' Thus did they turn into ridicule those eternal truths which he had taught under the form of parables to those whom he came from heaven to save ; and whilst repeating these scoffing words, they continued to strike him with their fists and sticks, and to spit in his face. Next they put a crown of reeds upon his head, took off his robe and scapular, and then threw an old torn mantle, which scarcely reached his knees, over his shoulders ; around his neck they hung a long iron chain, with an iron ring at each end, studded with sharp points, which bruised and tore his knees as he walked. They again pinioned his arms, put a reed into his hand, and covered his Divine countenance with spittle. They had already thrown all sorts of filth over his hair, as well as over his chest, and upon the old mantle. They bound his eyes with a dirty rag, and struck him, crying out at the same time in loud tones, *' Prophesy unto us, O Christ, who is he that struck thee ?'* He answered not one word, but sighed, and prayed inwardly for them.

After many more insults, they seized the chain which was hanging on his neck, dragged him towards the room into which the Council had withdrawn, and with their sticks forced him in, vociferating at the same time, ' March forward, thou King of Straw ! Show thyself to the Council with the insignia of the regal honours we have rendered unto thee.' A large body of councillors, with Caiphas at their head, were still in the room, and they looked with both delight and approbation at the shameful scene which was enacted, beholding with pleasure the most sacred ceremonies turned into derision. The pitiless guards covered him with mud and spittle, and with mock gravity exclaimed, ' Receive the prophetic unction—the regal unction.' Then they impiously parodied the baptismal ceremonies, and the pious act of Magdalen in emptying the vase of perfume on his head. ' How canst thou presume,' they exclaimed, ' to appear before the Council in such a condition? Thou dost purify others, and thou art not pure thyself; but we will soon purify thee.' They fetched a basin of dirty water, which they poured over his face and shoulders, whilst they bent their knees before him, and exclaimed, 'Behold thy precious unction, behold the spikenard worth three hundred pence; thou hast been baptised in the pool of Bethsaida.' They intended by this to throw into ridicule the act of respect and veneration shown by Magdalen, when she poured the precious ointment over his head, at the house of the Pharisee.

By their derisive words concerning his baptism in the pool of Bethsaida, they pointed out, although unintentionally, the resemblance between Jesus and the Paschal lamb, for the lambs were washed in the first place in the pond near the Probatica gate, and then brought to the pool of Bethsaida, where they underwent another purification before being taken to the Temple to be sacrificed. The enemies of Jesus likewise alluded to the man who had been infirm for thirty-eight years, and who was cured by Jesus at the pool of Bethsaida; for I saw this man either washed or baptised there; I say either washed or baptised, because I do not exactly remember the circumstances.

They then dragged Jesus round the room, before all the members of the Council, who continued to address him in reproachful and abusive language. Every countenance looked diabolical and enraged, and all around was dark, confused, and terrific. Our Lord, on the contrary, was from the moment that he declared himself to be the Son of God, generally surrounded with a halo of light. Many of the assembly appeared to have a confused knowledge of this fact, and to be filled with consternation at perceiving that neither outrages or ignominies could alter the majestic expression of his countenance.

The halo which shone around Jesus from the moment he declared himself to be the Christ, the Son of the Living God, served but to incite his enemies to greater fury, and yet it was so resplendent that they could not look at it, and I believe their intention in throwing the dirty rag over his head was to deaden its brightness.

CHAPTER X.

The Denial of St. Peter.

AT the moment when Jesus uttered the words, '*Thou hast said it*,' and the High Priest rent his garment, the whole room resounded with tumultuous cries. Peter and John, who had suffered intensely during the scene which had just been enacted, and which they had been obliged to witness in silence, could bear the sight no longer. Peter therefore got up to leave the room, and John followed soon after. The latter went to the Blessed Virgin, who was in the house of Martha with the holy women, but Peter's love for Jesus was so great, that he could not make up his mind to leave him; his heart was bursting, and he wept bitterly, although he endeavoured to restrain and hide his tears. It was impossible for him to remain in the tribunal, as his deep emotion at the sight of his beloved Master's sufferings would have betrayed him; therefore he went into the vestibule and approached the fire, around which soldiers and common people were sitting and talking in the most heartless and disgusting manner concerning the sufferings of Jesus, and relating all that they themselves had done to him. Peter was silent, but his silence and dejected demeanour made the bystanders suspect something. The portress came up to the fire in the midst of the conversation, cast a bold glance at Peter and said, '*Thou also wast with Jesus the Galilæan.*' These words startled and alarmed Peter; he trembled as to what might ensue if he owned the truth before his brutal companions, and therefore answered quickly, '*Woman, I know him not*,' got up, and left the vestibule. At this moment the cock crowed somewhere in the outskirts of the town. I do not remember hearing it, but I felt that it was crowing. As he went out, another maid-servant looked at him, and said to those who were with her, '*This man was also with him*,' and the persons she addressed immediately demanded of Peter whether her words were true, saying, ' Art thou not one

of this man's disciples?' Peter was even more alarmed
than before, and renewed his denial in these words, '*I
am not; I know not the man.*'

He left the inner court, and entered the exterior court;
he was weeping, and so great was his anxiety and grief,
that he did not reflect in the least on the words he had
just uttered. The exterior court was quite filled with persons, and some had climbed on to the top of the wall to
listen to what was going on in the inner court which they
were forbidden to enter. A few of the disciples were
likewise there, for their anxiety concerning Jesus was so
great that they could not make up their minds to remain
concealed in the caves of Hinnom. They came up to Peter,
and with many tears questioned him concerning their
loved Master, but he was so unnerved and so fearful of
betraying himself, that he briefly recommended them to
go away, as it was dangerous to remain, and left them
instantly. He continued to indulge his violent grief,
while they hastened to leave the town. I recognised among
these disciples, who were about sixteen in number, Bartholomew, Nathaniel, Saturninus, Judas Barsabeas, Simon,
who was afterwards bishop of Jerusalem, Zacheus, and
Manahem, the man who was born blind and cured by our
Lord.

Peter could not rest anywhere, and his love for Jesus
prompted him to return to the inner court, which he was
allowed to enter, because Joseph of Arimathea and Nicodemus had, in the first instance, taken him in. He did
not reënter the vestibule, but turned to the right and
went towards the round room which was behind the tribunal, and in which Jesus was undergoing every possible
insult and ignominy from his cruel enemies. Peter walked
timidly up to the door, and although perfectly conscious
that he was suspected by all present of being a partisan of
Jesus, yet he could not remain outside; his love for his
Master impelled him forward; he entered the room, advanced, and soon stood in the very midst of the brutal
throng who were feasting their cruel eyes on the sufferings
of Jesus. They were at that moment dragging him igno-

miniously backwards and forwards with the crown of straw upon his head; he cast a sorrowful and even severe glance upon Peter, which cut him to the heart, but as he was still much alarmed, and at that moment heard some of the bystanders call out, '*Who is that man?*' he went back again into the court, and seeing that the persons in the vestibule were watching him, came up to the fire and remained before it for some time. Several persons who had observed his anxious troubled countenance began to speak in opprobrious terms of Jesus, and one of them said to him, '*Thou also art one of his disciples; thou also art a Galilæan; thy very speech betrays thee.*' Peter got up, intending to leave the room, when a brother of Malchus came up to him and said, '*Did I not see thee in the garden with him?* didst thou not cut off my brother's ear?'

Peter became almost beside himself with terror; he began to curse and to swear '*that he knew not the man.*' and ran out of the vestibule into the outer court; the cock then crowed again, and Jesus, who at that moment was led across the court, cast a look of mingled compassion and grief upon his Apostle. This look of our Lord pierced Peter to the very heart,—it recalled to his mind in the most forcible and terrible manner the words addressed to him by our Lord on the previous evening: '*Before the cock crows twice, thou shalt thrice deny me.*' He had forgotten all his promises and protestations to our Lord, that he would die rather than deny him—he had forgotten the warning given to him by our Lord;—but when Jesus looked at him, he felt the enormity of his fault, and his heart was nigh bursting with grief. He had denied his Lord, when that beloved Master was outraged, insulted, delivered up into the hands of unjust judges,—when he was suffering all in patience and in silence. His feelings of remorse were beyond expression; he returned to the exterior court, covered his face and wept bitterly; all fear of being recognised was over;—he was ready to proclaim to the whole universe both his fault und his repentance.

What man will dare assert that he would have shown

more courage than Peter if, with his quick and ardent
temperament, he were exposed to such danger, trouble,
and sorrow, at a moment, too, when completely unnerved
between fear and grief, and exhausted by the sufferings of
this sad night ?   Our Lord left Peter to his own strength,
and he was weak, like all who forget the words: ' *Watch
and pray, that ye enter not into temptation.*'

CHAPTER XI.

Mary in the House of Caiphas.

THE Blessed Virgin was ever united to her Divine
Son by interior spiritual communications ; she was, therefore, fully aware of all that happened to him—she suffered
with him, and joined in his continual prayer for his murderers. But her maternal feelings prompted her to suppli-
cate Almighty God most ardently not to suffer the crime
to be completed, and to save her Son from such dreadful
torments. She eagerly desired to return to him; and
when John, who had left the tribunal at the moment the
frightful cry, ' *He is guilty of death,*' was raised, came to
the house of Lazarus to see after her, and to relate the
particulars of the dreadful scene he had just witnessed,
she, as also Magdalen and some of the other holy women,
begged to be taken to the place where Jesus was suffering.
John, who had only left our Saviour in order to console
her whom he loved best next to his Divine Master, instantly acceded to their request, and conducted them
through the streets, which were lighted up by the moon
alone, and crowded with persons hastening to their homes.
The holy women were closely veiled ; but the sobs which
they could not restrain made many who passed by observe
them, and their feelings were harrowed by the abusive
epithets they overheard bestowed upon Jesus by those
who were conversing on the subject of his arrest. The
Blessed Virgin, who ever beheld in spirit the opprobrious
treatment which her dear Son was receiving, continued

'to lay up *all these things in her heart;*' like him she suffered in silence; but more than once she became totally unconscious. Some disciples of Jesus, who were returning from the hall of Caiphas, saw her fainting in the arms of the holy women, and, touched with pity, stopped to look at her compassionately, and saluted her in these words : ' Hail! unhappy Mother—hail, Mother of the Most Holy One of Israel, the most afflicted of all mothers !' Mary raised her head, thanked them gratefully, and continued her sad journey.

When in the vicinity of Caiphas's house, their grief was renewed by the sight of a group of men who were busily occupied under a tent, making the cross ready for our Lord's crucifixion. The enemies of Jesus had given orders that the cross should be prepared directly after his arrest, that they might without delay execute the sentence which they hoped to persuade Pilate to pass on him. The Romans had already prepared the crosses of the two thieves, and the workmen who were making that of Jesus were much annoyed at being obliged to labour at it during the night; they did not attempt to conceal their anger at this, and uttered the most frightful oaths and curses, which pierced the heart of the tender Mother of Jesus through and through; but she prayed for these blind creatures who thus unknowingly blasphemed the Saviour who was about to die for their salvation, and prepared the cross for his cruel execution.

Mary, John, and the holy women traversed the outer court attached to Caiphas's house. They stopped under the archway of a door which opened into the inner court. Mary's heart was with her Divine Son, and she desired most ardently to see this door opened, that she might again have a chance of beholding him, for she knew that it alone separated her from the prison where he was confined. The door was at length opened, and Peter rushed out, his face covered with his mantle, wringing his hands, and weeping bitterly. By the light of the torches he soon recognised John and the Blessed Virgin, but the sight of them only renewed those dreadful feelings of remorse which the look of Jesus had awakened in his breast. Mary approached him instantly, and said, 'Simon, tell me, I entreat you, what is become of Jesus, my Son!' These words pierced his very heart; he could not even look at her, but turned away, and again wrung his hands. Mary drew close to him, and said in a voice trembling with emotion: 'Simon, son of John, why dost thou not answer me?'—'Mother!' exclaimed Peter, in a dejected tone, 'O, Mother, speak not to me—thy Son is suffering more than words can express: speak not to me! They have condemned him to death, and I have denied him three times.' John came up to ask a few more questions, but Peter ran out of the court as if beside himself, and did not stop for a single moment until he reached the cave at Mount Olivet—that cave on the stones of which the impression of the hands of our Saviour had been miraculously left. I believe it is the cave in which Adam took refuge to weep after his fall.

The Blessed Virgin was inexpressibly grieved at hearing of the fresh pang inflicted on the loving heart of her Divine Son, the pang of hearing himself denied by that disciple who had first acknowledged him as the Son of the Living God; she was unable to support herself, and fell down on the door-stone, upon which the impression of her feet and hands remains to the present day. I have seen the stones, which are preserved somewhere, but I cannot at this moment remember where. The door was not again shut, for the crowd was dispersing, and when the Blessed Virgin came to herself, she begged to be taken to some place as near as possible to her Divine Son. John, therefore, led her and the holy women to the front of the prison where Jesus was confined. Mary was with Jesus in spirit, and Jesus was with her; but this loving Mother wished to hear with her own ears the voice of her Divine Son. She listened and heard not only his moans, but also the abusive language of those around him. It was impossible for the holy women to remain in the court any longer without attracting attention. The grief of Magdalen was so violent that she was unable to conceal it ; and although the Blessed Virgin, by a special grace from Almighty God, maintained a calm and dignified exterior in the midst of her sufferings, yet even she was recognised, and overheard harsh words, such as these : ' *Is not that the Mother of the Galilæan ?* Her Son will most certainly be executed, but not before the festival, unless, indeed, he is the greatest of criminals.'

The Blessed Virgin left the court, and went up to the fireplace in the vestibule, where a certain number of persons were still standing. When she reached the spot where Jesus had said that he was the Son of God, and the wicked Jews cried out, ' *He is guilty of death,*' she again fainted, and John and the holy women carried her away, in appearance more like a corpse than a living person. The bystanders said not a word ; they seemed struck with astonishment, and silence, such as might have been produced in hell by the passage of a celestial being, reigned in that vestibule.

The holy women again passed the place where the cross was being prepared ; the workmen appeared to find as much difficulty in completing it as the judges had found in pronouncing sentence, and were obliged to fetch fresh wood every moment, for some bits would not fit, and others split; this continued until the different species of wood were placed in the cross according to the intentions of Divine Providence. I saw angels who obliged these men to recommence their work, and who would not let them rest, until all was accomplished in a proper manner ; but my remembrance of this vision is indistinct.

CHAPTER XII.

Jesus confined in the subterranean Prison.

THE Jews, having quite exhausted their barbarity, shut Jesus up in a little vaulted prison, the remains of which subsist to this day. Two of the archers alone remained with him, and they were soon replaced by two others.

He was still clothed in the old dirty mantle, and covered with the spittle and other filth which they had thrown over him; for they had not allowed him to put on his own clothes again, but kept his hands tightly bound together.

When our Lord entered this prison, he prayed most fervently that his Heavenly Father would accept all that he had already suffered, and all that he was about to suffer, as an expiatory sacrifice, not only for his executioners, but likewise for all who in future ages might have to suffer torments such as he was about to endure, and be tempted to impatience or anger.

The enemies of our Lord did not allow him a moment's respite, even in this dreary prison, but tied him to a pillar which stood in the centre, and would not allow him to lean upon it, although he was so exhausted from ill treatment, the weight of his chains, and his numerous falls, that he could scarcely support himself on his swollen and torn feet. Never for a moment did they cease insulting him; and when the first set were tired out, others replaced them.

It is quite impossible to describe all that the Holy of Holies suffered from these heartless beings; for the sight affected me so excessively that I became really ill, and I felt as if I could not survive it. We ought, indeed, to be ashamed of that weakness and susceptibility which renders us unable to listen composedly to the descriptions, or speak without repugnance, of those sufferings which our Lord endured so calmly and patiently for our salvation. The horror we feel is as great as that of a murderer who is forced to place his hands upon the wounds he himself has inflicted on his victim. Jesus endured all without opening his mouth; and it was man, sinful man, who perpetrated all these outrages against one who was at once their Brother, their Redeemer, and their God. I, too, am a great sinner, and my sins caused these sufferings. At the day of judgment, when the most hidden things will be manifested, we shall see the share we have had in the torments endured by the Son of God; we shall see how far we have caused them by the sins we so frequently commit, and which are, in fact, a species of consent which we give to, and a participation in, the tortures which were inflicted on Jesus by his cruel enemies. If, alas! we reflected seriously on this, we should repeat with much greater fervour the words which we find so often in prayer-books: 'Lord, grant that I may die, rather than ever wilfully offend thee again by sin.'

Jesus continued to pray for his enemies, and they being at last tired out left him in peace for a short time, when he leaned against the pillar to rest, and a bright light shone around him. The day was beginning to dawn, —the day of his Passion, of our Redemption,—and a faint ray penetrating the narrow vent-hole of the prison, fell upon the holy and immaculate Lamb, who had taken upon himself the sins of the world. Jesus turned towards the ray of light, raised his fettered hands, and, in the most touching manner, returned thanks to his Heavenly Father for the dawn of that day, which had been so long desired by the prophets, and for which he himself had so ardently sighed from the moment of his birth on earth, and concerning which he had said to his disciples, '*I have a baptism wherewith I am to be baptised, and how am I straitened until it be accomplished?*' I prayed with him; but I cannot give the words of his prayer, for I was so completely overcome, and touched to hear him return thanks to his Father for the terrible sufferings which he had already endured for me, and for the still greater which he was about to endure. I could only repeat over and over with the greatest fervour, ' Lord, I beseech thee, give me these sufferings: they belong to me : I have deserved them in punishment for my sins.' I was quite overwhelmed with feelings of love and compassion when I looked upon him thus welcoming the first dawn of the great day of his Sacrifice, and that ray of light which penetrated into his prison might, indeed, be compared to the visit of a judge who wishes to be reconciled to a criminal before the sentence of death which he has pronounced upon him is executed.

The archers, who were dozing, woke up for a moment, and looked at him with surprise : they said nothing, but appeared to be somewhat astonished and frightened. Our Divine Lord was confined in this prison during an hour, or thereabouts.

Whilst Jesus was in this dungeon, Judas, who had been wandering up and down the valley of Hinnom like a madman, directed his steps towards the house of Caiphas, with the thirty pieces of silver, the reward of his treachery, still hanging to his waist. All was silent around, and he addressed himself to some of the sentinels, without letting them know who he was, and asked what was going to be done to the Galilæan. ' He has been condemned to death, and he will certainly be crucified,' was the reply. Judas walked to and fro, and listened to the different conversations which were held concerning Jesus. Some spoke of the cruel treatment he had received, others of his astonishing patience, while others, again, discoursed concerning the solemn trial which was to take place in the morning before the great Council. Whilst the traitor was listening eagerly to the different opinions given, day dawned ; the members of the tribunal commenced their preparations, and Judas slunk behind the building that he might not be seen, for like Cain he sought to hide himself from human eyes, and despair was beginning to take possession of his soul. The place in which he took refuge happened to be the very spot where the workmen had been preparing the wood for making the cross of our Lord ; all was in readiness, and the men were asleep by its side. Judas was filled with horror at the sight : he shuddered and fled when he beheld the instrument of that cruel death to which for a paltry sum of money he had delivered up his Lord and Master ; he ran to and fro in perfect agonies of remorse, and finally hid himself in an adjoining cave, where he determined to await the trial which was to take place in the morning.

CHAPTER XIII.

The Morning Trial.

CAIPHAS, Annas, the ancients, and the scribes assembled again in the morning in the great hall of the tribunal, to have a legal trial, as meetings at night were not lawful, and could only be looked upon in the light of preparatory audiences. The majority of the members had slept in the house of Caiphas, where beds had been prepared for them, but some, and among them Nicodemus and Joseph of Arimathea, had gone home, and returned at the dawn of day. The meeting was crowded, and the members commenced their operations in the most hurried manner possible. They wished to condemn Jesus to death at once, but Nicodemus, Joseph, and some others opposed their wishes and demanded that the decision should be deferred until after the festival, for fear of causing an insurrection among the people, maintaining likewise that no criminal could be justly condemned upon charges which were not proved, and that in the case now before them all the witnesses contradicted one another. The High Priests and their adherents became very angry, and told Joseph and Nicodemus, in plain terms, that they were not surprised at their expressing displeasure at what had been done, because they were themselves partisans of the Galilæan and his doctrines, and were fearful of being convicted. The High Priest even went so far as to endeavour to exclude from the Council all those members who were in the slightest degree favourable to Jesus. These members protested that they washed their hands of all the future proceedings of the Council, and leaving the room went to the Temple, and from this day never again took their seats in the Council. Caiphas then ordered the guards to bring Jesus once more into his presence, and to prepare everything for taking him to Pilate's court directly he should have pronounced sentence. The emissaries of the Council hurried off to the prison, and with their usual brutality untied the hands of Jesus, dragged off the old mantle

which they had thrown over his shoulders, made him put
on his own soiled garment, and having fastened ropes
round his waist, dragged him out of the prison.   The appearance of Jesus, when he passed through the midst of
the crowd who were already assembled in the front of the
house, was that of a victim led to be sacrificed; his countenance was totally changed and disfigured from ill-usage,
and his garments stained and torn; but the sight of his
sufferings, far from exciting a feeling of compassion in the
hard hearted Jews, simply filled them with disgust, and
increased their rage.   Pity was, indeed, a feeling unknown
in their cruel breasts.

Caiphas, who did not make the slightest effort to conceal his hatred, addressed our Lord haughtily in these
words : *If thou be Christ, tell us plainly.*   Then Jesus
raised his head, and answered with great dignity and calmness, *If I shall tell you, you will not believe me ; and if I
shall also ask you, you will not answer me, nor let me go.
But hereafter the Son of Man shall be sitting on the right
hand of the power of God.*   The High Priests looked at
one another, and said to Jesus, with a disdainful laugh,
Art thou, then, the Son of God ?   And Jesus answered,
with the voice of eternal truth, *You say that I am.*
At these words they all exclaimed, *What need we any
further testimony ?   For we ourselves have heard it from
his own mouth.*

They all arose instantly and vied with each other as
to who should heap the most abusive epithets upon Jesus,
whom they termed a low-born miscreant, who aspired to
being their Messiah, and pretended to be entitled to sit
at the right hand of God.   They ordered the archers to
tie his hands again, and to fasten a chain round his neck
(this was usually done to criminals condemned to death),
and they then prepared to conduct him to Pilate's hall,
where a messenger had already been dispatched to beg
him to have all in readiness for trying a criminal, as it
was necessary to make no delay on account of the festival
day.

The Jewish Priests murmured among themselves at

being obliged to apply to the Roman governor for the confirmation of their sentence, but it was necessary, as they had not the right of condemning criminals excepting for things which concerned religion and the Temple alone, and they could not pass a sentence of death. They wished to prove that Jesus was an enemy to the emperor, and this accusation concerned those departments which were under Pilate's jurisdiction. The soldiers were all standing in front of the house, surrounded by a large body of the enemies of Jesus, and of common persons attracted by curiosity. The High Priests and a part of the Council walked at the head of the procession, and Jesus, led by archers, and guarded by soldiers, followed, while the mob brought up the rear. They were obliged to descend Mount Sion, and cross a part of the lower town to reach Pilate's palace, and many priests who had attended the Council went to the Temple directly afterwards, as it was necessary to prepare for the festival.

CHAPTER XIV.

The Despair of Judas

WHILST the Jews were conducting Jesus to Pilate, the traitor Judas walked about listening to the conversation of the crowd who followed, and his ears were struck by words such as these : ' They are taking him before Pilate ; the High Priests have condemned the Galilæan to death ; he will be crucified ; they will accomplish his death ; he has been already dreadfully ill-treated ; his patience is wonderful ; he answers not ; his only words are that he is the Messiah, and that he will be seated at the right hand of God ; they will crucify him on account of those words ; had he not said them they could not have condemned him to death. The miscreant who sold him was one of his disciples, and had a short time before eaten the Paschal lamb with him ; not for worlds would I have had to do with such an act ; however guilty the Galilæan may

be, he has not at all events sold his friend for money;
such an infamous character as this disciple is infinitely
more deserving of death.' Then, but too late, anguish,
despair, and remorse took possession of the mind of
Judas. Satan instantly prompted him to fly. He fled
as if a thousand furies were at his heel, and the bag
which was hanging at his side struck him as he ran, and
propelled him as a spur from hell; but he took it into his
hand to prevent its blows. He fled as fast as possible,
but where did he fly? Not towards the crowd, that he
might cast himself at the feet of Jesus, his merciful
Saviour, implore his pardon, and beg to die with him,—
not to confess his fault with true repentance before God,
but to endeavour to unburden himself before the world
of his crime, and of the price of his treachery. He ran
like one beside himself into the Temple, where several
members of the Council had gathered together after the
judgment of Jesus. They looked at one another with
astonishment; and then turned their haughty countenances, on which a smile of irony was visible, upon Judas.
He with a frantic gesture tore the thirty pieces of silver
from his side, and holding them forth with his right hand,
exclaimed in accents of the most deep despair, 'Take back
your silver—that silver with which you bribed me to betray this just man; take back your silver; release Jesus;
our compact is at an end; I have sinned grievously, for I
have betrayed innocent blood.' The priests answered him
in the most contemptuous manner, and, as if fearful of
contaminating themselves by the contact of the reward
of the traitor, would not touch the silver he tended, but
replied, 'What have we to do with thy sin? If thou
thinkest to have sold innocent blood, it is thine own
affair; we know what we have paid for, and we have
judged him worthy of death. Thou hast thy money, say
no more.' They addressed these words to him in the
abrupt tone in which men usually speak when anxious to
get rid of a troublesome person, and instantly arose and
walked away. These words filled Judas with such rage
and despair that he became almost frantic: his hair stood

on end on his head; he rent in two the bag which contained the thirty pieces of silver, cast them down in the Temple, and fled to the outskirts of the town.

I again beheld him rushing to and fro like a madman in the valley of Hinnom : Satan was by his side in a hideous form, whispering in his ear, to endeavour to drive him to despair, all the curses which the prophets had hurled upon this valley, where the Jews formerly sacrificed their children to idols.

It appeared as if all these maledictions were directed against him, as in these words, for instance : ' *They shall go forth, and behold the carcases of those who have sinned against me, whose worm dieth not, and whose fire shall never be extinguished.*' Then the devil murmured in his ears, ' Cain, where is thy brother Abel? What hast thou done ?—his blood cries to me for vengeance : thou art cursed upon earth, a wanderer for ever.' When he reached the torrent of Cedron, and saw Mount Olivet, he shuddered, turned away, and again the words vibrated in his ear, ' *Friend, whereto art thou come ? Judas, dost thou betray the Son of Man with a kiss ?*' Horror filled his soul, his head began to wander, and the arch fiend again whispered, ' It was here that David crossed the Cedron when he fled from Absalom. Absalom put an end to his life by hanging himself. It was of thee that David spoke when he said : "*And they repaid me evil for good; hatred for my love. May the devil stand at his right hand ; when he is judged, may he go out condemned. May his days be few, and his bishopric let another take. May the iniquity of his father be remembered in the sight of the Lord ; and let not the sin of his mother be blotted out, because he remembered not to show mercy, but persecuted the poor man and the beggar and the broken in heart, to put him to death. And he loved cursing, and it shall come unto him. And he put on cursing like a garment, and it went in like water into his entrails, and like oil into his bones. May it be unto him like a garment which covereth him ; and like a girdle, with which he is girded continually.*" '
Overcome by these terrible thoughts Judas rushed on, and

reached the foot of the mountain. It was a dreary, desolate spot filled with rubbish and putrid remains; discordant sounds from the city reverberated in his ears, and Satan continually repeated, 'They are now about to put him to death; thou hast sold him. Knowest thou not the words of the law, "*He who sells a soul among his brethren, and receives the price of it, let him die the death*"? Put an end to thy misery, wretched one; put an end to thy misery.' Overcome by despair Judas tore off his girdle, and hung himself on a tree which grew in a crevice of the rock, and after death his body burst asunder, and his bowels were scattered around.

CHAPTER XV.

Jesus is taken before Pilate.

THE malicious enemies of our Saviour led him through the most public part of the town to take him before Pilate. The procession wended its way slowly down the north side of the mountain of Sion, then passed through that section on the eastern side of the Temple, called Acre, towards the palace and tribunal of Pilate, which were seated on the north-west side of the Temple, facing a large square. Caiphas, Annas, and many others of the Chief Council, walked first in festival attire; they were followed by a multitude of scribes and many other Jews, among whom were the false witnesses, and the wicked Pharisees who had taken the most prominent part in accusing Jesus. Our Lord followed at a short distance; he was surrounded by a band of soldiers, and led by the archers. The multitude thronged on all sides and followed the procession, thundering forth the most fearful oaths and imprecations, while groups of persons were hurrying to and fro, pushing and jostling one another. Jesus was stripped of all save his under garment, which was stained and soiled by the filth which had been flung upon it; a long chain was hanging round his neck, which struck his knees as he

walked; his hands were pinioned as on the previous day,
and the archers dragged him by the ropes which were
fastened round his waist. He tottered rather than walked,
and was almost unrecognisable from the effects of his sufferings during the night;—he was colourless, haggard, his
face swollen and even bleeding, and his merciless persecutors continued to torment him each moment more and
more. They had gathered together a large body of the
dregs of the people, in order to make his present disgraceful
entrance into the city a parody on his triumphal entrance
on Palm Sunday. They mocked, and with derisive gestures called him king, and tossed in his path stones, bits
of wood, and filthy rags; they made game of, and by a
thousand taunting speeches mocked him, during this pretended triumphal entry.

In the corner of a building, not far from the house of
Caiphas, the afflicted Mother of Jesus, with John and
Magdalen, stood watching for him. Her soul was ever
united to his; but propelled by her love, she left no means
untried which could enable her really to approach him.
She remained at the Cenacle for some time after her midnight visit to the tribunal of Caiphas, powerless and speechless from grief; but when Jesus was dragged forth from
his prison, to be again brought before his judges, she arose,
cast her veil and cloak about her, and said to Magdalen
and John: 'Let us follow my Son to Pilate's court; I
must again look upon him.' They went to a place through
which the procession must pass, and waited for it. The
Mother of Jesus knew that her Son was suffering dreadfully, but never could she have conceived the deplorable,
the heartrending condition to which he was reduced by
the brutality of his enemies. Her imagination had depicted him to her as suffering fearfully, but yet supported
and illuminated by sanctity, love, and patience. Now,
however, the sad reality burst upon her. First in the procession appeared the priests, those most bitter enemies of
her Divine Son. They were decked in flowing robes; but
ah, terrible to say, instead of appearing resplendent in their
character of priests of the Most High, they were trans-

formed into priests of Satan, for no one could look upon
their wicked countenances without beholding there, portrayed in vivid colours, the evil passions with which their
souls were filled—deceit, infernal cunning, and a raging
anxiety to carry out that most tremendous of crimes, the
death of their Lord and Saviour, the only Son of God.
Next followed the false witnesses, his perfidious accusers,
surrounded by the vociferating populace; and last of all—
himself—her Son—Jesus, the Son of God, the Son of
Man, loaded with chains, scarcely able to support himself,
but pitilessly dragged on by his infernal enemies, receiving
blows from some, buffets from others, and from the whole
assembled rabble curses, abuse, and the most scurrilous
language. He would have been perfectly unrecognisable
even to her maternal eyes, stripped as he was of all save
a torn remnant of his garment, had she not instantly
marked the contrast between his behaviour and that of
his vile tormentors. He alone in the midst of persecution
and suffering looked calm and resigned, and far from returning blow for blow, never raised his hands but in acts
of supplication to his Eternal Father for the pardon of his
enemies. As he approached, she was unable to restrain
herself any longer, but exclaimed in thrilling accents:
'Alas! is that my Son? Ah, yes! I see that it is my
beloved Son. O, Jesus, my Jesus!' When the procession was almost opposite, Jesus looked upon her with an
expression of the greatest love and compassion; this look
was too much for the heartbroken mother: she became
for the moment totally unconscious, and John and Magdalen endeavoured to carry her home, but she quickly
roused herself, and accompanied the beloved disciple to
Pilate's palace.

The inhabitants of the town of Ophel were all gathered
together in an open space to meet Jesus, but far from
administering comfort, they added a fresh ingredient to
his cup of sorrow; they inflicted upon him that sharp
pang which must ever be felt by those who see their
friends abandon them in the hour of adversity. Jesus had
done much for the inhabitants of Ophel, but no sooner

did they see him reduced to such a state of misery and degradation, than their faith was shaken; they could no longer believe him to be a king, a prophet, the Messiah, and the Son of God. The Pharisees jeered and made game of them, on account of the admiration they had formerly expressed for Jesus. 'Look at your king now,' they exclaimed; 'do homage to him; have you no congratulations to offer him now that he is about to be crowned, and seated on his throne? All his boasted miracles are at an end; the High Priest has put an end to his tricks and witchcraft.'

Notwithstanding the remembrance which these poor people had of the miracles and wonderful cures which had been performed under their very eyes by Jesus; notwithstanding the great benefits he had bestowed upon them, their faith was shaken by beholding him thus derided and pointed out as an object of contempt by the High Priest and the members of the Sanhedrim, who were regarded in Jerusalem with the greatest veneration. Some went away doubting, while others remained and endeavoured to join the rabble, but they were prevented by the guards, who had been sent by the Pharisees, to prevent riots and confusion.

CHAPTER XVI.

Description of Pilate's Palace and the adjacent Buildings.

The palace of the Roman Governor, Pilate, was built on the north-west side of the mountain on which the Temple stood, and to reach it persons were obliged to ascend a flight of marble steps. It overlooked a large square surrounded by a colonnade, under which the merchants sat to sell their various commodities. A parapet, and an entrance at the north, south, east, and west sides alone broke the uniformity of this part of the market-place, which was called the forum, and built on higher ground than the adjacent streets, which sloped down from it. The palace of Pilate was not quite close, but separated

by a large court, the entrance to which at the eastern side
was through a high arch facing a street leading to the door
called the ' Probatica,' on the road to the Mount of Olives.
The southern entrance was through another arch, which
leads to Sion, in the neighbourhood of the fortress of Acre.
From the top of the marble steps of Pilate's palace, a person could see across the court as far as the forum, at the
entrance of which a few columns and stone seats were
placed.   It was at these seats that the Jewish priests
stopped, in order not to defile themselves by entering the
tribunal of Pilate, a line traced on the pavement of the
court indicating the precise boundary beyond which they
could not pass without incurring defilement.   There was
a large parapet near the western entrance, supported by
the sides of Pilate's Prætorium, which formed a species of
porch between it and the square.   That part of Pilate's
palace which he made use of when acting in the capacity
of judge, was called the Prætorium.   A number of columns
surrounded the parapet of which we have just spoken, and
in the centre was an uncovered portion, containing an
underground part, where the two thieves condemned to be
crucified with our Lord were confined, and this part was
filled with Roman soldiers.   The pillar upon which our
Lord was scourged was placed on the forum itself, not far
from this parapet and the colonnade.   There were many
other columns in this place ; those nearest to the palace
were made use of for the infliction of various corporal
punishments, and the others served as posts to which were
fastened the beasts brought for sale.   Upon the forum itself, opposite this building, was a platform filled with seats
made of stone ; and from this platform, which was called
Gabbatha, Pilate was accustomed to pronounce sentence
on great criminals.   The marble staircase ascended by per
sons going to the governor's palace led likewise to an uncovered terrace, and it was from this terrace that Pilate
gave audience to the priests and Pharisees, when they
brought forward their accusations against Jesus.   They all
stood before him in the forum, and refused to advance
further than the stone seats before mentioned.   A person

speaking in a loud tone of voice from the terrace could be easily heard by those in the forum.

Behind Pilate's palace there were many other terraces, and likewise gardens, and a country house. The gardens were between the palace of the governor and the dwelling of his wife, Claudia Procles. A large moat separated these buildings from the mountain on which the Temple stood, and on this side might be seen the houses inhabited by those who served in the Temple. The palace of Herod the elder was placed on the eastern side of Pilate's palace ; and it was in its inner court that numbers of the Innocents were massacred. At present the appearance of these two buildings is a little altered, as their entrances are changed. Four of the principal streets commenced at this part of the town, and ran in a southerly direction, three leading to the forum and Pilate's palace, and the fourth to the gate through which persons passed on their way to Bethsur. The beautiful house which belonged to Lazarus, and likewise that of Martha, were in a prominent part of this street.

One of these streets was very near to the Temple, and began at the gate which was called Probatica. The pool of Probatica was close to this gate on the right-hand side, and in this pool the sheep were washed for the first time, before being taken to the Temple ; while the second and more solemn washing took place in the pool of Bethsaida, which is near the south entrance to the Temple. The second of the above-mentioned streets contained a house belonging to St. Anne, the Mother of the Blessed Virgin, which she usually inhabited when she came up to Jerusalem with her family to offer sacrifice in the Temple. I believe it was in this house that the espousals of St. Joseph and the Blessed Virgin were celebrated.

The forum, as I have already explained, was built on higher ground than the neighbouring streets, and the aqueducts which ran through these streets flowed into the Probatica pool. On Mount Sion, directly opposite to the old castle of King David, stood a building very similar to the forum, while to the south-east might be seen the Cenacle, and a little towards the north the tribunals of

Annas and Caiphas. King David's castle was a deserted fortress, filled with courts, empty rooms, and stables, generally let to travellers. It had long been in this state of ruin, certainly before the time of our Lord's nativity. I saw the Magi with their numerous retinue enter it before going into Jerusalem.

When in meditation I behold the ruins of old castles and temples, see their neglected and forlorn state, and reflect on the uses to which they are now put, so different from the intentions of those who raised them, my mind always reverts to the events of our own days, when so many of the beautiful edifices erected by our pious and zealous ancestors are either destroyed, defaced, or used for worldly, if not wicked purposes. The little church of our convent, in which our Lord deigned to dwell, notwithstanding our unworthiness, and which was to me a paradise upon earth, is now without either roof or windows, and all the monuments are effaced or carried away. Our beloved convent, too, what will be done with it in a short time? that convent, where I was more happy in my little cell with my broken chair, than a king could be on his throne, for from its window I beheld that part of the church which contained the Blessed Sacrament. In a few years, perhaps, no one will know that it ever existed,—no one will know that it once contained hundreds of souls consecrated to God, who spent their days in imploring his mercy upon sinners. But God will know all, he never forgets,—the past and the future are equally present to him. He it is who reveals to me events which took place so long ago, and on the day of judgment, when all must be accounted for, and every debt paid, even to the farthing, he will remember both the good and the evil deeds performed in places long since forgotten. With God there is no exception of persons or places, his eyes see all, even the Vineyard of Naboth. It is a tradition among us that our convent was originally founded by two poor nuns, whose worldly possessions consisted in a jar of oil and a sack of beans. On the last day God will reward them for the manner in which they put out this small talent to interest, and for the large harvest which they reaped and presented to him. It is often said that poor souls remain in purgatory in punishment for what appears to us so small a crime as not having made restitution of a few coppers of which they had unlawful possession. May God therefore have mercy upon those who have seized the property of the poor, or of the Church.

CHAPTER XVII.

Jesus before Pilate.

IT was about eight in the morning, according to our method of counting time, when the procession reached the palace of Pilate. Annas, Caiphas, and the chiefs of the Sanhedrim stopped at a part between the forum and the entrance to the Prætorium, where some stone seats were placed for them. The brutal guards dragged Jesus to the foot of the flight of stairs which led to the judgment-seat of Pilate. Pilate was reposing in a comfortable chair, on a terrace which overlooked the forum, and a small three-legged table stood by his side, on which was placed the insignia of his office, and a few other things. He was surrounded by officers and soldiers dressed with the magnificence usual in the Roman army. The Jews and the priests did not enter the Prætorium, for fear of defiling themselves, but remained outside.

When Pilate saw the tumultuous procession enter, and perceived how shamefully the cruel Jews had treated their prisoner, he arose, and addressed them in a tone as contemptuous as could have been assumed by a victorious general towards the vanquished chief of some insignificant village : ' What are you come about so early ? Why have you ill-treated this prisoner so shamefully ? Is it not possible to refrain from thus tearing to pieces and beginning to execute your criminals even before they are judged ?' They made no answer, but shouted out to the guards, ' Bring him on—bring him to be judged !' and then, turning to Pilate, they said, 'Listen to our accusations against this malefactor; for we cannot enter the tribunal lest we defile ourselves.' Scarcely had they finished these words, when a voice was heard to issue from the midst of the dense multitude; it proceeded from a venerable-looking old man, of imposing stature, who exclaimed, 'You are right in not entering the Prætorium, for it has been sanctified by the blood of Innocents; there is but one Person who has a right to enter, and who alone can enter, because he alone is pure as the Innocents who were massacred there.' The person who uttered these words in a loud voice, and then disappeared among the crowd, was a rich man of the name of Zadoc, first-cousin to Obed, the husband of Veronica; two of his children were among the Innocents whom Herod had caused to be butchered at the birth of our Saviour. Since that dreadful moment he had given up the world, and, together with his wife, followed the rules of the Essenians. He had once seen our Saviour at the house of Lazarus, and there heard him discourse, and the sight of the barbarous manner in which he was dragged before Pilate recalled to his mind all he himself had suffered when his babes were so cruelly murdered before his eyes, and he determined to give this public testimony of his belief in the innocence of Jesus. The persecutors of our Lord were far too provoked at the haughty manner which Pilate assumed towards them, and at the humble position they were obliged to occupy, to take any notice of the words of a stranger.

The brutal guards dragged our Lord up the marble staircase, and led him to the end of the terrace, from whence Pilate was conferring with the Jewish priests. The Roman governor had often heard of Jesus, although he had never seen him, and now he was perfectly astonished at the calm dignity of deportment of a man brought before him in so pitiable a condition. The inhuman behaviour of the priests and ancients both exasperated him and increased his contempt for them, and he informed them pretty quickly that he had not the slightest intention of condemning Jesus without satisfactory proofs of the truth of their accusations. 'What accusation do you bring against this man?' said he, addressing the priests in the most scornful tone possible. '*If he were not a malefactor we would not have delivered him up to thee,*' replied the priests sullenly. '*Take him,*' said Pilate, '*and judge you him according to your law.*' 'Thou knowest well,' replied they, 'that *it is not lawful for us to condemn any man to death.*' The enemies of Jesus were furious—they wished to have the trial finished off, and their victim executed as quickly as possible, that they might be ready at the festival-day to sacrifice the Paschal lamb, not knowing, miserable wretches as they were, that he whom they had dragged before the tribunal of an idolatrous judge (into whose house they would not enter, for fear of defiling themselves before partaking of the figurative victim), that he, and he alone, was the true Paschal Lamb, of which the other was only the shadow.

Pilate, however, at last ordered them to produce their accusations. These accusations were three in number, and they brought forward ten witnesses to attest the truth of each. Their great aim was to make Pilate believe that Jesus was the leader of a conspiracy against the emperor, in order that he might condemn him to death as a rebel. They themselves were powerless in such matters, being allowed to judge none but religious offences. Their first endeavour was to convict him of seducing the people, exciting them to rebellion, and of being an enemy to public peace and tranquillity. To prove these charges they brought forward some false witnesses, and declared likewise that he violated the Sabbath, and even profaned it by curing the sick upon that day. At this accusation Pilate interrupted them, and said in a jeering tone, 'It is very evident you were none of you ill yourselves—had you been so you would not have complained of being cured on the Sabbath-day.' 'He seduces the people, and inculcates the most disgusting doctrines. He even says, that no person can attain eternal life unless they eat his flesh and drink his blood.' Pilate was quite provoked at the intense hatred which their words and countenances expressed, and, turning from them with a look of scorn, exclaimed, 'You most certainly must wish to follow his doctrines and to attain eternal life, for you are thirsting for both his body and blood.'

The Jews then brought forward the second accusation against Jesus, which was that he forbad the people to pay tribute to the emperor. These words roused the indignation of Pilate, as it was his place to see that all the taxes were properly paid, and he exclaimed in an angry tone, 'That is a lie! I must know more about it than you.' This obliged the enemies of our Lord to proceed to the third accusation, which they did in words such as these: 'Although this man is of obscure birth, he is the chief of a large party. When at their head, he denounces curses upon Jerusalem, and relates parables of double meaning concerning a king who is preparing a wedding feast for his son. The multitude whom he had gathered together on a mountain endeavoured once to make him their king; but it was sooner than he intended: his plans were not matured; therefore he fled and hid himself. Latterly he has come forward much more: it was but the other day that he entered Jerusalem at the head of a tumultuous assembly, who by his orders made the people rend the air with acclamations of "Hosanna to the Son of David! Blessed be the empire of our Father David, which is now beginning." He obliges his partisans to pay him regal honours, and tells them that he is the Christ, the Anointed of the Lord, the Messiah, the king promised to the Jews, and he wishes to be addressed by these fine titles.' Ten witnesses gave testimony concerning these things.

The last accusation—that of Jesus causing himself to be called king—made some impression upon Pilate; he became a little thoughtful, left the terrace and, casting a scrutinising glance on Jesus, went into the adjoining apartment, and ordered the guards to bring him alone into his presence. Pilate was not only superstitious, but likewise extremely weak-minded and susceptible. He had often, during the course of his pagan education, heard mention made of sons of his gods who had dwelt for a time upon earth ; he was likewise fully aware that the Jewish prophets had long foretold that one should appear in the midst of them who should be the Anointed of the Lord, their Saviour, and Deliverer from slavery ; and that many among the people believed this firmly. He remembered likewise that kings from the east had come to Herod, the predecessor of the present monarch of that name, to pay homage to a newly-born king of the Jews, and that Herod had on this account given orders for the massacre of the Innocents. He had often heard of the traditions concerning the Messiah and the king of the Jews, and even examined them with some curiosity ; although of course, being a pagan, without the slightest belief. Had he believed at all, he would probably have agreed with the Herodians, and with those Jews who expected a powerful and victorious king. With such impressions, the idea of the Jews accusing the poor miserable individual whom they had brought into his presence of setting himself up as the promised king and Messiah, of course appeared to him absurd ; but as the enemies of Jesus brought forward these charges in proof of treason against the emperor, he thought it proper to interrogate him privately concerning them.

' *Art thou the king of the Jews ?*' said Pilate, looking at our Lord, and unable to repress his astonishment at the divine expression of his countenance.

Jesus made answer, '*Sayest thou this thing of thyself, or have others told it thee of me ?*'

Pilate was offended that Jesus should think it possible for him to believe such a thing, and answered, '*Am I a Jew ? Thy own nation and the chief priests have delivered thee up to me* as deserving of death : *what hast thou done ?*'

Jesus answered majestically, ' *My kingdom is not of this world. If my kingdom were of this world, my servants would certainly strive that I should not be delivered to the Jews ; but now my kingdom is not from hence.*'

Pilate was somewhat moved by these solemn words, and said to him in a more serious tone, ' *Art thou a king, then ?*'

Jesus answered, ' *Thou sayest that I am a king. For*

*this was I born, and for this I came into the world, that I
should give testimony to the truth. Every one that is of the
truth heareth my voice.'*

Pilate looked at him, and rising from his seat said,
' The truth ! *what is truth ?'*

They then exchanged a few more words, which I do
not now remember, and Pilate returned to the terrace.
The answers and deportment of Jesus were far beyond his
comprehension ; but he saw plainly that his assumption
of royalty would not clash with that of the emperor, for
that it was to no worldly kingdom that he laid claim ;
whereas the emperor cared for nothing beyond this world.
He therefore again addressed the chief priests from the
terrace, and said, *'I find no cause in him.'* The enemies
of Jesus became furious, and uttered a thousand different
accusations against our Saviour. But he remained silent,
solely occupied in praying for his base enemies, and replied
not when Pilate addressed him in these words, *'Answerest
thou nothing? Behold in how many things they accuse
thee !'* Pilate was filled with astonishment, and said, ' I
see plainly that all they allege is false.' But his accusers,
whose anger continued to increase, cried out, ' You find
no cause in him ? Is it no crime to incite the people
to revolt in all parts of the kingdom ?—to spread his false
doctrines, not only here, but in Galilee likewise ?'

The mention of Galilee made Pilate pause : he reflected
for a moment, and then asked, ' Is this man a Galilæan,
and a subject of Herod's ?' They made answer, ' He is ;
his parents lived at Nazareth, and his present dwelling is
in Capharnaum.'

' Since that is the case,' replied Pilate, ' take him before Herod ; he is here for the festival, and can judge him
at once, as he is his subject.' Jesus was immediately led
out of the tribunal, and Pilate dispatched an officer to
Herod, to inform him that Jesus of Nazareth, who was his
subject, was about to be brought to him to be judged.
Pilate had two reasons for following this line of conduct ;
in the first place he was delighted to escape having to
pass sentence himself, as he felt very uncomfortable about

the whole affair; and in the second place he was glad of an opportunity of pleasing Herod, with whom he had had a disagreement, for he knew him to be very curious to see Jesus.

The enemies of our Lord were enraged at being thus dismissed by Pilate in the presence of the whole multitude, and gave vent to their anger by ill-treating him even more than before. They pinioned him afresh, and then ceased not overwhelming him with curses and blows as they led him hurriedly through the crowd, towards the palace of Herod, which was situated at no great distance from the forum. Some Roman soldiers had joined the procession.

During the time of the trial Claudia Procles, the wife of Pilate, had sent him frequent messages to intimate that she wished extremely to speak to him; and when Jesus was sent to Herod, she placed herself on a balcony and watched the cruel conduct of his enemies with mingled feelings of fear, grief, and horror.

CHAPTER XVIII.

The Origin of the Way of the Cross.

DURING the whole of the scene which we have just described, the Mother of Jesus, with Magdalen and John, had stood in a recess in the forum: they were overwhelmed with the most bitter sorrow, which was but increased by all they heard and saw. When Jesus was taken before Herod, John led the Blessed Virgin and Magdalen over the parts which had been sanctified by his footsteps. They again looked at the house of Caiphas, that of Annas, Ophel, Gethsemani, and the Garden of Olives; they stopped and contemplated each spot where he had fallen, or where he had suffered particularly; and they wept silently at the thought of all he had undergone. The Blessed Virgin knelt down frequently and kissed the ground where her Son had fallen, while Magdalen wrung her hands in bitter grief, and John, although he could not restrain his own tears, endeavoured to console his companions, supported, and led them on. Thus was the holy devotion of the 'Way of the Cross' first practised; thus were the Mysteries of the Passion of Jesus first honoured, even before that Passion was accomplished, and the Blessed Virgin, that model of spotless purity, was the first to show forth the deep veneration felt by the Church for our dear Lord. How sweet and consoling to follow this Immaculate Mother, passing to and fro, and bedewing the sacred spots with her tears. But, ah! who can describe the sharp, sharp sword of grief which then transfixed her tender soul? She who had once borne the Saviour of the world in her chaste womb, and suckled him for so long,—she who had truly conceived him who was the Word of God, in God from all eternity, and truly God,—she beneath whose heart, full of grace, he had deigned to dwell nine months, who had felt him living within her before he appeared among men to impart the blessing of salvation and teach them his heavenly doctrines; she suffered with Jesus, sharing with him not only the sufferings of his bitter Passion, but likewise that ardent desire of redeeming fallen man by an ignominious death, which consumed him.

In this touching manner did the most pure and holy Virgin lay the foundation of the devotion called the Way of the Cross; thus at each station, marked by the sufferings of her Son, did she lay up in her heart the inexhaustible merits of his Passion, and gather them up as precious stones or sweet-scented flowers to be presented as a choice offering to the Eternal Father in behalf of all true believers. The grief of Magdalen was so intense as to make her almost like an insane person. The holy and boundless love she felt for our Lord prompted her to cast herself at his feet, and there pour forth the feelings of her heart (as she once poured the precious ointment on his head as he sat at table); but when on the point of following this impulse, a dark gulf appeared to intervene between herself and him. The repentance she felt for her faults was immense, and not less intense was her gratitude for their pardon; but when she longed to offer acts of love and thanksgiving as precious incense at the feet of Jesus, she beheld him betrayed, suffering, and about to die for the expiation of her offences which he had taken upon himself, and this sight filled her with horror, and almost rent her soul asunder with feelings of love, repentance, and gratitude. The sight of the ingratitude of those for whom he was about to die increased the bitterness of these feelings tenfold, and every step, word, or movement demonstrated the agony of her soul. The heart of John was filled with love, and he suffered intensely, but he uttered not a word. He supported the Mother of his beloved Master in this her first pilgrimage through the stations of the Way of the Cross, and assisted her in giving the example of that devotion which has since been practised with so much fervour by the members of the Christian Church.

CHAPTER XIX.

Pilate and his Wife.

WHILST the Jews were leading Jesus to Herod, I saw Pilate go to his wife, Claudia Procles. She hastened to meet him, and they went together into a small garden-house which was on one of the terraces behind the palace. Claudia appeared to be much excited, and under the influence of fear. She was a tall, fine-looking woman, although extremely pale. Her hair was plaited and slightly ornamented, but partly covered by a long veil which fell gracefully over her shoulders. She wore earrings, a necklace, and her flowing dress was drawn together and held up by a species of clasp. She conversed with Pilate for a long time, and entreated him by all that he held sacred not to injure Jesus, that Prophet, that saint of saints; and she related the extraordinary dreams or visions which she had had on the previous night conrning him.

Whilst she was speaking I saw the greatest part of

these visions : the following were the most striking. In the first place, the principal events in the life of our Lord — the annunciation, the nativity, the adoration of the shepherds and that of the kings, the prophecy of Simeon and that of Anna, the flight into Egypt, the massacre of the Innocents, and our Lord's temptation in the wilderness. She had likewise been shown in her sleep the most striking features of the public life of Jesus. He always appeared to her environed with a resplendent light, but his malicious and cruel enemies were under the most horrible and disgusting forms imaginable. She saw his intense sufferings, his patience, and his inexhaustible love, likewise the anguish of his Mother, and her perfect resignation. These visions filled the wife of Pilate with the greatest anxiety and terror, particularly as they were accompanied by symbols which made her comprehend their meaning, and her tender feelings were harrowed by the sight of such dreadful scenes. She had suffered from them during the whole of the night ; they were sometimes obscure, but more often clear and distinct ; and when morning dawned and she was roused by the noise of the tumultuous mob who were dragging Jesus to be judged, she glanced at the procession and instantly saw that the unresisting victim in the midst of the crowd, bound, suffering, and so inhumanely treated as to be scarcely recognisable, was no other than that bright and glorious being who had been so often brought before her eyes in the visions of the past night. She was greatly affected by this sight, and immediately sent for Pilate, and gave him an account of all that had happened to her. She spoke with much vehemence and emotion ; and although there was a great deal in what she had seen which she could not understand, much less express, yet she entreated and implored her husband in the most touching terms to grant her request.

Pilate was both astonished and troubled by the words of his wife. He compared the narration with all he had previously heard concerning Jesus ; and reflected on the hatred of the Jews, the majestic silence of our Saviour, and the mysterious answers he had given to all his questions. He hesitated for some time, but was at last overcome by the entreaties of his wife, and told her that he had already declared his conviction of the innocence of Jesus, and that he would not condemn him, because he saw that the accusations were mere fabrications of his enemies. He spoke of the words of Jesus to himself, promised his wife that nothing should induce him to condemn this just man, and even gave her a ring before they parted as a pledge of his promise.

The character of Pilate was debauched and undecided, but his worst qualities were an extreme pride and meanness which made him never hesitate in the performance of an unjust action, provided it answered his ends. He was excessively superstitious, and when in any difficulty had recourse to charms and spells. He was much puzzled and alarmed about the trial of Jesus; and I saw him running backwards and forwards, offering incense first to one god and then to another, and imploring them to assist him; but Satan filled his imagination with still greater confusion; he first instilled one false idea and then another into his mind. He then had recourse to one of his favourite superstitious practices, that of watching the sacred chickens eat, but in vain,—his mind remained enveloped in darkness, and he became more and more undecided. He first thought that he would acquit our Saviour, whom he well knew to be innocent, but then he feared incurring the wrath of his false gods if he spared him, as he fancied he might be a species of demigod, and obnoxious to them. ' It is possible,' said he inwardly, ' that this man may really be that king of the Jews concerning whose coming there are so many prophecies. It was a king of the Jews whom the Magi came from the East to adore. Perhaps he is a secret enemy both of our gods and of the emperor; it might be most imprudent in me to spare his life. Who knows whether his death would not be a triumph to my gods ?' Then he remembered the wonderful dreams described to him by his wife, who had never seen Jesus, and he again changed, and decided that it would be safer

not to condemn him.   He tried to persuade himself that
he wished to pass a just sentence; but he deceived himself, for when he asked himself, ' What is the truth?' he
did not wait for the answer.   His mind was filled with
confusion, and he was quite at a loss how to act, as his
sole desire was to entail no risk upon himself.

CHAPTER XX.

Jesus before Herod.

THE palace of the Tetrarch Herod was built on the
north side of the forum, in the new town; not very far
from that of Pilate.   An escort of Roman soldiers, mostly
from that part of the country which is situated between
Switzerland and Italy, had joined the procession.   The
enemies of Jesus were perfectly furious at the trouble
they were compelled to take in going backwards and
forwards, and therefore vented their rage upon him.   Pilate's messenger had preceded the procession, consequently
Herod was expecting them.   He was seated on a pile of
cushions, heaped together so as to form a species of throne,
in a spacious hall, and surrounded by courtiers and warriors.   The Chief Priests entered and placed themselves
by his side, leaving Jesus at the entrance.   Herod was
much elated and pleased at Pilate's having thus publicly
acknowledged his right of judging the Galilæans, and
likewise rejoiced at seeing that Jesus who had never
deigned to appear before him reduced to such a state
of humiliation and degradation.   His curiosity had been
greatly excited by the high terms in which John the
Baptist had announced the coming of Jesus, and he had
likewise heard much about him from the Herodians, and
through the many spies whom he had sent into different
parts : he was therefore delighted at this opportunity of
interrogating him in the presence of his courtiers and of
the Jewish priests, hoping to make a grand display of his
own knowledge and talents.   Pilate having sent him word,

'that he could find no cause in the man,' he concluded that these words were intended as a hint that he (Pilate) wished the accusers to be treated with contempt and mistrust. He, therefore, addressed them in the most haughty distant manner possible, and thereby increased their rage and anger indescribably.

They all began at once to vociferate their accusations, to which Herod hardly listened, being intent solely on gratifying his curiosity by a close examination of Jesus, whom he had so often wished to see. But when he beheld him stripped of all clothing save the remnant of a mantle, scarcely able to stand, and his countenance totally disfigured from the blows he had received, and from the mud and missiles which the rabble had flung at his head, the luxurious and effeminate prince turned away in disgust, uttered the name of God, and said to the priests in a tone of mingled pity and contempt, 'Take him hence, and bring him not back into my presence in such a deplorable state.' The guards took Jesus into the outer court, and procured some water in a basin, with which they cleansed his soiled garments and disfigured countenance; but they could not restrain their brutality even while doing this, and paid no regard to the wounds with which he was covered.

Herod meantime accosted the priests in much the same strain as Pilate had done. 'Your behaviour vastly resembles that of butchers,' he said, 'and you commence your immolations pretty early in the morning.' The Chief Priests produced their accusations at once. Herod, when Jesus was again brought into his presence, pretended to feel some compassion, and offered him a glass of wine to recruit his strength; but Jesus turned his head away and refused this alleviation.

Herod then began to expatiate with great volubility on all he had heard concerning our Lord. He asked a thousand questions, and exhorted him to work a miracle in his presence; but Jesus answered not a word, and stood before him with his eyes cast down, which conduct both irritated and disconcerted Herod, although he endeavoured to con-

ceal his anger, and continued his interrogations. He at
first expressed surprise, and made use of persuasive words.
'Is it possible, Jesus of Nazareth,' he exclaimed, 'that it
is thou thyself that appearest before me as a criminal? I
have heard thy actions so much spoken of. Thou art not
perhaps aware that thou didst offend me grievously by
setting free the prisoners whom I had confined at Thirza,
but possibly thy intentions were good. The Roman
governor has now sent thee to me to be judged; what answer canst thou give to all these accusations? Thou art
silent? I have heard much concerning thy wisdom, and
the religion thou teachest, let me hear thee answer and
confound thy enemies. Art thou the king of the Jews?
Art thou the Son of God? Who art thou? Thou art
said to have performed wonderful miracles; work one now
in my presence. I have the power to release thee. Is it
true that thou hast restored sight to the blind, raised up
Lazarus from the dead, and fed two or three thousand
persons with a few loaves? Why dost thou not answer?
I recommend thee to work a miracle quickly before me;
perhaps thou mayest rejoice afterwards at having complied
with my wishes.'

Jesus still kept silence, and Herod continued to question him with even more volubility.

'Who art thou?' said he. 'From whence hast thou thy
power? How is it that thou dost no longer possess it?
Art thou he whose birth was foretold in such a wonderful
manner? Kings from the East came to my father to see
a newly-born king of the Jews: is it true that thou wast
that child? Didst thou escape when so many children
were massacred, and how was thy escape managed? Why
hast thou been for so many years unknown? Answer my
questions! Art thou a king? Thy appearance certainly
is not regal. I have been told that thou wast conducted
to the Temple in triumph a short time ago. What was the
meaning of such an exhibition?—speak out at once!—
Answer me!'

Herod continued to question Jesus in this rapid manner; but our Lord did not vouchsafe a reply. I was shown

(as indeed I already knew) that Jesus was thus silent because Herod was in a state of excommunication, both on
account of his adulterous marriage with Herodias, and of
his having given orders for the execution of St. John the
Baptist. Annas and Caiphas, seeing how indignant Herod
was at the silence of Jesus, immediately endeavoured to
take advantage of his feelings of wrath, and recommenced
their accusations, saying that he had called Herod himself
a fox; that his great aim for many years had been the
overthrow of Herod's family; that he was endeavouring
to establish a new religion, and had celebrated the Pasch
on the previous day. Although Herod was extremely enraged at the conduct of Jesus, he did not lose sight of the
political ends which he wished to forward. He was determined not to condemn our Lord, both because he experienced a secret and indefinable sensation of terror in
his presence, and because he still felt remorse at the
thought of having put John the Baptist to death, besides
which he detested the High Priests for not having allowed
him to take part in the sacrifices on account of his adulterous connection with Herodias.

But his principal reason for determining not to condemn Jesus was, that he wished to make some return to
Pilate for his courtesy, and he thought the best return
would be the compliment of showing deference to his decision and agreeing with him in opinion. But he spoke
in the most contemptuous manner to Jesus, and turning
to the guards and servants who surrounded him, and who
were about two hundred in number, said : 'Take away
this fool, and pay him that homage which is his due ; he
is mad, rather than guilty of any crime.'

Our Lord was immediately taken into a large court,
where every possible insult and indignity was heaped upon
him. This court was between the two wings of the palace,
and Herod stood a spectator on a platform for some time.
Annas and Caiphas were by his side, endeavouring to persuade him to condemn our Saviour. But their efforts were
fruitless, and Herod answered in a tone loud enough to be
heard by the Roman soldiers : ' No, I should act quite

wrongly if I condemned him.' His meaning was, that it would be wrong to condemn as guilty one whom Pilate had pronounced innocent, although he had been so courteous as to defer the final judgment to him.

When the High Priests and the other enemies of Jesus perceived that Herod was determined not to give in to their wishes, they dispatched emissaries to that division of the city called Acre, which was chiefly inhabited by Pharisees, to let them know that they must assemble in the neighbourhood of Pilate's palace, gather together the rabble, and bribe them to make a tumult, and demand the condemnation of our Lord. They likewise sent forth secret agents to alarm the people by threats of the divine vengeance if they did not insist on the execution of Jesus, whom they termed a sacrilegious blasphemer. These agents were ordered likewise to alarm them by intimating that if Jesus were not put to death, he would go over to the Romans, and assist in the extermination of the Jewish nation, for that it was to this he referred when he spoke of his future kingdom. They endeavoured to spread a report in other parts of the city, that Herod had condemned him, but still that it was necessary for the people likewise to express their wishes, as his partisans were to be feared ; for that if he were released he would join the Romans, make a disturbance on the festival day, and take the most inhuman revenge. Some among them circulated contradictory and alarming reports, in order to excite the people, and cause an insurrection; while others distributed money among the soldiers to bribe them to ill-treat Jesus, so as to cause his death, which they were most anxious should be brought about as quickly as possible, lest Pilate should acquit him.

Whilst the Pharisees were busying themselves in this manner, our Blessed Saviour was suffering the greatest outrages from the brutal soldiers to whom Herod had delivered him, that they might deride him as a fool. They dragged him into the court, and one of their number having procured a large white sack which had once been filled with cotton, they made a hole in its centre with a sword, and then tossed it over the head of Jesus, accompanying each action with bursts of the most contemptuous laughter. Another soldier brought the remnant of an old scarlet cloak, and passed it round his neck, while the rest bent their knee before him—shoved him—abused him—spat upon him—struck him on the cheek, because he had refused to answer their king, mocked him by pretending to pay homage—threw mud upon him—seized him by the waist, pretending to make him dance; then, having thrown him down, dragged him through a gutter which ran on the side of the court, thus causing his sacred head to strike against the columns and sides of the wall, and when at last they raised him up, it was only in order to recommence their insults. The soldiers and servants of Herod who were assembled in this court amounted to upwards of two hundred, and all thought to pay court to their monarch by torturing Jesus in some unheard-of way. Many were bribed by the enemies of our Lord to strike him on the head with their sticks, and they took advantage of the confusion and tumult to do so. Jesus looked upon them with compassion; excess of pain drew from him occasional moans and groans, but his enemies rejoiced in his sufferings, and mocked his moans, and not one among the whole assembly showed the slightest degree of compassion. I saw blood streaming from his head, and three times did the blows prostrate him, but angels were weeping at his side, and they anointed his head with heavenly balsam. It was revealed to me that had it not been for this miraculous assistance he must have died from those wounds. The Philistines at Gaza, who gave vent to their wrath by tormenting poor blind Samson, were far less barbarous than these cruel executioners of our Lord.

The priests were, however, impatient to return to the Temple; therefore, having made certain that their orders regarding Jesus would be obeyed, they returned to Herod, and endeavoured to persuade him to condemn our Lord. But he, being determined to do all in his power to please Pilate, refused to accede to their wishes, and sent Jesus back again clothed in the fool's garment.

CHAPTER XXI.

Jesus led back from the Court of Herod to that of Pilate.

THE enemies of Jesus were perfectly infuriated at being obliged to take Jesus back, still uncondemned, to Pilate, who had so many times declared his innocence. They led him round by a much longer road, in order in the first place to let the persons of that part of the town see him in the state of ignominy to which he was reduced, and in the second place to give their emissaries more time to stir up the populace.

This road was extremely rough and uneven; and the soldiers, encouraged by the Pharisees, scarcely refrained a moment from tormenting Jesus. The long garment with which he was clothed impeded his steps, and caused him to fall heavily more than once; and his cruel guards, as also many among the brutal populace, instead of assisting him in his state of exhaustion, endeavoured by blows and kicks to force him to rise.

To all these outrages Jesus offered not the smallest resistance; he prayed constantly to his Father for grace and strength that he might not sink under them, but accomplish the work of his Passion for our redemption.

It was about eight o'clock when the procession reached the palace of Pilate. The crowd was dense, and the Pharisees might be seen walking to and fro, endeavouring to incite and infuriate them still more. Pilate, who remembered an insurrection which had taken place the year before at the Paschal time, had assembled upwards of a thousand soldiers, whom he posted around the Prætorium, the Forum, and his palace.

The Blessed Virgin, her elder sister Mary (the daughter of Heli), Mary (the daughter of Cleophas), Magdalen, and about twenty of the holy women, were standing in a room from whence they could see all which took place, and at first John was with them.

The Pharisees led Jesus, still clothed in the fool's garment, through the midst of the insolent mob, and had done all in their power to gather together the most vile and wicked of miscreants from among the dregs of the people. A servant sent by Herod had already reached Pilate, with a message to the effect that his master had fully appreciated his polite deference to his opinion, but that he looked upon the far-famed Galilæan as no better than a fool, that he had treated him as such, and now sent him back. Pilate was quite satisfied at finding that Herod had come to the same conclusion as himself, and therefore returned a polite message. From that hour they became friends, having been enemies many years; in fact, ever since the falling-in of the aqueduct.* Jesus was

---

* The cause of the quarrel between Pilate and Herod was, according to the account of Sister Emmerich, simply this : Pilate had undertaken to build an aqueduct on the south-east side of the mountain on which the Temple stood, at the edge of the torrent into which the waters of the pool of Bethsaida emptied themselves, and this aqueduct was to carry off the refuse of the Temple. Herod, through the medium of one of his confidants, who was a member of the Sanhedrim, agreed to furnish him with the necessary materials, as also with twenty-eight architects, who were also Herodians. His aim was to set the Jews still more against the Roman governor, by causing the undertaking to fail. He accordingly came to a private understanding with the architects, who agreed to construct the aqueduct in such a manner that it would be certain to fall. When the work was almost finished, and a number of bricklayers from Ophel were busily employed in removing the scaffolding, the twenty-eight builders went on to the top of the Tower of Siloe to contemplate the crash which they knew must take place. Not only did the whole of the building crumble to pieces, fall, and kill ninety-three workmen, but even the tower containing the twenty-eight architects came down, and not one escaped death. This accident occurred a short time previous to the 8th of January, two years after Jesus had commenced preaching ; it took place on Herod's birthday, the same day that John the Baptist was beheaded in the Castle of Marcherunt. No Roman officer attended these festivities on account of the affair of the aqueduct, although Pilate had, with hypocritical politeness, been requested to take a part in them. Sister Emmerich saw some of the disciples of Jesus carry the news of this event into Samaria, where he was teaching, on the 8th of January. Jesus went from thence to Hebron, to comfort the family of John ; and she saw him, on the 13th of January, cure many among the workmen of Ophel who had been injured by the fall of the aqueduct. We have seen by the relation previously given how little gratitude they

again led to the house of Pilate. The archers dragged
him up the stairs with their usual brutality ; his feet
became entangled in his long robe, and he fell upon the
white marble steps, which were stained with blood from
his sacred head.   His enemies had again taken their seats
at the entrance of the forum ; the mob laughed at his fall,
and the archers struck their innocent victim, instead of
assisting him to rise.   Pilate was reclining on a species of
easy-chair, with a little table before him, and surrounded
with officers and persons who held strips of parchment
covered with writing in their hands.   He came forward
and said to the accusers of Jesus : ' *You have presented
unto me this man, as one that perverteth the people, and
behold I, having examined him before you, find no cause
in this man in those things wherein you accuse him.   No,
nor Herod neither.   For I sent you to him, and behold,*

---

showed him. The enmity of Herod towards Pilate was still farther
increased by the manner in which the latter revenged himself on
the followers of Herod. We will insert here a few details which
were communicated at different times to Sister Emmerich. On the
25th of March, of the second year of our Lord's preaching, when
Jesus and his disciples were in the neighbourhood of Bethania,
they were warned by Lazarus that Judas of Gaulon intended to
excite an insurrection against Pilate. On the 28th of March, Pilate issued a proclamation to the effect that he intended to impose
a tax, the proceeds of which were partly to cover the expenses he
had incurred in raising the building which had just fallen to the
ground. This announcement was followed by a sedition headed
by Judas of Gaulon, who always stood up for liberty, and who was
(unknown to himself) a tool in the hands of the Herodians. The
Herodians were rather like our Freemasons. On the 30th of March,
at ten o'clock P.M., Jesus, dressed in a dark garment, was teaching in the Temple, with his Apostles and thirty disciples. The revolt of the Galilæans against Pilate burst forth on this very day,
and the rebels set free fifty of their number who had been imprisoned the day before ; and many among the Romans were killed.
On the 6th of April, Pilate caused the Galilæans to be massacred
at the moment of offering sacrifice, by disguised soldiers whom he
had concealed in the Temple. Judas was killed with his companions. This massacre exasperated Herod still more against Pilate, and we have just seen by what means their reconciliation was
effected.

nothing worthy of death is done to him. I will chastise him, therefore, and release him.'

When the Pharisees heard these words, they became furious, and endeavoured to the utmost of their power to persuade the people to revolt, distributing money among them to effect this purpose. Pilate looked around with contempt, and addressed them in scornful words.

It happened to be the precise time when, according to an ancient custom, the people had the privilege of demanding the deliverance of one prisoner. The Pharisees had dispatched emissaries to persuade the people to demand the death, and not the life, of our Lord. Pilate hoped that they would ask for Jesus, and determined to give them to choose between him and a criminal called Barabbas, who had been convicted of a dreadful murder committed during a sedition, as also of many other crimes, and was, moreover, detested by the people.

There was considerable excitement among the crowd; a certain portion came forward, and their orators, addressing Pilate in a loud voice, said : ' Grant us the favour you have always granted on the festival day.' Pilate made answer : ' It is customary for me to deliver to you a criminal at the Paschal time ; *whom will you that I release to you, Barabbas, or Jesus that is called Christ ?'*

Although Pilate did not in his own mind feel at all certain that Jesus was the King of the Jews, yet he called him so, partly because his Roman pride made him take delight in humbling the Jews by calling such a despicable-looking person their king; and partly because he felt a kind of inward belief that Jesus might really be that miraculous king, that Messiah who had been promised. He saw plainly that the priests were incited by envy alone in their accusations against Jesus; this made him most anxious to disappoint them ; and the desire was increased by that glimmering of the truth which partly enlightened his mind. There was some hesitation among the crowd when Pilate asked this question, and a few voices answered, ' *Barabbas.*' A servant sent by Pilate's wife asked for him at this moment ; he left the platform, and the mes-

senger presented the pledge which he had given her, say·
ing at the same time : ' Claudia Procles begs you to remember your promise this morning.' The Pharisees and
the priests walked anxiously and hastily about among the
crowd, threatening some and ordering others, although, in
fact, little was required to incite the already infuriated
multitude.

Mary, with Magdalen, John, and the holy women,
stood in a corner of the forum, trembling and weeping ;
for although the Mother of Jesus was fully aware that the
redemption of man could not be brought about by any
other means than the death of her Son, yet she was filled
with the anguish of a mother, and with a longing desire
to save him from those tortures and from that death which
he was about to suffer. She prayed God not to allow
such a fearful crime to be perpetrated ; she repeated the
words of Jesus in the Garden of Olives : ' *If it is possible,
let this chalice pass away.*' She still felt a glimmering of
hope, because there was a report current that Pilate wished
to acquit Jesus. Groups of persons, mostly inhabitants of
Capharnaum, where Jesus had taught, and among whom
he had wrought so many miraculous cures, were congregated in her vicinity ; they pretended not to remember
either her or her weeping companions ; they simply cast
a glance now and then, as if by chance, at their closely-
veiled figures. Many thought, as did her companions
likewise, that these persons at least would reject Barabbas,
and beg for the life of their Saviour and Benefactor ; but
these hopes were, alas, fallacious.

Pilate sent back the pledge to his wife, as an assurance
of his intention to keep his promise. He again came forward on the platform, and seated himself at the little table.
The Chief Priests took their seats likewise, and Pilate once
more demanded : ' *Which of the two am I to deliver up to
you ?*' A general cry resounded through the hall : ' *Not
this man, but Barabbas !*' ' *But what am I to do with
Jesus, who is called Christ ?*' replied Pilate. All exclaimed in a tumultuous manner : ' *Let him be crucified !
let him be crucified !*' ' *But what evil has he done ?*' asked

Pilate for the third time. '*I find no cause in him. I will scourge and then acquit him.*' But the cry, '*Crucify him! Crucify him!*' burst from the crowd, and the sounds echoed like an infernal tempest; the High Priests and the Pharisees vociferated and hurried backwards and forwards as if insane. Pilate at last yielded; his weak pusillanimous character could not withstand such violent demonstrations; he delivered up Barabbas to the people, and condemned Jesus to be scourged.

CHAPTER XXII.

The Scourging of Jesus.

THAT most weak and undecided of all judges, Pilate, had several times repeated these dastardly words: '*I find no crime in him: I will chastise him, therefore, and let him go;*' to which the Jews had continued to respond, '*Crucify him! Crucify him!*' but he determined to adhere to his resolution of not condemning our Lord to death, and ordered him to be scourged according to the manner of the Romans. The guards were therefore ordered to conduct him through the midst of the furious multitude to the forum, which they did with the utmost brutality, at the same time loading him with abuse, and striking him with their staffs. The pillar where criminals were scourged stood to the north of Pilate's palace, near the guard-house, and the executioners soon arrived, carrying whips, rods, and ropes, which they tossed down at its base. They were six in number, dark, swarthy men, somewhat shorter than Jesus; their chests were covered with a piece of leather, or with some dirty stuff; their loins were girded, and their hairy, sinewy arms bare. They were malefactors from the frontiers of Egypt, who had been condemned for their crimes to hard labour, and were employed principally in making canals, and in erecting public buildings, the most criminal being selected to act as executioners in the Prætorium.

These cruel men had many times scourged poor criminals to death at this pillar. They resembled wild beasts or demons, and appeared to be half drunk. They struck our Lord with their fists, and dragged him by the cords with which he was pinioned, although he followed them without offering the least resistance, and, finally, they barbarously knocked him down against the pillar. This pillar, placed in the centre of the court, stood alone, and did not serve to sustain any part of the building; it was not very high, for a tall man could touch the summit by stretching out his arm; there was a large iron ring at the top, and both rings and hooks a little lower down. It is quite impossible to describe the cruelty shown by these ruffians towards Jesus: they tore off the mantle with which he had been clothed in derision at the court of Herod, and almost threw him prostrate again.

Jesus trembled and shuddered as he stood before the pillar, and took off his garments as quickly as he could, but his hands were bloody and swollen. The only return he made when his brutal executioners struck and abused him was, to pray for them in the most touching manner: he turned his face once towards his Mother, who was standing overcome with grief; this look quite unnerved her: she fainted, and would have fallen, had not the holy women who were there supported her. Jesus put his arms round the pillar, and when his hands were thus raised, the archers fastened them to the iron ring which was at the top of the pillar; they then dragged his arms to such a height that his feet, which were tightly bound to the base of the pillar, scarcely touched the ground. Thus was the Holy of holies violently stretched, without a particle of clothing, on a pillar used for the punishment of the greatest criminals; and then did two furious ruffians who were thirsting for his blood begin in the most barbarous manner to scourge his sacred body from head to foot. The whips or scourges which they first made use of appeared to me to be made of a species of flexible white wood, but perhaps they were composed of the sinews of the ox, or of strips of leather.

Our loving Lord, the Son of God, true God and true Man, writhed as a worm under the blows of these barbarians; his mild but deep groans might be heard from afar; they resounded through the air, forming a kind of touching accompaniment to the hissing of the instruments of torture. These groans resembled rather a touching cry of prayer and supplication, than moans of anguish. The clamour of the Pharisees and the people formed another species of accompaniment, which at times as a deafening thunder-storm deadened and smothered these sacred and mournful cries, and in their place might be heard the words, ' *Put him to death !*' ' *Crucify him !*' Pilate continued parleying with the people, and when he demanded silence in order to be able to speak, he was obliged to proclaim his wishes to the clamorous assembly by the sound of a trumpet, and at such moments you might again hear the noise of the scourges, the moans of Jesus, the imprecations of the soldiers, and the bleating of the Paschal lambs which were being washed in the Probatica pool, at no great distance from the forum. There was something peculiarly touching in the plaintive bleating of these lambs : they alone appeared to unite their lamentations with the suffering moans of our Lord.

The Jewish mob was gathered together at some distance from the pillar at which the dreadful punishment was taking place, and Roman soldiers were stationed in different parts round about. Many persons were walking to and fro, some in silence, others speaking of Jesus in the most insulting terms possible, and a few appearing touched, and I thought I beheld rays of light issuing from our Lord and entering the hearts of the latter. I saw groups of infamous, bold-looking young men, who were for the most part busying themselves near the watch-house in preparing fresh scourges, while others went to seek branches of thorns. Several of the servants of the High Priests went up to the brutal executioners and gave them money ; as also a large jug filled with a strong bright red liquid, which quite inebriated them, and increased their cruelty tenfold towards their innocent Victim. The two ruffians continued to strike our Lord with unremitting violence for a quarter of an hour, and were then succeeded by two others. His body was entirely covered with black, blue, and red marks; the blood was trickling down on the ground, and yet the furious cries which issued from among the assembled Jews showed that their cruelty was far from being satiated.

The night had been extremely cold, and the morning was dark and cloudy; a little hail had fallen, which surprised every one, but towards twelve o'clock the day became brighter, and the sun shone forth.

The two fresh executioners commenced scourging Jesus with the greatest possible fury; they made use of a different kind of rod,—a species of thorny stick, covered with knots and splinters. The blows from these sticks tore his flesh to pieces; his blood spouted out so as to stain their arms, and he groaned, prayed, and shuddered. At this moment, some strangers mounted on camels passed through the forum; they stopped for a moment, and were quite overcome with pity and horror at the scene before them, upon which some of the bystanders explained the cause of what they witnessed. Some of these travellers had been baptised by John, and others had heard the sermon of Jesus on the mountain. The noise and the tumult of the mob was even more deafening near the house of Pilate.

Two fresh executioners took the places of the last mentioned, who were beginning to flag; their scourges were composed of small chains, or straps covered with iron hooks, which penetrated to the bone, and tore off large pieces of flesh at every blow. What word, alas! could describe this terrible—this heartrending scene!

The cruelty of these barbarians was nevertheless not yet satiated; they untied Jesus, and again fastened him up with his back turned towards the pillar. As he was totally unable to support himself in an upright position, they passed cords round his waist, under his arms, and above his knees, and having bound his hands tightly into the rings which were placed at the upper part of the pillar, they recommenced scourging him with even greater fury than before ; and one among them struck him constantly on the face with a new rod. The body of our Lord was perfectly torn to shreds,—it was but one wound. He looked at his torturers with his eyes filled with blood, as if entreating mercy ; but their brutality appeared to increase, and his moans each moment became more feeble.

The dreadful scourging had been continued without intermission for three quarters of an hour, when a stranger of lowly birth, a relation to Ctesiphon, the blind man whom Jesus had cured, rushed from amidst the crowd, and approached the pillar with a knife shaped like a cutlass in his hand. ' Cease !' he exclaimed, in an indignant tone ; ' Cease ! scourge not this innocent man unto death !' The drunken miscreants, taken by surprise, stopped short, while he quickly severed the cords which bound Jesus to the pillar, and disappeared among the crowd. Jesus fell almost without consciousness on the ground, which was bathed with his blood. The executioners left him there, and rejoined their cruel companions, who were amusing themselves in the guard-house with drinking, and plaiting the crown of thorns.

Our Lord remained for a short time on the ground, at the foot of the pillar, bathed in his own blood, and two or three bold-looking girls came up to gratify their curiosity by looking at him. They gave a glance, and were turning away in disgust, but at the moment the pain of the wounds of Jesus was so intense that he raised his bleeding head and looked at them. They retired quickly, and the soldiers and guards laughed and made game of them.

During the time of the scourging of our Lord, I saw weeping angels approach him many times ; I likewise heard the prayers he constantly addressed to his Father for the pardon of our sins—prayers which never ceased during the whole time of the infliction of this cruel punishment. Whilst he lay bathed in his blood I saw an angel present to him a vase containing a bright-looking beverage which appeared to reinvigorate him in a certain degree. The archers soon returned, and after giving him some blows with their sticks, bade him rise and follow them. He raised himself with the greatest difficulty, as his trembling limbs could scarcely support the weight of his body; they did not give him sufficient time to put on his clothes, but threw his upper garment over his naked shoulders and led him from the pillar to the guard-house, where he wiped the blood which trickled down his face with a corner of his garment. When he passed before the benches on which the High Priests were seated, they cried out, ' Put him to death ! Crucify him ! crucify him !' and then turned away disdainfully. The executioners led him into the interior of the guard-house, which was filled with slaves, archers, hodmen, and the very dregs of the people, but there were no soldiers.

The great excitement among the populace alarmed Pilate so much, that he sent to the fortress of Antonia for a reinforcement of Roman soldiers, and posted these well-disciplined troops round the guard-house; they were permitted to talk and to deride Jesus in every possible way, but were forbidden to quit their ranks. These soldiers, whom Pilate had sent for to intimidate the mob, numbered about a thousand.

CHAPTER XXIII.

Mary during the Flagellation of our Lord.

I saw the Blessed Virgin in a continual ecstasy during the time of the scourging of her Divine Son ; she saw and suffered with inexpressible love and grief all the torments he was enduring. She groaned feebly, and her eyes were red with weeping. A large veil covered her person, and she leant upon Mary of Heli, her eldest sister,* who was

* Mary of Heli is often spoken of in this relation. According to Sister Emmerich, she was the daughter of St. Joachim and St. Anne, and was born nearly twenty years before the Blessed Virgin. She was not the child of promise, and is called Mary of Heli, by which she is distinguished from the other of the same name, be-

old and extremely like their mother, Anne. Mary of Cleophas, the daughter of Mary of Heli, was there also. The friends of Jesus and Mary stood around the latter; they wore large veils, appeared overcome with grief and anxiety, and were weeping as if in the momentary expectation of death. The dress of Mary was blue; it was long, and partly covered by a cloak made of white wool, and her veil was of rather a yellow white. Magdalen was totally beside herself from grief, and her hair was floating loosely under her veil.

When Jesus fell down at the foot of the pillar, after the flagellation, I saw Claudia Procles, the wife of Pilate, send some large pieces of linen to the Mother of God. I know not whether she thought that Jesus would be set free, and that his Mother would then require linen to dress his wounds, or whether this compassionate lady was aware of the use which would be made of her present. At the termination of the scourging, Mary came to herself for a time, and saw her Divine Son all torn and mangled, being led away by the archers after the scourging: he wiped his eyes, which were filled with blood, that he might look at his Mother, and she stretched out her hands towards him, and continued to look at the bloody traces of his footsteps. I soon after saw Mary and Magdalen approach the pillar where Jesus had been scourged; the mob were at a distance, and they were partly concealed by the other holy women, and by a few kind-hearted persons who had joined them; they knelt down on the ground near the pillar, and wiped up the sacred blood with the linen which Claudia Procles had sent. John was not at that time with the holy women, who were about twenty in number. The sons

---

cause she was the daughter of Joachim, or Heliachim. Her husband bore the name of Cleophas, and her daughter that of Mary of Cleophas. This daughter was, however, older than her aunt, the Blessed Virgin, and had been married first to Alpheus, by whom she had three sons, afterwards the Apostles Simon, James the Less and Thaddeus. She had one son by her second husband, Sabat and another called Simon, by her third husband, Jonas. Simon was afterwards Bishop of Jerusalem.

of Simeon and of Obed, and Veronica, as also the two nephews of Joseph of Arimathea—Aram and Themni— were in the Temple, and appeared to be overwhelmed with grief. It was not more than nine o'clock A.M. when the scourging terminated.

CHAPTER XXIV.

Interruption of the Visions of the Passion by the Appearance of St. Joseph under the form of a Child.

DURING the whole time of the visions which we have just narrated (that is to say, from the 18th of February until the 8th of March), Sister Emmerich continued to suffer all the mental and bodily tortures which were once endured by our Lord. Being totally immersed in these meditations, and, as it were, dead to exterior objects, she wept and groaned like a person in the hands of an exe- cutioner, trembled, shuddered, and writhed on her couch, while her face resembled that of a man about to expire under torture, and a bloody sweat often trickled over her chest and shoulders. She generally perspired so profusely that her bed and clothes were saturated. Her sufferings from thirst were likewise fearful, and she might truly be compared to a person perishing in a desert from the want of water. Generally speaking, her mouth was so parched in the morning, and her tongue so contracted and dried up, that she could not speak, but was obliged by signs and inarticulate sounds to beg for relief. Her constant state of fever was probably brought on by the great pains she endured, added to which she likewise often took upon herself the illnesses and temporal calamities merited by others. It was always necessary for her to rest for a time before relating the different scenes of the Passion, nor was it always that she could speak of what she had seen, and she was even often obliged to discontinue her narrations for the day. She was in this state of suffering on Satur- day the 8th of March, and with the greatest difficulty and suffering described the scourging of our Lord which she had seen in the vision of the previous night, and which appeared to be present to her mind during the greatest part of the following day. Towards evening, however, a change took place, and there was an interruption in the course of meditations on the Passion which had latterly followed one another so regularly. We will describe this interruption, in order, in the first place, to give our readers a more full comprehension of the interior life of this most extraordinary person ; and, in the second, to enable them to pause for a time to rest their minds, as I well know that meditations on the Passion of our Lord exhaust the weak, even when they remember that it was for their salvation that he suffered and died.

The life of Sister Emmerich, both as regarded her spiritual and intellectual existence, invariably harmonised with the spirit of the Church at different seasons of the year. It harmonised even more strongly than man's natural life does with the seasons, or with the hours of the day, and this caused her to be (if we may thus express ourselves) a realisation of the existence and of the various intentions of the Church. Her union with its spirit was so complete, that no sooner did a festival day begin (that is to say, on the eve), than a perfect change took place within her, both intellectually and spiritually. As soon as the spiritual sun of these festival days of the Church was set, she directed all her thoughts towards that which would rise on the following day, and disposed all her prayers, good works, and sufferings for the attainment of the special graces attached to the feast about to commence, like a plant which absorbs the dew, and revels in the warmth and light of the first rays of the sun. These changes did not, as will readily be believed, always take place at the exact moment when the sound of the Angelus announced the commencement of a festival, and summoned the faithful to prayer ; for this bell is often, either through ignorance or negligence, rung at the wrong time ; but they commenced at the time when the feast really began.

If the Church commemorated a sorrowful mystery, she

appeared depressed, faint, and almost powerless; but the instant the celebration of a joyful feast commenced, both body and soul revived to a new life, as if refreshed by the dew of new graces, and she continued in this calm, quiet, and happy state, quite released from every kind of suffering, until the evening. These things took place in her soul quite independently of her will; but as she had had from infancy the most ardent desire of being obedient to Jesus and to his Church, God had bestowed upon her those special graces which give a natural facility for practising obedience. Every faculty of her soul was directed towards the Church, in the same manner as a plant which, even if put into a dark cellar, naturally turns its leaves upwards, and appears to seek the light.

On Saturday, 8th of March 1823, after sunset, Sister Emmerich had, with the greatest difficulty, portrayed the different events of the scourging of our Lord, and the writer of these pages thought that her mind was occupied in the contemplation of the 'crowning with thorns,' when suddenly her countenance, which was previously pale and haggard, like that of a person on the point of death, became bright and serene, and she exclaimed in a coaxing tone, as if speaking to a child, 'O, that dear little boy! Who is he?—Stay, I will ask him. His name is Joseph. He has pushed his way through the crowd to come to me. Poor child, he is laughing; he knows nothing at all of what is going on. How light his clothing is! I fear he must be cold, the air is so sharp this morning. Wait, my child; let me put something more over you.' After saying these words in such a natural tone of voice that it was almost impossible for those present not to turn round and expect to see the child, she held up a dress which was near her, as would be done by a kind-hearted person wishing to clothe a poor frozen child. The friend who was standing by her bedside had not sufficient time to ask her to explain the words she had spoken, for a sudden change took place, both in her whole appearance and manner, when her attendant pronounced the word *obedience*,—one of the vows by which she had consecrated herself to our

Lord. She instantly came to herself, and, like an obedient
child awakening from a sound sleep and starting up at
the voice of its mother, she stretched forth her hand, took
the rosary and crucifix which were always at her side,
arranged her dress, rubbed her eyes, and sat up. She
was then carried from her bed to a chair, as she could
neither stand nor walk ; and it being the time for making
her bed, her friend left the room in order to write out
what he had heard during the day.

On Sunday, the 9th of March, the friend asked her
attendant what Sister Emmerich meant the evening before when she spoke of a child called Joseph. The attendant answered, ' She spoke of him again many times
yesterday evening ; he is the son of a cousin of mine, and
a great favourite of hers. I fear that her talking so much
about him is a sign that he is going to have an illness,
for she said so many times that the poor child was almost
without clothing, and that he must be cold.'

The friend remembered having often seen this little
Joseph playing on the bed of Sister Emmerich, and he
supposed that she was dreaming about him on the previous day. When the friend went to see her later in the
day to endeavour to obtain a continuation of the narrations of the Passion, he found her, contrary to his expectation, more calm, and apparently better in health than on
the previous day. She told him that she had seen nothing
more after the scourging of our Lord ; and when he questioned her concerning what she had said about little Joseph, she could not remember having spoken of the child
at all. He then asked the reason of her being so calm,
serene, and apparently well in health ; and she answered,
' I always feel thus when Mid-Lent comes, for then the
Church sings with Isaias in the introit at Mass ; " Rejoice,
O, Jerusalem, and come together all you that love her ;
rejoice with joy, you that have been in sorrow, that you
may exult and be filled from the breasts of your consolation." Mid-Lent Sunday is consequently a day of rejoicing ; and you may likewise remember that, in the
gospel of this day, the Church relates how our Lord fed

five thousand men with five loaves and two fishes, of which twelve baskets of fragments remained, consequently we ought to rejoice.'

She likewise added, that our Lord had deigned to visit her on that day in the Holy Communion, and that she always felt especial spiritual consolation when she received him on that particular day of the year. The friend cast his eyes on the calendar of the diocese of Munster, and saw that on that day they not only kept Mid-Lent Sunday, but likewise the Feast of St. Joseph, the foster-father of our Lord; he was not aware of this before, because in other places the feast of St. Joseph is kept on the 19th, and he remarked this circumstance to Sister Emmerich, and asked her whether she did not think that was the cause of her speaking about Joseph. She answered that she was perfectly aware of its being the feast of the foster-father of Jesus, but that she had not been thinking of the child of that name. However, a moment after, she suddenly remembered what her thoughts had been the day before, and explained to her friend that the moment the feast of St. Joseph began, her visions of the sorrowful mysteries of the Passion ceased, and were superseded by totally different scenes, in which St. Joseph appeared under the form of a child, and that it was to him that the words we have mentioned above were addressed.

We found that when she received these communications the vision was often in the form of a child, especially in those cases when an artist would have made use of that simile to express his ideas. If, for instance, the accomplishment of some Scripture prophecy was being shown to her, she often saw by the side of the illustration a child, who clearly designated the characteristics of such or such a prophet, by his position, his dress, and the manner in which he held in his hand and waved to and fro the prophetic roll appended to a staff.

Sometimes, when she was in extreme suffering, a beautiful child, dressed in green, with a calm and serene countenance, would approach, and seat himself in a posture of resignation at the side of her bed, allowing himself to be moved from one side to the other, or even put down on to the ground, without the smallest opposition and constantly looking at her affectionately and consoling her. If, when quite prostrate from illness and the sufferings of others which she had taken upon herself, she entered into communication with a saint, either by participation in the celebration of his feast, or from his relics being brought to her, she sometimes saw passages of the childhood of this saint, and at others the most terrible scenes of his martyrdom. In her greatest sufferings she was usually consoled, instructed, or reproved (whichever the occasion called for) by apparitions under the form of children. Sometimes, when totally overcome by trouble and distress, she would fall asleep, and be carried back in imagination to the scenes and perils of her childhood. She sometimes dreamed, as her exclamations and gestures demonstrated, that she was once more a little country girl of five years old, climbing over a hedge, caught in the briars, and weeping with fear.

These scenes of her childhood were always events which had really occurred, and the words which escaped her showed what was passing in her mind. She would exclaim (as if repeating the words of others): ' Why do you call out so?' ' I will not hold the hedge back until you are quiet and ask me gently to do so.' She had obeyed this injunction when she was a child and caught in the hedge, and she followed the same rule when grown up and suffering from the most terrible trials. She often spoke and joked about the thorn hedge, and the patience and prayer which had then been recommended to her, which admonition she, in after-life, had frequently neglected, but which had never failed her when she had recourse to it. This symbolical coincidence of the events of her childhood with those of her riper years shows that, in the individual no less than in humanity at large, prophetic types may be found. But, to the individual as well as to mankind in general, a Divine Type has been given in the person of our Redeemer, in order that both the one and the other, by walking in his footsteps and with his assistance, may surpass human nature and attain to perfect wisdom and grace with God and man.   Thus it is that the will of God is done on earth as in heaven, and that his kingdom is attained by ' men of good will.'

She then gave a short account of the visions which had, on the previous night, interrupted her visions of the Passion at the commencement of the feast of St. Joseph.

CHAPTER XXV.

Description of the personal Appearance of the Blessed Virgin.

WHILE these sad events were taking place I was in Jerusalem, sometimes in one locality and sometimes in another ; I was quite overcome, my sufferings were intense, and I felt as if about to expire.   During the time of the scourging of my adorable Spouse, I sat in the vicinity, in a part which no Jew dared approach, for fear of defiling himself; but I did not fear defilement, I was only anxious for a drop of our Lord's blood to fall upon me, to purify me.   I felt so completely heartbroken that I thought I must die as I could not relieve Jesus, and each blow which he received drew from me such sobs and moans that I felt quite astonished at not being driven away.   When the executioners took Jesus into the guard-house, to crown him with thorns, I longed to follow that I might again contemplate him in his sufferings.   Then it was that the Mother of Jesus, accompanied by the holy women, approached the pillar and wiped up the blood with which it and the ground around were saturated. The door of the guard-house was open, and I heard the brutal laughter of the heartless men who were busily employed in finishing off the crown of thorns which they had prepared for our Lord.   I was too much affected to weep, but I endeavoured to drag myself near to the place where our Lord was to be crowned with thorns.

I once more saw the Blessed Virgin ; her countenance was wan and pale, her eyes red with weeping, but the simple dignity of her demeanour cannot be described. Notwithstanding her grief and anguish, notwithstanding the fatigue which she had endured (for she had been wandering ever since the previous evening through the streets of Jerusalem, and across the Valley of Josaphat), her appearance was placid and modest, and not a fold of her dress out of place. She looked majestically around, and her veil fell gracefully over her shoulders. She moved quietly, and although her heart was a prey to the most bitter grief, her countenance was calm and resigned. Her dress was moistened by the dew which had fallen upon it during the night, and by the tears which she had shed in such abundance; otherwise it was totally unsoiled. Her beauty was great, but indescribable, for it was super-human—a mixture of majesty, sanctity, simplicity, and purity.

The appearance of Mary Magdalen was totally different; she was taller and more robust, the expression of her countenance showed greater determination, but its beauty was almost destroyed by the strong passions which she had so long indulged, and by the violent repentance and grief she had since felt. It was painful to look upon her; she was the very picture of despair, her long dishevelled hair was partly covered by her torn and wet veil, and her appearance was that of one completely absorbed by woe, and almost beside herself from sorrow. Many of the inhabitants of Magdalum were standing near, gazing at her with surprise and curiosity, for they had known her in former days, first in prosperity and afterwards in degradation and consequent misery. They pointed, they even cast mud upon her, but she saw nothing, knew nothing, and felt nothing, save her agonising grief.

CHAPTER XXVI.

The Crowning with Thorns.

No sooner did Sister Emmerich recommence the narrative of her visions on the Passion than she again became extremely ill, oppressed with fever, and so tormented by violent thirst that her tongue was perfectly parched and contracted; and on the Monday after Mid-Lent Sunday, she was so exhausted that it was not without great difficulty, and after many intervals of rest, that she narrated all which our Lord suffered in his crowning with thorns. She was scarcely able to speak, because she herself felt every sensation which she described in the following account:

Pilate harangued the populace many times during the time of the scourging of Jesus, but they interrupted him once, and vociferated, ' He shall be executed, even if we die for it.' When Jesus was led into the guard-house, they all cried out again, ' Crucify him, crucify him !'

After this there was silence for a time. Pilate occupied himself in giving different orders to the soldiers, and the servants of the High Priests brought them some refreshments; after which Pilate, whose superstitious tendencies made him uneasy in mind, went into the inner part of his palace in order to consult his gods, and to offer them incense.

When the Blessed Virgin and the holy women had gathered up the blood of Jesus, with which the pillar and the adjacent parts were saturated, they left the forum and went into a neighbouring small house, the owner of which I do not know. John was not, I think, present at the scourging of Jesus.

A gallery encircled the inner court of the guard-house where our Lord was crowned with thorns, and the doors were open. The cowardly ruffians, who were eagerly waiting to gratify their cruelty by torturing and insulting our Lord, were about fifty in number, and the greatest part slaves or servants of the jailers and soldiers. The mob gathered round the building, but were soon displaced by a thousand Roman soldiers, who were drawn up in good order and stationed there. Although forbidden to leave their ranks, these soldiers nevertheless did their utmost by laughter and applause to incite the cruel executioners to redouble their insults ; and as public applause gives fresh energy to a comedian, so did their words of encouragement increase tenfold the cruelty of these men.

In the middle of the court there stood the fragment of a pillar, and on it was placed a very low stool which these cruel men maliciously covered with sharp flints and bits of broken potsherds. Then they tore off the garments of Jesus, thereby reopening all his wounds ; threw over his shoulders an old scarlet mantle which barely reached his knees ; dragged him to the seat prepared, and pushed him roughly down upon it, having first placed the crown of thorns upon his head. The crown of thorns was made of three branches plaited together, the greatest part of the thorns being purposely turned inwards so as to pierce our Lord's head. Having first placed these twisted branches on his forehead, they tied them tightly together at the back of his head, and no sooner was this accomplished to their satisfaction than they put a large reed into his hand, doing all with derisive gravity as if they were really crowning him king. They then seized the reed, and struck his head so violently that his eyes were filled with blood ; they knelt before him, derided him, spat in his face, and buffeted him, saying at the same time, ' *Hail, King of the Jews !*' Then they threw down his stool, pulled him up again from the ground on which he had fallen, and reseated him with the greatest possible brutality.

It is quite impossible to describe the cruel outrages which were thought of and perpetrated by these monsters under human form. The sufferings of Jesus from thirst, caused by the fever which his wounds and sufferings had brought on, were intense.* He trembled all over, his

* These meditations on the sufferings of Jesus filled Sister Emmerich with such feelings of compassion that she begged of God

flesh was torn piecemeal, his tongue contracted, and the
only refreshment he received was the blood which trickled
from his head on to his parched lips. This shameful scene
was protracted a full half-hour, and the Roman soldiers
continued during the whole time to applaud and encourage
the perpetration of still greater outrages.

CHAPTER XXVII.

Ecce Homo.

THE cruel executioners then reconducted our Lord to
Pilate's palace, with the scarlet cloak still thrown over
his shoulders, the crown of thorns on his head, and the
reed in his fettered hands. He was perfectly unrecognisable, his eyes, mouth, and beard being covered with blood,
his body but one wound, and his back bowed down as
that of an aged man, while every limb trembled as he
walked. When Pilate saw him standing at the entrance
of his tribunal, even he (hard-hearted as he usually was)
started, and shuddered with horror and compassion, whilst
the barbarous priests and the populace, far from being
moved to pity, continued their insults and mockery. When
Jesus had ascended the stairs, Pilate came forward, the
trumpet was sounded to announce that the governor
was about to speak, and he addressed the Chief Priests
and the bystanders in the following words : ' *Behold, I
bring him forth to you, that you may know that I find no
cause in him.*'

The archers then led Jesus up to Pilate, that the

---

to allow her to suffer as he had done. She instantly became feverish and parched with thirst, and, by morning, was speechless from
the contraction of her tongue and of her lips. She was in this
state when her friend came to her in the morning, and she looked
like a victim which had just been sacrificed. Those around succeeded, with some difficulty, in moistening her mouth with a little
water, but it was long before she could give any further details
concerning her meditations on the Passion.

people might again feast their cruel eyes on him, in the state of degradation to which he was reduced. Terrible and heartrending, indeed, was the spectacle he presented, and an exclamation of horror burst from the multitude, followed by a dead silence, when he with difficulty raised his wounded head, crowned as it was with thorns, and cast his exhausted glance on the excited throng. Pilate exclaimed, as he pointed him out to the people; ' *Ecce homo ! Behold the man !*' The hatred of the High Priests and their followers was, if possible, increased at the sight of Jesus, and they cried out, ' Put him to death ; *crucify him.*' ' Are you not content ?' said Pilate. ' The punishment he has received is, beyond question, sufficient to deprive him of all desire of making himself king.' But they cried out the more, and the multitude joined in the cry, ' Crucify him, crucify him !' Pilate then sounded the trumpet to demand silence, and said : ' *Take you him and crucify him, for I find no cause in him.*' ' *We have a law, and according to that law he ought to die,*' replied the priests, ' *because he made himself the Son of God.*' These words, ' *he made himself the Son of God,*' revived the fears of Pilate ; he took Jesus into another room, and asked him ; ' *Whence art thou ?*' But Jesus made no answer. ' *Speakest thou not to me ?*' said Pilate ; ' *knowest thou not that I have power to crucify thee, and power to release thee ?*' ' *Thou shouldst not have any power against me,*' replied Jesus, ' *unless it were given thee from above ; therefore he that hath delivered me to thee hath the greater sin.*'

The undecided, weak conduct of Pilate filled Claudia Procles with anxiety; she again sent him the pledge, to remind him of his promise, but he only returned a vague, superstitious answer, importing that he should leave the decision of the case to the gods. The enemies of Jesus, the High Priests and the Pharisees, having heard of the efforts which were being made by Claudia to save him, caused a report to be spread among the people, that the partisans of our Lord had seduced her. that he would be released, and then join the Romans and bring about the destruction of Jerusalem, and the extermination of Jews.

Pilate was in such a state of indecision and uncertainty as to be perfectly beside himself; he did not know what step to take next, and again addressed himself to the enemies of Jesus, declaring that ' *he found no crime in him*,' but they demanded his death still more clamorously. He then remembered the contradictory accusations which had been brought against Jesus, the mysterious dreams of his wife, and the unaccountable impression which the words of Jesus had made on himself, and therefore determined to question him again in order thus to obtain some information which might enlighten him as to the course he ought to pursue; he therefore returned to the Prætorium, went alone into a room, and sent for our Saviour. He glanced at the mangled and bleeding Form before him, and exclaimed inwardly : ' Is it possible that he can be God?' Then he turned to Jesus, and adjured him to tell him if he was God, if he was that king who had been promised to the Jews, where his kingdom was, and to what class of gods he belonged. I can only give the sense of the words of Jesus, but they were solemn and severe. He told him ' that his kingdom was not of this world,' and he likewise spoke strongly of the many hidden crimes with which the conscience of Pilate was defiled ; warned him of the dreadful fate which would be his, if he did not repent ; and finally declared that he himself, the Son of Man, would come at the last day, to pronounce a just judgment upon him.

Pilate was half frightened and half angry at the words of Jesus ; he returned to the balcony, and again declared that he would release Jesus ; but they cried out : ' *If thou release this man, thou art not Cæsar's friend. For whosoever maketh himself a king speaketh against Cæsar.*' Others said that they would accuse him to the Emperor of having disturbed their festival ; that he must make up his mind at once, because they were obliged to be in the Temple by ten o'clock at night. The cry, ' *Crucify him ! crucify him !*' resounded on all sides ; it reëchoed even from the flat roofs of the houses near the forum, where many persons were assembled. Pilate saw that all his efforts were vain, that he could make no impression on the infuriated mob; their yells and imprecations were deafening, and he began to fear an insurrection. Therefore he took water, and washed his hands before the people, saying, '*I am innocent of the blood of this just man; look you to it.*' A frightful and unanimous cry then came from the dense multitude, who were assembled from all parts of Palestine, '*His blood be upon us, and upon our children.*'

CHAPTER XXVIII.

Reflections on the Visions.

WHENEVER, during my meditations on the Passion of our Lord, I imagine I hear that frightful cry of the Jews, '*His blood be upon us, and upon our children,*' visions of a wonderful and terrible description display before my eyes at the same moment the effect of that solemn curse. I fancy I see a gloomy sky covered with clouds, of the colour of blood, from which issue fiery swords and darts, lowering over the vociferating multitude; and this curse, which they have entailed upon themselves, appears to me to penetrate even to the very marrow of their bones,— even to the unborn infants. They appear to me encompassed on all sides by darkness; the words they utter take, in my eyes, the form of black flames, which recoil upon them, penetrating the bodies of some, and only playing around others.

The last-mentioned were those who were converted after the death of Jesus, and who were in considerable numbers, for neither Jesus nor Mary ever ceased praying, in the midst of their sufferings, for the salvation of these miserable beings.

When, during visions of this kind, I turn my thoughts to the holy souls of Jesus and Mary, and to those of the enemies of Christ, all that takes place within them is shown me under various forms. I see numerous devils among the crowd, exciting and encouraging the Jews, whispering in their ears, entering their mouths, inciting them still more against Jesus, but nevertheless trembling at the sight of his ineffable love and heavenly patience. Innumerable angels surrounded Jesus, Mary, and the small number of saints who were there. The exterior of these angels denotes the office they fill; some represent consolation, others prayer, or some of the works of mercy.

I likewise often see consolatory, and at other times menacing voices, under the appearance of bright or coloured gleams of light, issuing from the mouths of these different apparitions; and I see the feelings of their souls, their interior sufferings, and in a word, their every thought, under the appearance of dark or bright rays. I then understand everything perfectly, but it is impossible for me to give an explanation to others; besides which, I am so ill, and so totally overcome by the grief which I feel for my own sins and for those of the world, I am so overpowered by the sight of the sufferings of our Lord, that I can hardly imagine how it is possible for me to relate events with the slightest coherency. Many of these things, but more especially the apparitions of devils and of angels, which are related by other persons who have had visions of the Passion of Jesus Christ, are fragments of symbolical interior perceptions of this species, which vary according to the state of the soul of the spectator. Hence the numerous contradictions, because many things are naturally forgotten or omitted.

Sister Emmerich sometimes spoke on these subjects, either during the time of her visions on the Passion, or before they commenced; but she more often refused to speak at all concerning them, for fear of causing confusion in the visions. It is easy to see how difficult it must have been for her, in the midst of such a variety of apparitions, to preserve any degree of connection in her narrations. Who can therefore be surprised at finding some omissions and confusion in her descriptions?

CHAPTER XXIX.

Jesus condemned to be crucified.

PILATE, who did not desire to know the truth, but was solely anxious to get out of the difficulty without harm to himself, became more undecided than ever; his conscience whispered—' Jesus is innocent ;' his wife said, ' he is holy ;' his superstitious feelings made him fear that Jesus was the enemy of his gods ; and his cowardice filled him with dread lest Jesus, if he was a god, should wreak his vengeance upon his judge. He was both irritated and alarmed at the last words of Jesus, and he made another attempt for his release ; but the Jews instantly threatened to lay an accusation against him before the Emperor. This menace terrified him, and he determined to accede to their wishes, although firmly convinced in his own mind of the innocence of Jesus, and perfectly conscious that by pronouncing sentence of death upon him he should violate every law of justice, besides breaking the promise he had made to his wife in the morning. Thus did he sacrifice Jesus to the enmity of the Jews, and endeavour to stifle remorse by washing his hands before the people, saying, ' *I am innocent of the blood of this just man ; look you to it.*' Vainly dost thou pronounce these words, O Pilate ! for his blood is on thy head likewise; thou canst not wash his blood from thy soul, as thou dost from thy hands.

Those fearful words, ' *His blood be upon us and upon our children*,' had scarcely ceased to resound, when Pilate commenced his preparations for passing sentence. He called for the dress which he wore on state occasions, put a species of diadem, set in precious stones, on his head, changed his mantle, and caused a staff to be carried before him. He was surrounded with soldiers, preceded by officers belonging to the tribunal, and followed by Scribes, who carried rolls of parchments and books used for inscribing names and dates. One man walked in front, who carried the trumpet. The procession marched in this order from Pilate's palace to the forum, where an elevated seat, used

on these particular occasions, was placed opposite to the
pillar where Jesus was scourged. This tribunal was called
Gabbatha; it was a kind of round terrace, ascended by
means of staircases; on the top was a seat for Pilate, and
behind this seat a bench for those in minor offices, while
a number of soldiers were stationed round the terrace and
upon the staircases. Many of the Pharisees had left the
palace and were gone to the Temple, so that Annas, Caiphas, and twenty-eight priests alone followed the Roman
governor on to the forum, and the two thieves were taken
there at the time that Pilate presented our Saviour to the
people, saying : ' *Ecce homo!*'

Our Lord was still clothed in his purple garment, his
crown of thorns upon his head, and his hands manacled,
when the archers brought him up to the tribunal, and
placed him between the two malefactors. As soon as
Pilate was seated, he again addressed the enemies of Jesus,
in these words, ' *Behold your King !*'

But the cries of ' *Crucify him ! Crucify him !*' resounded on all sides.

' *Shall I crucify your King ?*' said Pilate.

' *We have no King but Cæsar !*' responded the High
Priests.

Pilate found it was utterly hopeless to say anything
more, and therefore commenced his preparations for passing sentence. The two thieves had received their sentence
of crucifixion some time before ; but the High Priests had
obtained a respite for them, in order that our Lord might
suffer the additional ignominy of being executed with two
criminals of the most infamous description. The crosses
of the two thieves were by their sides ; that intended for
our Lord was not brought, because he was not as yet
sentenced to death.

The Blessed Virgin, who had retired to some distance
after the scourging of Jesus, again approached to hear the
sentence of death pronounced upon her Son and her God.
Jesus stood in the midst of the archers, at the foot of the
staircase leading up to the tribunal. The trumpet was
sounded to demand silence, and then the cowardly, the

base judge, in a tremulous undecided voice, pronounced the sentence of death on the Just Man. The sight of the cowardice and duplicity of this despicable being, who was nevertheless puffed up with pride at his important position, almost overcame me, and the ferocious joy of the executioners—the triumphant countenances of the High Priests, added to the deplorable condition to which our loving Saviour was reduced, and the agonising grief of his beloved Mother—still further increased my pain. I looked up again, and saw the cruel Jews almost devouring their victim with their eyes, the soldiers standing coldly by, and multitudes of horrible demons passing to and fro and mixing in the crowd. I felt that I ought to have been in the place of Jesus, my beloved Spouse, for the sentence would not then have been unjust; but I was so overcome with anguish, and my sufferings were so intense, that I cannot exactly remember all that I did see. However, I will relate all as nearly as I can.

After a long preamble, which was composed principally of the most pompous and exaggerated eulogy of the Emperor Tiberias, Pilate spoke of the accusations which had been brought against Jesus by the High Priests. He said that they had condemned him to death for having disturbed the public peace, and broken their laws by calling himself the Son of God and King of the Jews; and that the people had unanimously demanded that their decree should be carried out. Notwithstanding his oft-repeated conviction of the innocence of Jesus, this mean and worthless judge was not ashamed of saying that he likewise considered their decision a just one, and that he should therefore pronounce sentence—which he did in these words : 'I condemn Jesus of Nazareth, the King of the Jews, to be crucified ;' and he ordered the executioners to bring the cross. I think I remember likewise that he took a long stick in his hands, broke it, and threw the fragments at the feet of Jesus.

On hearing these words of Pilate the Mother of Jesus became for a few moments totally unconscious, for she was now certain that her beloved Son must die the most ignominious and the most painful of all deaths. John and the holy women carried her away, to prevent the heartless beings who surrounded them from adding crime to crime by jeering at her grief; but no sooner did she revive a little than she begged to be taken again to each spot which had been sanctified by the sufferings of her Son, in order to bedew them with her tears; and thus did the Mother of our Lord, in the name of the Church, take possession of those holy places.

Pilate then wrote down the sentence, and those who stood behind him copied it out three times. The words which he wrote were quite different from those he had pronounced; I could see plainly that his mind was dreadfully agitated—an angel of wrath appeared to guide his hand. The substance of the written sentence was this: 'I have been compelled, for fear of an insurrection, to yield to the wishes of the High Priests, the Sanhedrim, and the people, who tumultuously demanded the death of Jesus of Nazareth, whom they accused of having disturbed the public peace, and also of having blasphemed and broken their laws. I have given him up to them to be crucified, although their accusations appeared to be groundless. I have done so for fear of their alleging to the Emperor that I encourage insurrections, and cause dissatisfaction among the Jews by denying them the rights of justice.'

He then wrote the inscription for the cross, while his clerks copied out the sentence several times, that these copies might be sent to distant parts of the country.

The High Priests were extremely dissatisfied at the words of the sentence, which they said were not true; and they clamorously surrounded the tribunal to endeavour to persuade him to alter the inscription, and not to put *King of the Jews,* but *that he said, I am the King of the Jews.*

Pilate was vexed, and answered impatiently, '*What I have written I have written!*'

They were likewise anxious that the cross of our Lord should not be higher than those of the two thieves, but it was necessary for it to be so, because there would otherwise not have been sufficient place for Pilate's inscription; they therefore endeavoured to persuade him not to have this obnoxious inscription put up at all. But Pilate was determined, and their words made no impression upon him; the cross was therefore obliged to be lengthened by a fresh bit of wood. Consequently the form of the cross was peculiar — the two arms stood out like the branches of a tree growing from the stem, and the shape was very like that of the letter Y, with the lower part lengthened so as to rise between the arms, which had been put on separately, and were thinner than the body of the cross. A piece of wood was likewise nailed at the bottom of the cross for the feet to rest upon.

During the time that Pilate was pronouncing the iniquitous sentence, I saw his wife, Claudia Procles, send him back the pledge which he had given her, and in the evening she left his palace and joined the friends of our Lord, who concealed her in a subterraneous vault in the house of Lazarus at Jerusalem. Later in the same day, I likewise saw a friend of our Lord engrave the words, *Judex injustus*, and the name of Claudia Procles, on a green-looking stone, which was behind the terrace called Gabbatha—this stone is still to be found in the foundations of a church or house at Jerusalem, which stands on the spot formerly called Gabbatha. Claudia Procles became a Christian, followed St. Paul, and became his particular friend.

No sooner had Pilate pronounced sentence than Jesus was given up into the hands of the archers, and the clothes which he had taken off in the court of Caiphas were brought for him to put on again. I think some charitable persons had washed them, for they looked clean. The ruffians who surrounded Jesus untied his hands for his dress to be changed, and roughly dragged off the scarlet mantle with which they had clothed him in mockery, thereby reopening all his wounds; he put on his own linen under-garment with trembling hands, and they threw his scapular over his shoulders. As the crown of thorns was too large and prevented the seamless robe, which his

Mother had made for him, from going over his head, they
pulled it off violently, heedless of the pain thus inflicted
upon him. His white woollen dress was next thrown over
his shoulders, and then his wide belt and cloak. After
this, they again tied round his waist a ring covered with
sharp iron points, and to it they fastened the cords by
which he was led, doing all with their usual brutal cruelty.

The two thieves were standing, one on the right and
the other on the left of Jesus, with their hands tied and
a chain round their necks; they were covered with black
and livid marks, the effects of the scourging of the previous day. The demeanour of the one who was afterwards converted was quiet and peaceable, while that of
the other, on the contrary, was rough and insolent, and
he joined the archers in abusing and insulting Jesus, who
looked upon his two companions with love and compassion, and offered up his sufferings for their salvation. The
archers gathered together all the implements necessary for
the crucifixions, and prepared everything for the terrible
and painful journey to Calvary.

Annas and Caiphas at last left off disputing with
Pilate, and angrily retired, taking with them the sheets
of parchment on which the sentence was written; they
went away in haste, fearing that they should get to the
Temple too late for the Paschal sacrifice. Thus did the
High Priests, unknowingly to themselves, leave the true
Paschal Lamb. They went to a temple made of stone,
to immolate and to sacrifice that lamb which was but a
symbol, and they left the true Paschal Lamb, who was
being led to the Altar of the Cross by the cruel executioners; they were most careful not to contract exterior
defilement, while their souls were completely defiled by
anger, hatred, and envy. They had said, '*His blood be
upon us and upon our children!*' And by these words
they had performed the ceremony, and had placed the
hand of the sacrificer upon the head of the Victim. Thus
were the two paths formed—the one leading to the altar
belonging to the Jewish law, the other leading to the
Altar of Grace: Pilate, that proud and irresolute pagan,

that slave of the world, who trembled in the presence of the true God, and yet adored his false gods, took a middle path, and returned to his palace.

The iniquitous sentence was given at about ten in the morning.

CHAPTER XXX.

The Carriage of the Cross.

WHEN Pilate left the tribunal a portion of the soldiers followed him, and were drawn up in files before the palace ; a few accompanying the criminals. Eight-and-twenty armed Pharisees came to the forum on horseback, in order to accompany Jesus to the place of execution, and among these were the six enemies of Jesus, who had assisted in arresting him in the Garden of Olives. The archers led Jesus into the middle of the court, the slaves threw down the cross at his feet, and the two arms were forthwith tied on to the centre piece. Jesus knelt down by its side, encircled it with his sacred arms, and kissed it three times, addressing, at the same time, a most touching prayer of thanksgiving to his Heavenly Father for that work of redemption which he had begun. It was the custom among pagans for the priest to embrace a new altar, and Jesus in like manner embraced his cross, that august altar on which the bloody and expiatory sacrifice was about to be offered. The archers soon made him rise, and then kneel down again, and almost without any assistance, place the heavy cross on his right shoulder, supporting its great weight with his right hand. I saw angels come to his assistance, otherwise he would have been unable even to raise it from the ground. Whilst he was on his knees, and still praying, the executioners put the arms of the crosses, which were a little curved and not as yet fastened to the centre pieces, on the backs of the two thieves, and tied their hands tightly to them. The middle parts of the crosses were carried by slaves, as the transverse pieces were not to be fastened to them until just before the time of execu-

tion.   The trumpet sounded to announce the departure of
Pilate's horsemen, and one of the Pharisees belonging to
the escort came up to Jesus, who was still kneeling, and
said, ' Rise, we have had a sufficiency of thy fine speeches;
rise and set off.'   They pulled him roughly up, for he was
totally unable to rise without assistance, and he then felt
upon his shoulders the weight of that cross which we must
carry after him, according to his true and holy command
to follow him.   Thus began that triumphant march of the
King of Kings, a march so ignominious on earth, and so
glorious in heaven.

By means of ropes, which the executioners had fastened
to the foot of the cross, two archers supported it to prevent
its getting entangled in anything, and four other soldiers
took hold of the ropes, which they had fastened to Jesus
underneath his clothes.   The sight of our dear Lord trembling beneath his burden, reminded me forcibly of Isaac,
when he carried the wood destined for his own sacrifice up
the mountain.   The trumpet of Pilate was sounded as the
signal for departure, for he himself intended to go to Calvary at the head of a detachment of soldiers, to prevent
the possibility of an insurrection.   He was on horseback, in armour, surrounded by officers and a body of
cavalry, and followed by about three hundred of the in-
fantry, who came from the frontiers of Italy and Switzerland.   The procession was headed by a trumpeter, who
sounded his trumpet at every corner and proclaimed the
sentence.   A number of women and children walked behind the procession with ropes, nails, wedges, and baskets
filled with different articles, in their hands ; others, who
were stronger, carried poles, ladders, and the centre pieces
of the crosses of the two thieves, and some of the Pharisees
followed on horseback.   A boy who had charge of the inscription which Pilate had written for the cross, likewise
carried the crown of thorns (which had been taken off the
head of Jesus) at the end of a long stick, but he did not
appear to be wicked and hard-hearted like the rest.   Next
I beheld our Blessed Saviour and Redeemer—his bare feet
swollen and bleeding—his back bent as though he were

about to sink under the heavy weight of the cross, and his whole body covered with wounds and blood. He appeared to be half fainting from exhaustion (having had neither refreshment or sleep since the supper of the previous night), weak from loss of blood, and parched with thirst produced by fever and pain. He supported the cross on his right shoulder with his right hand, the left hung almost powerless at his side, but he endeavoured now and then to hold up his long garment to prevent his bleeding feet from getting entangled in it. The four archers who held the cords which were fastened round his waist, walked at some distance from him, the two in front pulled him on, and the two behind dragged him back, so that he could not get on at all without the greatest difficulty. His hands were cut by the cords with which they had been bound; his face bloody and disfigured; his hair and beard saturated with blood; the weight of the cross and of his chains combined to press and make the woollen dress cleave to his wounds, and reopen them : derisive and heartless words alone were addressed to him, but he continued to pray for his persecutors, and his countenance bore an expression of combined love and resignation. Many soldiers under arms walked by the side of the procession, and after Jesus came the two thieves, who were likewise led, the arms of their crosses, separate from the middle, being placed upon their backs, and their hands tied tightly to the two ends. They were clothed in large aprons, with a sort of sleeveless scapular which covered the upper part of their bodies, and they had straw caps upon their heads. The good thief was calm, but the other was, on the contrary, furious, and never ceased cursing and swearing. The rear of the procession was brought up by the remainder of the Pharisees on horseback, who rode to and fro to keep order. Pilate and his courtiers were at a certain distance behind; he was in the midst of his officers clad in armour, preceded by a squadron of cavalry, and followed by three hundred foot soldiers ; he crossed the forum, and then entered one of the principal streets, for he was marching through the town in order to prevent any insurrection among the people.

Jesus was conducted by a narrow back street, that the procession might not inconvenience the persons who were going to the Temple, and likewise in order that Pilate and his band might have the whole principal street entirely to themselves. The crowd had dispersed and started in different directions almost immediately after the reading of the sentence, and the greatest part of the Jews either returned to their own houses, or to the Temple, to hasten their preparations for sacrificing the Paschal Lamb; but a certain number were still hurrying on in disorder to see the melancholy procession pass; the Roman soldiers prevented all persons from joining the procession, therefore the most curious were obliged to go round by back streets, or to quicken their steps so as to reach Calvary before Jesus. The street through which they led Jesus was both narrow and dirty; he suffered much in passing through it, because the archers were close and harassed him. Persons stood on the roofs of the houses, and at the windows, and insulted him with opprobrious language; the slaves who were working in the streets threw filth and mud at him; even the children, incited by his enemies, had filled their pinafores with sharp stones, which they throw down before their doors as he passed, that he might be obliged to walk over them.

CHAPTER XXXI.

The first Fall of Jesus.

THE street of which we have just spoken, after turning a little to the left, became rather steep, as also wider, a subterranean aqueduct proceeding from Mount Sion passed under it, and in its vicinity was a hollow which was often filled with water and mud after rain, and a large stone was placed in its centre to enable persons to pass over more easily. When Jesus reached this spot, his strength was perfectly exhausted; he was quite unable to move; and as the archers dragged and pushed him without showing the slightest compassion, he fell quite down against this

stone, and the cross fell by his side. The cruel executioners were obliged to stop, they abused and struck him
unmercifully, but the whole procession came to a stand-
still, which caused a degree of confusion. Vainly did he
hold out his hand for some one to assist him to rise : ' Ah !'
he exclaimed, ' all will soon be over ;' and he prayed for
his enemies. ' Lift him up,' said the Pharisees, ' otherwise he will die in our hands.' There were many women
and children following the procession ; the former wept,
and the latter were frightened. Jesus, however, received
support from above, and raised his head ; but these cruel
men, far from endeavouring to alleviate his sufferings, put
the crown of thorns again on his head before they pulled
him out of the mud, and no sooner was he once more on
his feet than they replaced the cross on his back. The
crown of thorns which encircled his head increased his
pain inexpressibly, and obliged him to bend on one side to
give room for the cross, which lay heavily on his shoulders.

CHAPTER XXXII.

The second Fall of Jesus.

THE afflicted Mother of Jesus had left the forum,
accompanied by John and some other women, immediately after the unjust sentence was pronounced. She had
employed herself in walking to many of the spots sanctified by our Lord and watering them with her tears ; but
when the sound of the trumpet, the rush of people, and
the clang of the horsemen announced that the procession
was about to start for Calvary, she could not resist her
longing desire to behold her beloved Son once more, and
she begged John to take her to some place through which
he must pass. John conducted her to a palace, which had
an entrance in that street which Jesus traversed after his
first fall ; it was, I believe, the residence of the high priest
Caiphas, whose tribunal was in the division called Sion.
John asked and obtained leave from a kind-hearted serv-

ant to stand at the entrance mentioned above, with Mary
and her companions.   The Mother of God was pale, her
eyes were red with weeping, and she was closely wrapped
in a cloak of a bluish-gray colour.   The clamour and insulting speeches of the enraged multitude might be plainly
heard ; and a herald at that moment proclaimed in a loud
voice, that three criminals were about to be crucified.
The servant opened the door ; the dreadful sounds became
more distinct every moment ; and Mary threw herself on
her knees.   After praying fervently, she turned to John
and said, 'Shall I remain? ought I to go away? shall I
have strength to support such a sight?'   John made answer, 'If you do not remain to see him pass, you will grieve
afterwards.'   They remained therefore near the door, with
their eyes fixed on the procession, which was still distant,
but advancing by slow degrees.   When those who were
carrying the instruments for the execution approached,
and the Mother of Jesus saw their insolent and triumphant looks, she could not control her feelings, but joined
her hands as if to implore the help of heaven ; upon which
one among them said to his companions : 'What woman
is that who is uttering such lamentations?'   Another answered : 'She is the Mother of the Galilæan.'   When the
cruel men heard this, far from being moved to compassion,
they began to make game of the grief of this most afflicted
Mother : they pointed at her, and one of them took the
nails which were to be used for fastening Jesus to the
cross, and presented them to her in an insulting manner ;
but she turned away, fixed her eyes upon Jesus, who was
drawing near, and leant against the pillar for support, lest
she should again faint from grief, for her cheeks were as
pale as death, and her lips almost blue.   The Pharisees
on horseback passed by first, followed by the boy who
carried the inscription.   Then came her beloved Son.   He
was almost sinking under the heavy weight of his cross,
and his head, still crowned with thorns, was drooping in
agony on his shoulder.   He cast a look of compassion and
sorrow upon his Mother, staggered, and fell for the second
time upon his hands and knees.   Mary was perfectly ago-

nised at this sight; she forgot all else; she saw neither
soldiers nor executioners; she saw nothing but her dearly-
loved Son; and, springing from the doorway into the
midst of the group who were insulting and abusing him,
she threw herself on her knees by his side and embraced
him. The only words I heard were, 'Beloved Son!' and
'Mother!' but I do not know whether these words were
really uttered, or whether they were only in my own
mind.

A momentary confusion ensued. John and the holy
women endeavoured to raise Mary from the ground, and
the archers reproached her, one of them saying, 'What
hast thou to do here, woman? He would not have been
in our hands if he had been better brought up.'

A few of the soldiers looked touched; and, although
they obliged the Blessed Virgin to retire to the doorway,
not one laid hands upon her. John and the women surrounded her as she fell half fainting against a stone, which
was near the doorway, and upon which the impression of
her hands remained. This stone was very hard, and was
afterwards removed to the first Catholic church built in
Jerusalem, near the Pool of Bethsaida, during the time
that St. James the Less was Bishop of that city. The
two disciples who were with the Mother of Jesus carried
her into the house, and the door was shut. In the mean
time the archers had raised Jesus, and obliged him to
carry the cross in a different manner. Its arms being un-
fastened from the centre, and entangled in the ropes with
which he was bound, he supported them on his arm, and
by this means the weight of the body of the cross was a
little taken off, as it dragged more on the ground. I saw
numbers of persons standing about in groups, the greatest
part amusing themselves by insulting our Lord in different
ways, but a few veiled females were weeping.

CHAPTER XXXIII.

Simon of Cyrene.—Third Fall of Jesus.

THE procession had reached an arch formed in an old wall belonging to the town, opposite to a square, in which three streets terminated, when Jesus stumbled against a large stone which was placed in the middle of the archway, the cross slipped from his shoulder, he fell upon the stone, and was totally unable to rise. Many respectable-looking persons who were on their way to the Temple stopped, and exclaimed compassionately : ' Look at that poor man, he is certainly dying !' but his enemies showed no compassion. This fall caused a fresh delay, as our Lord could not stand up again, and the Pharisees said to the soldiers : ' We shall never get him to the place of execution alive, if you do not find some one to carry his cross.' At this moment Simon of Cyrene, a pagan, happened to pass by, accompanied by his three children. He was a gardener, just returning home after working in a garden near the eastern wall of the city, and carrying a bundle of lopped branches. The soldiers perceiving by his dress that he was a pagan, seized him, and ordered him to assist Jesus in carrying his cross. He refused at first, but was soon compelled to obey, although his children, being frightened, cried and made a great noise, upon which some women quieted and took charge of them. Simon was much annoyed, and expressed the greatest vexation at being obliged to walk with a man in so deplorable a condition of dirt and misery ; but Jesus wept, and cast such a mild and heavenly look upon him that he was touched, and instead of continuing to show reluctance, helped him to rise, while the executioners fastened one arm of the cross on his shoulders, and he walked behind our Lord, thus relieving him in a great measure from its weight; and when all was arranged, the procession moved forward. Simon was a stout-looking man, apparently about forty years of age. His children were dressed in tunics made of a variegated material ; the two eldest, named Rufus and

Alexander, afterwards joined the disciples; the third was much younger, but a few years later went to live with St. Stephen. Simon had not carried the cross after Jesus any length of time before he felt his heart deeply touched by grace.

CHAPTER XXXIV.

The Veil of Veronica.

WHILE the procession was passing through a long street, an incident took place which made a strong impression upon Simon. Numbers of respectable persons were hurrying towards the Temple, of whom many got out of the way when they saw Jesus, from a Pharisaical fear of defilement, while others, on the contrary, stopped and expressed pity for his sufferings. But when the procession had advanced about two hundred steps from the spot where Simon began to assist our Lord in carrying his cross, the door of a beautiful house on the left opened, and a woman of majestic appearance, holding a young girl by the hand, came out, and walked up to the very head of the procession. Seraphia was the name of the brave woman who thus dared to confront the enraged multitude; she was the wife of Sirach, one of the councillors belonging to the Temple, and was afterwards known by the name of Veronica, which name was given from the words *vera icon* (true portrait), to commemorate her brave conduct on this day.

Seraphia had prepared some excellent aromatic wine, which she piously intended to present to our Lord to refresh him on his dolorous way to Calvary. She had been standing in the street for some time, and at last went back into the house to wait. She was, when I first saw her, enveloped in a long veil, and holding a little girl of nine years of age, whom she had adopted, by the hand; a large veil was likewise hanging on her arm, and the little girl endeavoured to hide the jar of wine when the procession approached. Those who were marching at the head of the procession tried to push her back; but she made her way through the mob, the soldiers, and the archers, reached Jesus, fell on her knees before him, and presented the veil, saying at the same time, 'Permit me to wipe the face of my Lord.' Jesus took the veil in his left hand, wiped his bleeding face, and returned it with thanks. Seraphia kissed it, and put it under her cloak. The girl then timidly offered the wine, but the brutal soldiers would not allow Jesus to drink it. The suddenness of this courageous act of Seraphia had surprised the guards, and caused a momentary although unintentional halt, of which she had taken advantage to present the veil to her Divine Master. Both the Pharisees and the guards were greatly exasperated, not only by the sudden halt, but much more by the public testimony of veneration which was thus paid to Jesus, and they revenged themselves by striking and abusing him, while Seraphia returned in haste to her house.

No sooner did she reach her room than she placed the woollen veil on a table, and fell almost senseless on her knees. A friend who entered the room a short time after, found her thus kneeling, with the child weeping by her side, and saw, to his astonishment, the bloody countenance of our Lord imprinted upon the veil, a perfect likeness, although heartrending and painful to look upon. He roused Seraphia, and pointed to the veil. She again knelt down before it, and exclaimed through her tears, 'Now I shall indeed leave all with a happy heart, for my Lord has given me a remembrance of himself.' The texture of this veil was a species of very fine wool; it was three times the length of its width, and was generally worn on the shoulders. It was customary to present these veils to persons who were in affliction, or over-fatigued, or ill, that they might wipe their faces with them, and it was done in order to express sympathy or compassion. Veronica kept this veil until her death, and hung it at the head of her bed; it was then given to the Blessed Virgin, who left it to the Apostles, and they afterwards passed it on to the Church.

Seraphia and John the Baptist were cousins, her father

and Zacharias being brothers. When Joachim and Anna brought the Blessed Virgin, who was then only four years old, up to Jerusalem, to place her among the virgins in the Temple, they lodged in the house of Zacharias, which was situated near the fish-market. Seraphia was at least five years older than the Blessed Virgin, was present at her marriage with St. Joseph, and was likewise related to the aged Simeon, who prophesied when the Child Jesus was put into his arms. She was brought up with his sons, both of whom, as well as Seraphia, he imbued with his ardent desire of seeing our Lord. When Jesus was twelve years old, and remained teaching in the Temple, Seraphia, who was not then married, sent food for him every day to a little inn, a quarter of a mile from Jerusalem, where he dwelt when he was not in the Temple. Mary went there for two days, when on her way from Bethlehem to Jerusalem to offer her Child in the Temple. The two old men who kept this inn were Essenians, and well acquainted with the Holy Family; it contained a kind of foundation for the poor, and Jesus and his disciples often went there for a night's lodging.

Seraphia married rather late in life; her husband, Sirach, was descended from the chaste Susannah, and was a member of the Sanhedrim. He was at first greatly opposed to our Lord, and his wife suffered much on account of her attachment to Jesus, and to the holy women, but Joseph of Arimathea and Nicodemus brought him to a better state of feeling, and he allowed Seraphia to follow our Lord. When Jesus was unjustly accused in the court of Caiphas, the husband of Seraphia joined with Joseph and Nicodemus in attempts to obtain the liberation of our Lord, and all three resigned their seats in the Council.

Seraphia was about fifty at the time of the triumphant procession of our Lord when he entered into Jerusalem on Palm Sunday, and I then saw her take off her veil and spread it on the ground for him to walk upon. It was this same veil, which she presented to Jesus, at this his second procession, a procession which outwardly appeared

to be far less glorious, but was in fact much more so.
This veil obtained for her the name of Veronica, and it is
still shown for the veneration of the faithful.

CHAPTER XXXV.

The fourth and fifth Falls of Jesus.—The Daughters of Jerusalem.

THE procession was still at some distance from the
south-west gate, which was large, and attached to the
fortifications, and the street was rough and steep; it had
first to pass under a vaulted arch, then over a bridge, and
finally under a second arch. The wall on the left side of
the gate runs first in a southerly direction, then deviates a
little to the west, and finally runs to the south behind
Mount Sion. When the procession was near this gate,
the brutal archers shoved Jesus into a stagnant pool, which
was close to it; Simon of Cyrene, in his endeavours to
avoid the pool, gave the cross a twist, which caused Jesus
to fall down for the fourth time in the midst of the dirty
mud, and Simon had the greatest difficulty in lifting up
the cross again. Jesus then exclaimed in a tone which,
although clear, was moving and sad: ' *Jerusalem, Jeru-*
salem, how often would I have gathered together thy
children as the hen doth gather her chickens under her
wings, and thou wouldst not ?' When the Pharisees heard
these words, they became still more angry, and recom-
mencing their insults and blows endeavoured to force him
to get up out of the mud. Their cruelty to Jesus so exasperated Simon of Cyrene that he at last exclaimed, ' If
you continue this brutal conduct, I will throw down
the cross and carry it no farther. I will do so if you kill
me for it.'

A narrow and stony path was visible as soon as the
gate was passed, and this path ran in a northerly direction,
and led to Calvary. The high road from which it deviates
divided shortly after into three branches, one to the south-
west, which led to Bethlehem, through the vale of Gihon;

a second to the south towards Emmaus and Joppa; a third, likewise to the south-west, wound round Calvary, and terminated at the gate which led to Bethsur. A person standing at the gate through which Jesus was led might easily see the gate of Bethlehem. The officers had fastened an inscription upon a post which stood at the commencement of the road to Calvary, to inform those who passed by that Jesus and the two thieves were condemned to death. A group of women had gathered together near this spot, and were weeping and lamenting; many carried young children in their arms; the greatest part were young maidens and women from Jerusalem, who had preceded the procession, but a few came from Bethlehem, from Hebron, and from other neighbouring places, in order to celebrate the Pasch.

Jesus was on the point of again falling, but Simon, who was behind, perceiving that he could not stand, hastened to support him; he leant upon Simon, and was thus saved from falling to the ground. When the women and children of whom we have spoken above, saw the deplorable condition to which our Lord was reduced, they uttered loud cries, wept, and, according to the Jewish custom, presented him cloths to wipe his face. Jesus turned towards them and said : ' *Daughters of Jerusalem, weep not over me, but weep for yourselves and for your children. For behold the days shall come wherein they will say, Blessed are the barren, and the wombs that have not borne, and the paps that have not given suck. Then shall they begin to say to the mountains, Fall upon us, and to the hills, Cover us. For if in the green wood they do these things, what shall be done in the dry ?*' He then addressed a few words of consolation to them, which I do not exactly remember.

The procession made a momentary halt. The executioners, who set off first, had reached Calvary with the instruments for the execution, and were followed by a hundred of the Roman soldiers who had started with Pilate; he only accompanied the procession as far as the gateway, and returned to the town.

CHAPTER XXXVI.

Jesus on Mount Golgotha.—Sixth and seventh Falls of Jesus.

THE procession again moved on; the road was very steep and rough between the walls of the town and Calvary, and Jesus had the greatest difficulty in walking with his heavy burden on his shoulders; but his cruel enemies, far from feeling the slightest compassion, or giving the least assistance, continued to urge him on by the infliction of hard blows, and the utterance of dreadful curses. At last they reached a spot where the pathway turned suddenly to the south; here he stumbled and fell for the sixth time. The fall was a dreadful one, but the guards only struck him the harder to force him to get up, and no sooner did he reach Calvary than he sank down again for the seventh time.

Simon of Cyrene was filled with indignation and pity; notwithstanding his fatigue, he wished to remain that he might assist Jesus, but the archers first reviled, and then drove him away, and he soon after joined the body of disciples. The executioners then ordered the workmen and the boys who had carried the instruments for the execution to depart, and the Pharisees soon arrived, for they were on horseback, and had taken the smooth and easy road which ran to the east of Calvary. There was a fine view of the whole town of Jerusalem from the top of Calvary. This top was circular, and about the size of an ordinary riding-school, surrounded by a low wall, and with five separate entrances. This appeared to be the usual number in those parts, for there were five roads at the baths, at the place where they baptised, at the pool of Bethsaida, and there were likewise many towns with five gates. In this, as in many other peculiarities of the Holy Land, there was a deep prophetic signification; that number five, which so often occurred, was a type of those five sacred wounds of our Blessed Saviour, which were to open to us the gates of Heaven.

The horsemen stopped on the west side of the mount,

where the declivity was not so steep; for the side up which the criminals were brought was both rough and steep. About a hundred soldiers were stationed on different parts of the mountain, and as space was required, the thieves were not brought to the top, but ordered to halt before they reached it, and to lie on the ground with their arms fastened to their crosses. Soldiers stood around and guarded them, while crowds of persons who did not fear defiling themselves, stood near the platform or on the neighbouring heights; these were mostly of the lower classes—strangers, slaves, and pagans, and a number of them were women.

It wanted about a quarter to twelve when Jesus, loaded with his cross, sank down at the precise spot where he was to be crucified. The barbarous executioners dragged him up by the cords which they had fastened round his waist, and then untied the arms of the cross, and threw them on the ground. The sight of our Blessed Lord at this moment was, indeed, calculated to move the hardest heart to compassion; he stood or rather bent over the cross, being scarcely able to support himself; his heavenly countenance was pale and wan as that of a person on the verge of death, although wounds and blood disfigured it to a frightful degree; but the hearts of these cruel men were, alas! harder than iron itself, and far from showing the slightest commiseration, they threw him brutally down, exclaiming in a jeering tone, 'Most powerful king, we are about to prepare thy throne.' Jesus immediately placed himself upon the cross, and they measured him and marked the places for his feet and hands, whilst the Pharisees continued to insult their unresisting Victim. When the measurement was finished, they led him to a cave cut in the rock, which had been used formerly as a cellar, opened the door, and pushed him in so roughly that had it not been for the support of angels, his legs must have been broken by so hard a fall on the rough stone floor. I most distinctly heard his groans of pain, but they closed the door quickly, and placed guards before it, and the archers continued their preparations for the crucifixion. The

centre of the platform mentioned above was the most elevated part of Calvary,—it was a round eminence, about
two feet high, and persons were obliged to ascend two or
three steps to reach its top. The executioners dug the
holes for the three crosses at the top of this eminence, and
placed those intended for the thieves one on the right and
the other on the left of our Lord's; both were lower and
more roughly made than his. They then carried the cross
of our Saviour to the spot where they intended to crucify
him, and placed it in such a position that it would easily
fall into the hole prepared for it. They fastened the two
arms strongly on to the body of the cross, nailed the board
at the bottom which was to support the feet, bored the
holes for the nails, and cut different hollows in the wood
in the parts which would receive the head and back of our
Lord, in order that his body might rest against the cross,
instead of being suspended from it. Their aim in this was
the prolongation of his tortures, for if the whole weight of
his body was allowed to fall upon the hands the holes
might be quite torn open, and death ensue more speedily
than they desired. The executioners then drove into the
ground the pieces of wood which were intended to keep
the cross upright, and made a few other similar preparations.

CHAPTER XXXVII.

The Departure of Mary and the holy Women of Calvary.

ALTHOUGH the Blessed Virgin was carried away fainting after the sad meeting with her Son loaded with his
cross, yet she soon recovered consciousness; for love, and
the ardent desire of seeing him once more, imparted to
her a supernatural feeling of strength. Accompanied by
her companions she went to the house of Lazarus, which
was at the bottom of the town, and where Martha, Magdalen, and many holy women were already assembled.
All were sad and depressed, but Magdalen could not restrain her tears and lamentations. They started from this

house, about seventeen in number, to make the way ot the cross, that is to say, to follow every step Jesus had taken in this most painful journey. Mary counted each footstep, and being interiorly enlightened, pointed out to her companions those places which had been consecrated by peculiar sufferings. Then did the sharp sword predicted by aged Simeon impress for the first time in the heart of Mary that touching devotion which has since been so constantly practised in the Church. Mary imparted it to her companions, and they in their turn left it to future generations,—a most precious gift indeed, bestowed by our Lord on his beloved Mother, and which passed from her heart to the hearts of her children through the revered voice of tradition.

When these holy women reached the house of Veronica they entered it, because Pilate and his officers were at that moment passing through the street, on their way home. They burst forth into unrestrained tears when they beheld the countenance of Jesus imprinted on the veil, and they returned thanks to God for the favour he had bestowed on his faithful servant. They took the jar of aromatic wine which the Jews had prevented Jesus from drinking, and set off together towards Golgotha. Their number was considerably increased, for many pious men and women whom the sufferings of our Lord had filled with pity had joined them, and they ascended the west side of Calvary, as the declivity there was not so great. The Mother of Jesus, accompanied by her niece, Mary (the daughter of Cleophas), John, and Salome went quite up to the round platform ; but Martha, Mary of Heli, Veronica, Johanna, Chusa, Susanna, and Mary, the mother of Mark, remained below with Magdalen, who could hardly support herself. Lower down on the mountain there was a third group of holy women, and there were a few scattered individuals between the three groups, who carried messages from one to the other. The Pharisees on horseback rode to and fro among the people, and the five entrances were guarded by Roman soldiers. Mary kept her eyes fixed on the fatal spot, and stood as if entranced,—it was indeed a sight calculated to appal and rend the heart of a mother. There lay the terrible cross, the hammers, the ropes, the nails, and alongside of these frightful instruments of torture stood the brutal executioners, half drunk, and almost without clothing, swearing and blaspheming, whilst making their preparations. The sufferings of the Blessed Virgin were greatly increased by her not being able to see her Son ; she knew that he was still alive, and she felt the most ardent desire once more to behold him, while the thought of the torments he still had to endure made her heart ready to burst with grief.

A little hail had been falling at times during the morning, but the sun came out again after ten o'clock, and a thick red fog began to obscure it towards twelve.

CHAPTER XXXVIII.

The Nailing of Jesus to the Cross.

THE preparations for the crucifixion being finished four archers went to the cave where they had confined our Lord and dragged him out with their usual brutality, while the mob looked on and made use of insulting language, and the Roman soldiers regarded all with indifference, and thought of nothing but maintaining order. When Jesus was again brought forth, the holy women gave a man some money, and begged him to pay the archers anything they might demand if they would allow Jesus to drink the wine which Veronica had prepared ; but the cruel executioners, instead of giving it to Jesus, drank it themselves. They had brought two vases with them, one of which contained vinegar and gall, and the other a mixture which looked like wine mixed with myrrh and absinthe ; they offered a glass of the latter to our Lord, which he tasted, but would not drink.

There were eighteen archers on the platform ; the six who had scourged Jesus, the four who had conducted him to Calvary, the two who held the ropes which supported the cross, and six others who came for the purpose of crucifying him. They were strangers in the pay of either the Jews or the Romans, and were short thick-set men, with most ferocious countenances, rather resembling wild beasts than human beings, and employing themselves alternately in drinking and in making preparations for the crucifixion.

This scene was rendered the more frightful to me by the sight of demons, who were invisible to others, and I saw large bodies of evil spirits under the forms of toads, serpents, sharp-clawed dragons, and venomous insects, urging these wicked men to still greater cruelty, and perfectly darkening the air. They crept into the mouths and into the hearts of the assistants, sat upon their shoulders, filled their minds with wicked images, and incited them to revile and insult our Lord with still greater brutality. Weeping angels, however, stood around Jesus, and the sight of their tears consoled me not a little, and they were accompanied by little angels of glory, whose heads alone I saw. There were likewise angels of pity and angels of consolation among them; the latter frequently approached the Blessed Virgin and the rest of the pious persons who were assembled there, and whispered words of comfort which enabled them to bear up with firmness.

The executioners soon pulled off our Lord's cloak, the belt to which the ropes were fastened, and his own belt, when they found it was impossible to drag the woollen garment which his Mother had woven for him over his head, on account of the crown of thorns; they tore off this most painful crown, thus reopening every wound, and seizing the garment, tore it mercilessly over his bleeding and wounded head. Our dear Lord and Saviour then stood before his cruel enemies, stripped of all save the short scapular which was on his shoulders, and the linen which girded his loins. His scapular was of wool; the wool had stuck to the wounds, and indescribable was the agony of pain he suffered when they pulled it roughly off. He shook like the aspen as he stood before them, for he was so weakened from suffering and loss of blood that he could not support himself for more than a few moments; he was covered with open wounds, and his shoulders and back were torn to the bone by the dreadful scourging he had endured. He was about to fall when the executioners, fearing that he might die, and thus deprive them of the barbarous pleasure of crucifying him, led him to a large stone and placed him roughly down upon it, but no sooner was he seated than they aggravated his sufferings by putting the crown of thorns again upon his head. They then offered him some vinegar and gall, from which, however, he turned away in silence. The executioners did not allow him to rest long, but bade him rise and place himself on the cross that they might nail him to it. Then seizing his right arm they dragged it to the hole prepared for the nail, and having tied it tightly down with a cord, one of them knelt upon his sacred chest, a second held his hand flat, and a third taking a long thick nail, pressed it on the open palm of that adorable hand, which had ever been open to bestow blessings and favours on the ungrateful Jews, and with a great iron hammer drove it through the flesh, and far into the wood of the cross. Our Lord uttered one deep but suppressed groan, and his blood gushed forth and sprinkled the arms of the archers. I counted the blows of the hammer, but my extreme grief made me forget their number. The nails were very large, the heads about the size of a crown piece, and the thickness that of a man's thumb, while the points came through at the back of the cross. The Blessed Virgin stood motionless; from time to time you might distinguish her plaintive moans; she appeared as if almost fainting from grief, and Magdalen was quite beside herself. When the executioners had nailed the right hand of our Lord, they perceived that his left hand did not reach the hole they had bored to receive the nail, therefore they tied ropes to his left arm, and having steadied their feet against the cross, pulled the left hand violently until it reached the place prepared for it. This dreadful process caused our Lord indescribable agony, his breast heaved, and his legs were quite contracted. They again knelt upon him, tied down his arms, and drove the second nail into his left hand; his blood flowed afresh, and his feeble groans were once more heard between the blows of the hammer, but nothing could move the hard-hearted executioners to the slightest pity. The arms of Jesus, thus unnaturally stretched out, no longer covered the arms of the cross, which were sloped; there was a wide space between them and his armpits. Each additional torture and insult inflicted on our Lord caused a fresh pang in the heart of his Blessed Mother; she became white as a corpse, but as the Pharisees endeavoured to increase her pain by insulting words and gestures, the disciples led her to a group of pious women who were standing a little farther off.

The executioners had fastened a piece of wood at the lower part of the cross under where the feet of Jesus would be nailed, that thus the weight of his body might not rest upon the wounds of his hands, as also to prevent the bones of his feet from being broken when nailed to the cross. A hole had been pierced in this wood to receive the nail when driven through his feet, and there was likewise a little hollow place for his heels. These precautions were taken lest his wounds should be torn open by the weight of his body, and death ensue before he had suffered all the tortures which they hoped to see him endure. The whole body of our Lord had been dragged upward, and contracted by the violent manner with which the executioners had stretched out his arms, and his knees were bent up; they therefore flattened and tied them down tightly with cords; but soon perceiving that his feet did not reach the bit of wood which was placed for them to rest upon, they became infuriated. Some of their number proposed making fresh holes for the nails which pierced his hands, as there would be considerable difficulty in removing the bit of wood, but the others would do nothing of the sort, and continued to vociferate, ' He will not stretch himself out, but we will help him ;' they accompanied these words with the most fearful oaths and imprecations, and having fastened a rope to his right leg, dragged it violently until it reached the wood, and then tied it down as tightly as possible. The agony which Jesus suffered from this violent tension was indescribable ; the words 'My God, my God,' escaped his lips, and the executioners increased his pain by tying his chest and arms to the cross, lest the hands should be torn from the nails. They then fastened his left foot on to his right foot, having first bored a hole through them with a species of piercer, because they could not be placed in such a position as to be nailed together at once. Next they took a very long nail and drove it completely through both feet into the cross below, which operation was more than usually painful, on account of his body being so unnaturally stretched out ; I counted at least six and thirty blows of the hammer. During the whole time of the crucifixion our Lord never ceased praying, and repeating those passages in the Psalms which he was then accompanying, although from time to time a feeble moan caused by excess of suffering might be heard. In this manner he had prayed when carrying his cross, and thus he continued to pray until his death. I heard him repeat all these prophecies ; I repeated them after him, and I have often since noted the different passages when reading the Psalms, but I now feel so exhausted with grief that I cannot at all connect them.

When the crucifixion of Jesus was finished, the commander of the Roman soldiers ordered Pilate's inscription to be nailed on the top of the cross. The Pharisees were much incensed at this, and their anger was increased by the jeers of the Roman soldiers, who pointed at their crucified king ; they therefore hastened back to Jerusalem, determined to use their best endeavours to persuade the governor to allow them to substitute another inscription.

It was about a quarter past twelve when Jesus was crucified ; and at the moment the cross was lifted up, the Temple resounded with the blast of trumpets, which were always blown to announce the sacrifice of the Paschal Lamb.

CHAPTER XXXIX.

Erection of the Cross.

WHEN the executioners had finished the crucifixion of our Lord, they tied ropes to the trunk of the cross, and fastened the ends of these ropes round a long beam which was fixed firmly in the ground at a little distance, and by means of these ropes they raised the cross. Some of their number supported it while others shoved its foot towards the hole prepared for its reception—the heavy cross fell into this hole with a frightful shock—Jesus uttered a faint cry, and his wounds were torn open in the most fearful manner, his blood again burst forth, and his half dislocated bones knocked one against the other. The archers pushed the cross to get it thoroughly into the hole, and caused it to vibrate still more by planting five stakes around to support it.

A terrible, but at the same time a touching sight it was to behold the cross raised up in the midst of the vast concourse of persons who were assembled all around; not only insulting soldiers, proud Pharisees, and the brutal Jewish mob were there, but likewise strangers from all parts. The air resounded with acclamations and derisive cries when they beheld it towering on high, and after vibrating for a moment in the air, fall with a heavy crash into the hole cut for it in the rock. But words of love and compassion resounded through the air at the same moment; and need we say that these words, these sounds, were emitted by the most saintly of human beings—Mary—John—the holy women, and all who were pure of heart? They bowed down and adored the 'Word made flesh,' nailed to the cross; they stretched forth their hands as if desirous of giving assistance to the Holy of Holies, whom they beheld nailed to a cross and in the power of his furious enemies. But when the solemn sound of the fall of the cross into the hole prepared for it in the rock was heard, a dead silence ensued, every heart was filled with an undefinable feeling of awe—a feeling never before experienced, and for

which no one could account, even to himself; all the in-
mates of hell shook with terror, and vented their rage by
endeavouring to stimulate the enemies of Jesus to still
greater fury and brutality; the souls in Limbo were filled
with joy and hope, for the sound was to them a harbinger
of happiness, the prelude to the appearance of their Deliverer. Thus was the blessed cross of our Lord planted
for the first time on the earth; and well might it be compared to the tree of life in Paradise, for the wounds of
Jesus were as sacred fountains, from which flowed four
rivers destined both to purify the world from the curse of
sin, and to give it fertility, so as to produce fruit unto salvation.

The eminence on which the cross was planted was
about two feet higher than the surrounding parts; the feet
of Jesus were sufficiently near the ground for his friends
to be able to reach to kiss them, and his face was turned to
the north-west.

CHAPTER XL.

Crucifixion of the Thieves.

DURING the time of the crucifixion of Jesus, the two
thieves were left lying on the ground at some distance off;
their arms were fastened to the crosses on which they were
to be executed, and a few soldiers stood near on guard.
The accusation which had been proved against them was
that of having assassinated a Jewish woman who, with her
children, was travelling from Jerusalem to Joppa. They
were arrested, under the disguise of rich merchants, at a
castle in which Pilate resided occasionally, when employed
in exercising his troops, and they had been imprisoned for
a long time before being brought to trial. The thief placed
on the left-hand side was much older than the other; a
regular miscreant, who had corrupted the younger. They
were commonly called Dismas and Gesmas, and as I forget
their real names I shall distinguish them by these terms,

calling the good one Dismas, and the wicked one Gesmas. Both the one and the other belonged to a band of robbers who infested the frontiers of Egypt; and it was in a cave inhabited by these robbers that the Holy Family took refuge when flying into Egypt, at the time of the massacre of the Innocents. The poor leprous child, who was instantly cleansed by being dipped in the water which had been used for washing the infant Jesus, was no other than this Dismas, and the charity of his mother, in receiving and granting hospitality to the Holy Family, had been rewarded by the cure of her child; while this outward purification was an emblem of the inward purification which was afterwards accomplished in the soul of Dismas on Mount Calvary, through that Sacred Blood which was then shed on the cross for our redemption. Dismas knew nothing at all about Jesus, but as his heart was not hardened, the sight of the extreme patience of our Lord moved him much. When the executioners had finished putting up the cross of Jesus, they ordered the thieves to rise without delay, and they loosened their fetters in order to crucify them at once, as the sky was becoming **very** cloudy and bore every appearance of an approaching **storm**. After giving them some myrrh and vinegar, they stripped off their ragged clothing, tied ropes round their arms, and by the help of small ladders dragged them up to their places on the cross. The executioners then bound the arms of the thieves to the cross, with cords made of the bark of trees, and fastened their wrists, elbows, knees, and feet in like manner, drawing the cords so tight that their joints cracked, and the blood burst out. They uttered piercing cries, and the good thief exclaimed as they were drawing him up, 'This torture is dreadful, but if they had treated us as they treated the poor Galilæan, we should have been dead long ago.'

The executioners had divided the garments of Jesus, in order to draw lots for them; his mantle, which was narrow at the top, was very wide at the bottom, and lined over the chest, thus forming a pocket between the lining and the material itself; the lining they pulled out, tore into bands, and divided. They did the same with his long white robe, belt, scapular, and under-garment, which was completely saturated with his Sacred Blood. Not being able to agree as to who was to be the possessor of the seamless robe woven by his Mother, which could not be cut up and divided, they brought out a species of chess-board marked with figures, and were about to decide the point by lots, when a messenger, sent by Nicodemus and Joseph of Arimathea, informed them that there were persons ready to purchase all the clothes of Jesus; they therefore gathered them together and sold them in a bundle. Thus did the Christians get possession of these precious relics.

CHAPTER XLI.

Jesus hanging on the Cross between two Thieves.

THE tremendous concussion caused by the fall of the cross into the hole prepared for it drove the sharp points of the crown of thorns, which was still upon the head of our dear Saviour, still deeper into his sacred flesh, and blood ran down again in streams, both from it and from his hands and feet. The archers then placed ladders against the sides of the cross, mounted them and un-fastened the ropes with which they had bound our Lord to the cross, previous to lifting it up, fearing that the shock might tear open the wounds in his hands and feet, and that then the nails would no longer support his body. His blood had become, in a certain degree, stagnated by his horizontal position and the pressure of the cords, but when these were withdrawn, it resumed its usual course, and caused such agonising sensations throughout his countless wounds, that he bowed his head, and remained as if dead for more than seven minutes. A pause ensued; the executioners were occupied with the division of his garments; the trumpets in the temple no longer re-sounded; and all the actors in this fearful tragedy appeared to be exhausted, some by grief, and others by the efforts they had made to compass their wicked ends, and by the joy which they felt now at having at last succeeded in bringing about the death of him whom they had so long envied. With mixed feelings of fear and compassion I cast my eyes upon Jesus,—Jesus my Redeemer,—the Redeemer of the world. I beheld him motionless, and almost lifeless. I felt as if I myself must expire; my heart was overwhelmed between grief, love, and horror; my mind was half wandering, my hands and feet burning with a feverish heat; each vein, nerve, and limb was racked with inexpressible pain; I saw nothing distinctly, excepting my beloved Spouse hanging on the cross. I contemplated his disfigured countenance, his head encircled with that terrible crown of thorns, which prevented his raising it even for a moment without the most intense suffering, his mouth parched and half open from exhaustion, and his hair and beard clotted with blood. His chest was torn with stripes and wounds, and his elbows, wrists, and shoulders so violently distended as to be almost dislocated; blood constantly trickled down from the gaping wounds in his hands, and the flesh was so torn from his ribs that you might almost count them. His legs and thighs, as also his arms, were stretched out almost to dislocation, the flesh and muscles so completely laid bare that every bone was visible, and his whole body covered with black, green, and reeking wounds. The blood which flowed from his wounds was at first red, but it became by degrees light and watery, and the whole appearance of his body was that of a corpse ready for interment. And yet, notwithstanding the horrible wounds with which he was covered, notwithstanding the state of ignominy to which he was reduced, there still remained that inexpressible look of dignity and goodness which had ever filled all beholders with awe.

The complexion of our Lord was fair, like that of Mary, and slightly tinted with red; but his exposure to the weather during the last three years had tanned him considerably. His chest was wide, but not hairy like that of St. John Baptist; his shoulders broad, and his arms and thighs sinewy; his knees were strong and hardened, as is usually the case with those who have either walked or knelt much, and his legs long, with very strong muscles; his feet were well formed, and his hands beautiful, the fingers being long and tapering, and although not delicate like those of a woman, still not resembling those of a man who had laboured hard. His neck was rather long, with a well-set and finely proportioned head; his forehead large and high; his face oval; his hair, which was far from thick, was of a golden brown colour, parted in the middle and falling over his shoulders; his beard was not any great length, but pointed and divided under the chin. When I contemplated him on the cross, his hair was almost all torn off, and what remained was matted and clotted with blood; his body was one wound, and every limb seemed as if dislocated.

The crosses of the two thieves were placed, the one to the right and the other to the left of Jesus; there was sufficient space left for a horseman to ride between them. Nothing can be imagined more distressing than the appearance of the thieves on their crosses; they suffered terribly, and the one on the left-hand side never ceased cursing and swearing. The cords with which they were tied were very tight, and caused great pain; their countenances were livid, and their eyes inflamed and ready to start from the sockets. The height of the crosses of the two thieves was much less than that of our Lord.

CHAPTER XLII.

First Word of Jesus on the Cross.

As soon as the executioners had crucified the two thieves and divided the garments of Jesus between them, they gathered up their tools, addressed a few more insulting words to our Lord, and went away. The Pharisees, likewise, rode up to Jesus, looked at him scornfully, made use of some opprobrious expressions, and then left the place. The Roman soldiers, of whom a hundred had been posted round Calvary, were marched away, and their places filled by fifty others, the command of whom was given to Abenadar, an Arab by birth, who afterwards took the name of Ctésiphon in baptism; and the second in command was Cassius, who, when he became a Christian, was known by the name of Longinus : Pilate frequently made use of him as a messenger. Twelve Pharisees, twelve Sadducees, as many Scribes, and a few Ancients, accompanied by those Jews who had been endeavouring to persuade Pilate to change the inscription on the Cross of Jesus, then came up : they were furious, as the Roman governor had given them a direct refusal. They rode round the platform, and drove away the Blessed Virgin, whom St. John led to the holy women. When they passed the Cross of Jesus, they shook their heads disdainfully at him, exclaiming at the same time, '*Vah! thou that destroyest the temple of God, and in three days buildest it up again, save thyself, coming down from the Cross. Let Christ, the King of Israel, come down now from the Cross, that we may see and believe.*' The soldiers, likewise, made use of deriding language.

The countenance and whole body of Jesus became even more colourless : he appeared to be on the point of fainting, and Gesmas (the wicked thief) exclaimed, 'The demon by whom he is possessed is about to leave him.' A soldier then took a sponge, filled it with vinegar, put it on a reed, and presented it to Jesus, who appeared to drink. 'If thou art the King of the Jews,' said the soldier, '*save thyself, coming down from the Cross.*' These things took place during the time that the first band of soldiers was being relieved by that of Abenadar. Jesus raised his head a little, and said, '*Father, forgive them, for they know not what they do.*' And Gesmas cried out, 'If thou art the Christ, save thyself and us.' Dismas (the good thief) was silent, but he was deeply moved at the prayer of Jesus for his enemies. When Mary heard the voice of her Son, unable to restrain herself, she rushed forward, followed by John, Salome, and Mary of Cleophas, and approached the Cross, which the kind-hearted centurion did not prevent. The prayers of Jesus obtained for the good thief a most powerful grace; he suddenly remembered that it was Jesus and Mary who had cured him of leprosy in his childhood, and he exclaimed in a loud and clear voice, 'How can you insult him when he prays for you? He has been silent, and suffered all your outrages with patience; he is truly a Prophet—he is our King—he is the Son of God.' This unexpected reproof from the lips of a miserable malefactor who was dying on a cross caused a tremendous commotion among the spectators; they gathered up stones, and wished to throw them at him; but the centurion Abenadar would not allow it.

The Blessed Virgin was much comforted and strengthened by the prayer of Jesus, and Dismas said to Gesmas, who was still blaspheming Jesus, ' *Neither dost thou fear God, seeing thou art under the same condemnation. And we indeed justly, for we receive the due reward of our deeds; but this man hath done no evil.* Remember thou art now at the point of death, and repent.' He was enlightened and touched : he confessed his sins to Jesus, and said : 'Lord, if thou condemnest me it will be with justice.' And Jesus replied, 'Thou shalt experience my mercy.' Dismas, filled with the most perfect contrition, began instantly to thank God for the great graces he had received, and to reflect over the manifold sins of his past life. All these events took place between twelve and the half-hour shortly after the crucifixion; but such a surprising change had taken place in the appearance of nature during that time as to astonish the beholders and fill their minds with awe and terror.

CHAPTER XLIII.

Eclipse of the Sun.—Second and third Word of Jesus on the Cross.

A LITTLE hail had fallen at about ten o'clock,—when Pilate was passing sentence,—and after that the weather cleared up, until towards twelve, when the thick red-looking fog began to obscure the sun. Towards the sixth

hour, according to the manner of counting of the Jews, the
sun was suddenly darkened. I was shown the exact cause
of this wonderful phenomenon ; but I have unfortunately
partly forgotten it, and what I have not forgotten I cannot find words to express ; but I was lifted up from the
earth, and beheld the stars and the planets moving about
out of their proper spheres. I saw the moon like an immense ball of fire rolling along as if flying from the earth.
I was then suddenly taken back to Jerusalem, and I beheld the moon reappear behind the Mountain of Olives,
looking pale and full, and advancing rapidly towards the
sun, which was dim and overshrouded by a fog. I saw to
the east of the sun a large dark body which had the appearance of a mountain, and which soon entirely hid the
sun. The centre of this body was dark yellow, and a red
circle like a ring of fire was round it. The sky grew darker
and the stars appeared to cast a red and lurid light. Both
men and beasts were struck with terror ; the enemies of
Jesus ceased reviling him, while the Pharisees endeavoured
to give philosophical reasons for what was taking place,
but they failed in their attempt, and were reduced to silence. Many were seized with remorse, struck their breasts,
and cried out, ' May his blood fall upon his murderers !'
Numbers of others, whether near the Cross or at a distance, fell on their knees and entreated forgiveness of Jesus,
who turned his eyes compassionately upon them in the
midst of his sufferings. However, the darkness continued
to increase, and every one excepting Mary and the most
faithful among the friends of Jesus left the Cross. Dismas
then raised his head, and in a tone of humility and hope
said to Jesus, ' *Lord, remember me when thou shalt come
into thy kingdom.*' And Jesus made answer, ' *Amen, I
say to thee, This day thou shalt be with me in Paradise.*'
Magdalen, Mary of Cleophas, and John stood near the
Cross of our Lord and looked at him, while the Blessed
Virgin, filled with intense feelings of motherly love, entreated her Son to permit her to die with him ; but he,
casting a look of ineffable tenderness upon her, turned to
John and said, ' *Woman, behold thy son ;*' then he said to

John, ' *Behold thy mother.*' John looked at his dying
Redeemer, and saluted this beloved mother (whom he
henceforth considered as his own) in the most respectful
manner.   The Blessed Virgin was so overcome by grief at
these words of Jesus that she almost fainted, and was
carried to a short distance from the Cross by the holy
women.

I do not know whether Jesus really pronounced these
words, but I felt interiorly that he gave Mary to John as
a mother, and John to Mary as a son.   In similar visions
a person is often conscious of things which are not written,
and words can only express a portion of them, although
to the individual to whom they are shown they are so
clear as not to require explanation.   For this reason it did
not appear to me in the least surprising that Jesus should
call the Blessed Virgin ' *Woman,*' instead of ' Mother.'   I
felt that he intended to demonstrate that she was *that
woman* spoken of in Scripture who was to crush the head
of the serpent, and that then was the moment in which
that promise was accomplished in the death of her Son.
I knew that Jesus, by giving her as a mother to John,
gave her also as a mother to all *who believe in him, who
become children of God, and are not born of flesh and blood,
or of the will of man, but of God.*   Neither did it appear
to me surprising that the most pure, the most humble,
and the most obedient among women, who, when saluted
by the angel as ' *full of grace,*' immediately replied, ' *Behold the handmaid of the Lord, be it done to me according
to thy word,*' and in whose sacred womb the *Word* was
instantly *made flesh,*—that she, when informed by her dying Son that she was to become the spiritual mother of
another son, should repeat the same words with humble
obedience, and immediately adopt as her children all the
children of God, the brothers of Jesus Christ.   These
things are much easier to feel by the grace of God than
to be expressed in words.   I remember my celestial Spouse
once saying to me, ' Everything is imprinted in the hearts
of those children of the Church who believe, hope, and
love.'

CHAPTER XLIV.

The Fear felt by the Inhabitants of Jerusalem.—Fourth Word of Jesus on the Cross.

IT was about half-past one o'clock when I was taken into Jerusalem to see what was going on there. The inhabitants were perfectly overcome with terror and anxiety; the streets dark and gloomy, and some persons were feeling their way about, while others, seated on the ground with their heads veiled, struck their breasts, or went up to the roofs of their houses, looked at the sky, and burst forth in bitter lamentations. Even the animals uttered mournful cries, and hid themselves; the birds flew low, and fell to the ground. I saw Pilate conferring with Herod on the alarming state of things: they were both extremely agitated, and contemplated the appearance of the sky from that terrace upon which Herod was standing when he delivered up Jesus to be insulted by the infuriated rabble. 'These events are not in the common course of nature,' they both exclaimed: 'they must be caused by the anger of the gods, who are displeased at the cruelty which has been exercised towards Jesus of Nazareth.' Pilate and Herod, surrounded by guards, then directed their hasty trembling steps through the forum to Herod's palace. Pilate turned away his head when he passed Gabbatha, from whence he had condemned Jesus to be crucified. The square was almost empty; a few persons might be seen reëntering their houses as quickly as possible, and a few others running about and weeping, while two or three small groups might be distinguished in the distance. Pilate sent for some of the Ancients and asked them what they thought the astcunding darkness could possibly portend, and said that he himself considered it a terrific proof of the anger of their God at the crucifixion of the Galilæan, who was most certainly their prophet and their king: he added that he had nothing to reproach himself with on that head, for he had washed his hands of the whole affair, and was, therefore, quite innocent. The Ancients were as hardened as ever, and replied, in a sullen tone, that there was nothing unnatural in the course of events, that they might be easily accounted for by philosophers, and that they did not repent of anything they had done. However, many persons were converted, and among others those soldiers who fell to the ground at the words of our Lord when they were sent to arrest him in the Garden of Olives.

The rabble assembled before Pilate's house, and instead of the cry of '*Crucify him, crucify him!*' which had resounded in the morning, you might have heard vociferations of 'Down with the iniquitous judge!' 'May the blood of the just man fall upon his murderers!' Pilate was much alarmed; he sent for additional guards, and endeavoured to cast all the blame upon the Jews. He again declared that the crime was not his; that he was no subject of this Jesus, whom they had put to death unjustly, and who was their king, their prophet, their Holy One; that they alone were guilty, as it must be evident to all that he condemned Jesus solely from compulsion.

The Temple was thronged with Jews, who were intent on the immolation of the Paschal lamb; but when the darkness increased to such a degree that it was impossible to distinguish the countenance of one from that of the other, they were seized with fear, horror, and dread, which they expressed by mournful cries and lamentations. The High Priests endeavoured to maintain order and quiet. All the lamps were lighted; but the confusion became greater every moment, and Annas appeared perfectly paralysed with terror. I saw him endeavouring to hide first in one place, and then in another. When I left the Temple, and walked through the streets, I remarked that, although not a breath of wind was stirring, yet both the doors and windows of the houses were shaking as if in a storm, and the darkness was becoming every moment more dense.

The consternation produced by the sudden darkness at Mount Calvary was indescribable. When it first commenced, the confusion of the noise of the hammers, the vociferations of the rabble, the cries of the two thieves on being fastened to their crosses, the insulting speeches of the Pharisees, the evolutions of the soldiers, and the drunken shouts of the executioners, had so completely engrossed the attention of every one, that the change which was gradually coming over the face of nature was not remarked; but as the darkness increased, every sound ceased, each voice was hushed, and remorse and terror took possession of every heart, while the bystanders retired one by one to a distance from the Cross. Then it was that Jesus gave his Mother to St. John, and that she, overcome by grief, was carried away to a short distance. As the darkness continued to grow more and more dense, the silence became perfectly astounding; every one appeared terror-struck; some looked at the sky, while others, filled with remorse, turned towards the Cross, smote their breasts, and were converted. Although the Pharisees were in reality quite as much alarmed as other persons, yet they endeavoured at first to put a bold face on the matter, and declared that they could see nothing unaccountable in these events; but at last even they lost assurance, and were reduced to silence. The disc of the sun was of a dark-yellow tint, rather resembling a mountain when viewed by moonlight, and it was surrounded by a bright fiery ring; the stars appeared, but the light they cast was red and lurid; the birds were so terrified as to drop to the ground; the beasts trembled and moaned; the horses and the asses of the Pharisees crept as close as possible to one another, and put their heads between their legs. The thick fog penetrated everything.

Stillness reigned around the Cross. Jesus hung upon it alone; forsaken by all,—disciples, followers, friends, his Mother even was removed from his side; not one person of the thousands upon whom he had lavished benefits was near to offer him the slightest alleviation in his bitter agony,—his soul was overspread with an indescribable feeling of bitterness and grief,—all within him was dark, gloomy, and wretched. The darkness which reigned around

was but symbolical of that which overspread his interior;
he turned, nevertheless, to his Heavenly Father, he prayed
for his enemies, he offered the chalice of his sufferings for
their redemption, he continued to pray as he had done
during the whole of his Passion, and repeated portions of
those Psalms the prophecies of which were then receiving
their accomplishment in him.   I saw angels standing
around.   Again I looked at Jesus—my beloved Spouse—
on his Cross, agonising and dying, yet still in dreary solitude.   He at that moment endured anguish which no mortal pen can describe,—he felt that suffering which would
overwhelm a poor weak mortal if deprived at once of all
consolation, both divine and human, and then compelled,
without refreshment, assistance, or light, to traverse the
stormy desert of tribulation upheld by faith, hope, and
charity alone.

His sufferings were inexpressible; but it was by them
that he merited for us the grace necessary to resist those
temptations to despair which will assail us at the hour of
death,—that tremendous hour when we shall feel that we
are about to leave all that is dear to us here below.   When
our minds, weakened by disease, have lost the power of
reasoning, and even our hopes of mercy and forgiveness
are become, as it were, enveloped in mist and uncertainty,
—then it is that we must fly to Jesus, unite our feelings
of desolation with that indescribable dereliction which he
endured upon the Cross, and be certain of obtaining a
glorious victory over our infernal enemies.   Jesus then
offered to his Eternal Father his poverty, his dereliction,
his labours, and, above all, the bitter sufferings which our
ingratitude had caused him to endure in expiation for our
sins and weaknesses; no one, therefore, who is united to
Jesus in the bosom of his Church must despair at the
awful moment preceding his exit from this life, even if
he be deprived of all sensible light and comfort; for he
must then remember that the Christian is no longer obliged
to enter this dark desert alone and unprotected, as Jesus
has cast his own interior and exterior dereliction on the
Cross into this gulf of desolation, consequently he will not

be left to cope alone with death, or be suffered to leave this world in desolation of spirit, deprived of heavenly consolation. All fear of loneliness and despair in death must therefore be cast away; for Jesus, who is our true light, *the Way, the Truth, and the Life,* has preceded us on that dreary road, has overspread it with blessings, and raised his Cross upon it, one glance at which will calm our every fear. Jesus then (if we may so express ourselves) made his last testament in the presence of his Father, and bequeathed the merits of his Death and Passion to the Church and to sinners. Not one erring soul was forgotten; he thought of each and every one; praying, likewise, even for those heretics who have endeavoured to prove that, being God, he did not suffer as a man would have suffered in his place. The cry which he allowed to pass his lips in the height of his agony was intended not only to show the excess of the sufferings he was then enduring, but likewise to encourage all afflicted souls who acknowledge God as their Father to lay their sorrows with filial confidence at his feet. It was towards three o'clock when he cried out in a loud voice, '*Eloi, Eloi, lamma sabacthani?*' '*My God, my God, why hast thou forsaken me?*' These words of our Lord interrupted the dead silence which had continued so long; the Pharisees turned towards him, and one of them said, '*Behold, he calleth Elias;*' and another, '*Let us see whether Elias will come to deliver him.*' When Mary heard the voice of her divine Son, she was unable to restrain herself any longer, but rushed forwards, and returned to the foot of the Cross, followed by John, Mary the daughter of Cleophas, Mary Magdalen, and Salome. A troop of about thirty horsemen from Judæa and the environs of Joppa, who were on their way to Jerusalem for the festival, passed by just at the time when all was silent round the Cross, both assistants and spectators being transfixed with terror and apprehension. When they beheld Jesus hanging on the Cross, saw the cruelty with which he had been treated, and remarked the extraordinary signs of God's wrath which overspread the face of nature, they were filled with horror,

and exclaimed, 'If the Temple of God were not in Jerusalem, the city should be burned to the ground for having
taken upon itself so fearful a crime.' These words from
the lips of strangers—strangers too who bore the appearance of persons of rank—made a great impression on the
bystanders, and loud murmurs and exclamations of grief
were heard on all sides; some individuals gathered together in groups, more freely to indulge their sorrow, although a certain portion of the crowd continued to blas-
pheme and revile all around them. The Pharisees were
compelled to assume a more humble tone, for they feared
an insurrection among the people, being well aware of the
great existing excitement among the inhabitants of Jerusalem. They therefore held a consultation with Abenadar,
the centurion, and agreed with him that the gate of the
city, which was in the vicinity, should be closed, in order
to prevent farther communication, and that they should
send to Pilate and Herod for 500 men to guard against
the chance of an insurrection, the centurion, in the mean
time, doing all in his power to maintain order, and preventing the Pharisees from insulting Jesus, lest it should
exasperate the people still more.

Shortly after three o'clock the light reappeared in a
degree, the moon began to pass away from the disc of the
sun, while the sun again shone forth, although its appearance was dim, being surrounded by a species of red mist;
by degrees it became more bright, and the stars vanished,
but the sky was still gloomy. The enemies of Jesus soon
recovered their arrogant spirit when they saw the light returning; and it was then that they exclaimed, '*Behold,
he calleth Elias.*'

CHAPTER XLV.

Fifth, sixth, and seventh Words of Jesus on the Cross.—His Death.

THE light continued to return by degrees, and the
livid exhausted countenance of our Lord again became

visible   His body was become much more white from the
quantity of blood he had lost; and I heard him exclaim,
'*I am pressed as the grape, which is trodden in the wine-
press. My blood shall be poured out until water cometh,
but wine shall here be made no more.*' I cannot be sure
whether he really prouounced these words, so as to be
heard by others, or whether they were only an answer
given to my interior prayer. I afterwards had a vision relating to these words, and in it I saw Japhet making wine
in this place.

Jesus was almost fainting; his tongue was parched,
and he said : '*I thirst.*' The disciples who were standing round the Cross looked at him with the deepest expression of sorrow, and he added, 'Could you not have
given me a little water?' By these words he gave them
to understand that no one would have prevented them
from doing so during the darkness. John was filled with
remorse, and replied : 'We did not think of doing so, O
Lord.' Jesus pronounced a few more words, the import
of which was : 'My friends and my neighbours were also
to forget me, and not give me to drink, that so what was
written concerning me might be fulfilled.' This omission
had afflicted him very much. The disciples then offered
money to the soldiers to obtain permission to give him a
little water : they refused to give it, but dipped a sponge
in vinegar and gall, and were about to offer it to Jesus,
when the centurion Abenadar, whose heart was touched
with compassion, took it from them, squeezed out the gall,
poured some fresh vinegar upon it, and fastening it to a
reed, put the reed at the end of a lance, and presented it
for Jesus to drink. I heard our Lord say several other
things, but I only remember these words: '*When my voice
shall be silent, the mouths of the dead shall be opened.*'
Some of the bystanders cried out : 'He blasphemeth
again.' But Abenadar compelled them to be silent.

The hour of our Lord was at last come; his death-
struggle had commenced; a cold sweat overspread every
limb. John stood at the foot of the Cross, and wiped the
feet of Jesus with his scapular. Magdalen was crouched

to the ground in a perfect frenzy of grief behind the Cross. The Blessed Virgin stood between Jesus and the good thief, supported by Salome and Mary of Cleophas, with her eyes rivetted on the countenance of her dying Son. Jesus then said : '*It is consummated ;*' and, raising his head, cried out in a loud voice, '*Father, into thy hands I commend my spirit.*' These words, which he uttered in a clear and thrilling tone, resounded through heaven and earth ; and a moment after, he bowed down his head and gave up the ghost. I saw his soul, under the appearance of a bright meteor, penetrate the earth at the foot of the Cross. John and the holy women fell prostrate on the ground. The centurion Abenadar had kept his eyes steadfastly fixed on the disfigured countenance of our Lord, and was perfectly overwhelmed by all that had taken place. When our Lord pronounced his last words, before expiring, in a loud tone, the earth trembled, and the rock of Calvary burst asunder, forming a deep chasm between the Cross of our Lord and that of Gesmas. The voice of God—that solemn and terrible voice—had reëchoed through the whole universe ; it had broken the solemn silence which then pervaded all nature. All was accomplished. The soul of our Lord had left his body : his last cry had filled every breast with terror. The convulsed earth had paid homage to its Creator : the sword of grief had pierced the hearts of those who loved him. This moment was the moment of grace for Abenadar : his horse trembled under him ; his heart was touched; it was rent like the hard rock ; he threw his lance to a distance, struck his breast, and cried out : ' Blessed be the Most High God, the God of Abraham, of Isaac, and of Jacob ; *indeed this Man was the Son of God !*' His words convinced many among the soldiers, who followed his example, and were likewise converted.

Abenadar became from this moment a new man ; he adored the true God, and would no longer serve his enemies. He gave both his horse and his lance to a subaltern of the name of Longinus, who, having addressed a few words to the soldiers, mounted his horse, and took the command upon himself. Abenadar then left Calvary, and went through the Valley of Gihon to the caves in the Valley of Hinnom, where the disciples were hidden, announced the death of our Lord to them, and then went to the town, in order to see Pilate. No sooner had Abenadar rendered public testimony of his belief in the divinity of Jesus, than a large number of soldiers followed his example, as did also some of the bystanders, and even a few Pharisees. Many struck their breasts, wept, and returned home, while others rent their garments, and cast dust on their heads, and all were filled with horror and fear. John arose ; and some of the holy women who were at a short distance came up to the Blessed Virgin, and led her away from the foot of the Cross.

When Jesus, the Lord of life and death, gave up his soul into the hands of his Father, and allowed death to take possession of his body, this sacred body trembled and turned lividly white ; the countless wounds which were covered with congealed blood appeared like dark marks ; his cheeks became more sunken, his nose more pointed, and his eyes, which were obscured with blood, remained but half open. He raised his weary head, which was still crowned with thorns, for a moment, and then dropped it again in agony of pain ; while his parched and torn lips, only partially closed, showed his bloody and swollen tongue. At the moment of death his hands, which were at one time contracted round the nails, opened and returned to their natural size, as did also his arms ; his body became stiff, and the whole weight was thrown upon the feet, his knees bent, and his feet twisted a little on one side.

What words can, alas, express the deep grief of the Blessed Virgin? Her eyes closed, a death-like tint overspread her countenance ; unable to stand, she fell to the ground, but was soon lifted up, and supported by John, Magdalen, and the others. She looked once more upon her beloved Son—that Son whom she had conceived by the Holy Ghost, the flesh of her flesh, the bone of her bone, the heart of her heart—hanging on a cross between two thieves ; crucified, dishonoured, contemned by those whom he came on earth to save; and well might she at this moment be termed 'the queen of martyrs.'

The sun still looked dim and suffused with mist; and during the time of the earthquake the air was close and oppressive, but by degrees it became more clear and fresh.

It was about three o'clock when Jesus expired. The Pharisees were at first much alarmed at the earthquake; but when the first shock was over they recovered themselves, began to throw stones into the chasm, and tried to measure its depth with ropes. Finding, however, that they could not fathom its bottom, they became thoughtful, listened anxiously to the groans of the penitents, who were lamenting and striking their breasts, and then left Calvary. Many among the spectators were really converted, and the greatest part returned to Jerusalem perfectly overcome with fear. Roman soldiers were placed at the gates, and in other principal parts of the city, to prevent the possibility of an insurrection. Cassius remained on Calvary with about fifty soldiers. The friends of Jesus stood round the Cross, contemplated our Lord, and wept; many among the holy women had returned to their homes, and all were silent and overcome with grief.

CHAPTER XLVI.

The Earthquake.—Apparitions of the Dead in Jerusalem.

I saw the soul of Jesus, at the moment he expired, appear under the form of a bright orb, and accompanied by angels, among whom I distinguished the angel Gabriel penetrate the earth at the foot of the Cross. I likewise saw these angels cast a number of evil spirits into the great abyss, and I heard Jesus order several of the souls in Limbo to reënter the bodies in which they once dwelt, in order that the sight might fill sinners with a salutary terror, and that these souls might render a solemn testimony to his divinity.

The earthquake which produced the deep chasm at

Calvary did much damage in different parts of Palestine, but its effects were even more fatal in Jerusalem. Its inhabitants were just beginning to be a little reassured by the return of light, when their terror was reawakened with double force by the shocks of the earthquake, and the terrible noise and confusion caused by the downfall of houses and walls on all sides, which panic was still farther increased by the sudden appearance of dead persons, confronting the trembling miscreants who were flying to hide themselves, and addressing them in the most severe and reproachful language.

The High Priests had recommenced the sacrifice of the Paschal lamb (which had been stopped by the unexpected darkness), and they were triumphing at the return of light, when suddenly the ground beneath them trembled, the neighbouring buildings fell down, and the veil of the Temple was rent in two from the top to the bottom. Excess of terror at first rendered those on the outside speechless, but after a time they burst forth into cries and lamentations. The confusion in the interior of the Temple was not, however, as great as would naturally have been expected, because the strictest order and decorum were always enforced there, particularly with regard to the regulations to be followed by those who entered to make their sacrifice, and those who left after having offered it. The crowd was great, but the ceremonies were so solemnly carried out by the priests, that they totally engrossed the minds of the assistants. First came the immolation of the lamb, then the sprinkling of its blood, accompanied by the chanting of canticles and the sounding of trumpets. The priests were endeavouring to continue the sacrifices, when suddenly an unexpected and most appalling pause ensued; terror and astonishment were depicted on each countenance; all was thrown into confusion; not a sound was heard; the sacrifices ceased; there was a general rush to the gates of the Temple; every one endeavoured to fly as quickly as possible. And well might they fly, well might they fear and tremble; for in the midst of the multitude there suddenly appeared persons who had been dead and buried for many years! These persons looked at them sternly, and reproved them most severely for the crime they had committed that day, in bringing about the death of 'the just man,' and calling down his blood upon their heads. Even in the midst of this confusion, some attempts were, however, made by the priests to preserve order; they prevented those who were in the inner part of the Temple from rushing forward, pushing their way through the crowds who were in advance of them, and descending the steps which led out of the Temple: they even continued the sacrifices in some parts, and endeavoured to calm the fears of the people.

The appearance of the Temple at this moment can only be described by comparing it to an ant-hill on which persons have thrown stones, or which has been disturbed by a stick being driven into its centre. The ants in those parts on which the stones have fallen, or which the stick has disturbed, are filled with confusion and terror; they run to and fro and do nothing; while the ants in those parts which have not been disturbed continue to labour quietly, and even begin to repair the damaged parts.

The High Priest Caiphas and his retinue did not lose their presence of mind, and by the outward tranquillity which their diabolical hardness of heart enabled them to preserve, they calmed the confusion in a great degree, and then did their utmost to prevent the people from looking upon these stupendous events as testimonies of the innocence of Jesus. The Roman garrison belonging to the fortress of Antonia likewise made great efforts to maintain order; consequently, the disturbance of the festival was not followed by an insurrection, although every heart was fixed with fear and anxiety, which anxiety the Pharisees endeavoured (and in some instances with success) to calm.

I remember a few other striking incidents: in the first place, the two columns which were placed at the entrance of their Holy of Holies, and to which a magnificent curtain was appended, were shaken to the very foundations; the column on the left side fell down in a southerly, and that on the right side in a northerly direction, thus rending the veil in two from the top to the bottom with a fearful sound, and exposing the Holy of Holies uncovered to the public gaze. A large stone was loosened and fell from the wall at the entrance of the sanctuary, near where the aged Simeon used to kneel, and the arch was broken. The ground was heaved up, and many other columns were thrown down in other parts of the Temple.

An apparition of the High Priest Zacharias, who was slain between the porch and the altar, was seen in the sanctuary. He uttered fearful menaces, spoke of the death of the second Zacharias,* and of that of St. John Baptist, as also of the violent deaths of the other prophets. The two sons of the High Priest Simon, surnamed the Just (ancestors of the aged Simeon who prophesied when Jesus was presented in the Temple), made their appearance in the part usually occupied by the doctors of the law; they also spoke in terrific terms of the deaths of the prophets, of the sacrifice of the old law which was now about to cease, and they exhorted all present to be converted, and to embrace the doctrines which had been preached by him whom they had crucified. The prophet Jeremiah likewise appeared; he stood near the altar, and proclaimed, in a menacing tone, that the ancient sacrifice was at an end, and that a new one had commenced. As these apparitions took place in parts where none but priests were allowed to enter, Caiphas and a few others were alone cognisant of them, and they endeavoured, as far as possible, either to deny their reality, or to conceal them. These prodigies were followed by others still more extraordinary. The doors of the sanctuary flew open of themselves, and a voice was heard to utter these words: ' Let us leave this place;' and I saw all the angels of the Lord instantly leave the Temple. The thirty-two Pharisees

---

* The Zacharias here referred to was the father of John the Baptist, who was tortured and afterwards put to death by Herod, because he would not betray John into the hands of the tyrant. He was buried by his friends within the precincts of the Temple.

who went to Calvary a short time before our Lord expired were almost all converted at the foot of the Cross. They returned to the Temple in the midst of the confusion, and were perfectly thunderstruck at all which had taken place there. They spoke most sternly, both to Annas and to Caiphas, and left the Temple. Annas had always been the most bitter of the enemies of Jesus, and had headed every proceeding against him; but the supernatural events which had taken place had so completely unnerved him that he knew not where to hide himself. Caiphas was, in reality, excessively alarmed, and filled with anxiety, but his pride was so great that he concealed his feelings as far as possible, and endeavoured to reassure Annas. He succeeded for a time; but the sudden appearance of a person who had been dead many years marred the effect of his words, and Annas became again a prey to the most fearful terror and remorse.

Whilst these things were going on in the Temple, the confusion and panic were not less in Jerusalem. Dead persons were walking about, and many walls and buildings had been shaken by the earthquake, and parts of them fallen down. The superstition of Pilate rendered him even more accessible to fear; he was perfectly paralysed and speechless with terror; his palace was shaken to the very foundation, and the earth quaked beneath his feet. He ran wildly from room to room, and the dead constantly stood before him, reproaching him with the unjust sentence he had passed upon Jesus. He thought that they were the gods of the Galilæan, and took refuge in an inner room, where he offered incense, and made vows to his idols to invoke their assistance in his distress. Herod was equally alarmed; but he shut himself up in his palace, out of the sight of every one.

More than a hundred persons who had died at different epochs reëntered the bodies they had occupied when on earth, made their appearance in different parts of Jerusalem, and filled the inhabitants with inexpressible consternation. Those souls which had been released by Jesus from Limbo uncovered their faces and wandered to and fro in the streets, and although their bodies were the same as those which they had animated when on earth, yet these bodies did not appear to touch the ground as they walked. They entered the houses of their descendants, proclaimed the innocence of Jesus, and reproved those who had taken part in his death most severely. I saw them passing through the principal streets; they were generally in couples, and appeared to me to glide through the air without moving their feet. The countenances of some were pale; others of a yellow tint; their beards were long, and their voices sounded strange and sepulchral. Their grave-clothes were such as it was customary to use at the period of their decease. When they reached the place where sentence of death was proclaimed on Jesus before the procession started for Calvary, they paused for a moment, and exclaimed in a loud voice : 'Glory be to Jesus for ever and ever, and destruction to his enemies !' Towards four o'clock all the dead returned to their graves. The sacrifices in the Temple had been so interrupted, and the confusion caused by the different prodigies was so great, that very few persons ate the Paschal lamb on that evening.

CHAPTER XLVII.

The Request of Joseph of Arimathea to be allowed to have the Body of Jesus.

SCARCELY had the commotion which the town had been thrown into begun to subside in a degree, when the Jews belonging to the Council sent to Pilate to request that the legs of the criminals might be broken, in order to put an end to their lives before the Sabbath-day dawned. Pilate immediately dispatched executioners to Calvary to carry out their wishes.

Joseph of Arimathea then demanded an audience ; he had heard of the death of Jesus, and he and Nicodemus had determined to bury him in a new sepulchre which he had made at the end of his garden, not far from Calvary.

Pilate was still filled with anxiety and solicitude, and was much astonished at seeing a person holding a high position like Joseph so anxious for leave to give honourable burial to a criminal whom he had sentenced to be ignominiously crucified. He sent for the centurion Abenadar, who returned to Jerusalem after he had conferred with the disciples who were hidden in the caverns, and asked him whether the King of the Jews was really dead. Abenadar gave Pilate a full account of the death of our Lord, of his last words, and of the loud cry he uttered immediately before death, and of the earthquake which had rent the great chasm in the rock. The only thing at which Pilate expressed surprise was that the death of Jesus should have taken place so quickly, as those who were crucified usually lived much longer; but although he said so little, every word uttered by Joseph increased his dismay and remorse. He instantly gave Joseph an order, by which he was authorised to take down the body of the King of the Jews from the Cross, and to perform the rites of sepulture at once. Pilate appeared to endeavour, by his readiness in granting this request, to wish to make up, in a degree, for his previous cruel and unjust conduct, and he was likewise very glad to do what he was certain would annoy the priests extremely, as he knew their wish was to have Jesus buried ignominiously between the two thieves. He dispatched a messenger to Calvary to see his orders executed. I believe the messenger was Abenadar, for I saw him assisting in taking Jesus down from the Cross.

When Joseph of Arimathea left Pilate's palace, he instantly rejoined Nicodemus, who was waiting for him at the house of a pious woman, which stood opposite to a large street, and was not far from that alley where Jesus was so shamefully ill-treated when he first commenced carrying his Cross. The woman was a vendor of aromatic herbs, and Nicodemus had purchased many perfumes which were necessary for embalming the body of Jesus from her. She procured the more precious kinds from other places, and Joseph went away to procure a fine winding-sheet. His servants then fetched ladders, hammers, pegs, jars of

water, and sponges, from a neighbourhing shed, and placed
them in a hand-barrow similar to that on which the disciples of John the Baptist put his body when they carried
it off from the castle of Macherus.

CHAPTER XLVIII.

The Opening of the Side of Jesus.—Death of the two Thieves.

WHILST these events were taking place in Jerusalem,
silence reigned around Calvary. The crowd which had
been for a time so noisy and tumultuous was dispersed;
all were panic-stricken; in some that panic had produced
sincere repentance, but on others it had had no beneficial
effects. Mary, John, Magdalen, Mary of Cleophas, and
Salome had remained, either standing or sitting before the
Cross, closely veiled and weeping silently. A few soldiers
were leaning over the terrace which enclosed the platform;
Cassius rode up and down; the sky was lowering, and all
nature wore a garb of mourning. Six archers soon after
made their appearance, bringing with them ladders, spades,
ropes, and large iron staves for the purpose of breaking
the legs of the criminals, in order to hasten their deaths.
When they approached our Lord's Cross, his friends retired
a few paces back, and the Blessed Virgin was seized with
fear lest they should indulge their hatred of Jesus by insulting even his dead body. Her fears were not quite un-
founded, for when they first placed their ladders against
the Cross they declared that he was only pretending to be
dead; in a few moments, however, seeing that he was cold
and stiff, they left him, and removed their ladders to the
crosses on which the two thieves were still hanging alive.
They took up their iron staves and broke the arms of the
thieves above and below the elbow; while another archer
at the same moment broke their legs, both above and
below the knee. Gesmas uttered frightful cries, therefore
the executioner finished him off by three heavy blows of a
cudgel on his chest. Dismas gave a deep groan, and ex-

pired : he was the first among mortals who had the happiness of rejoining his Redeemer. The cords were then loosened, the two bodies fell to the ground, and the executioners dragged them to a deep morass, which was between Calvary and the walls of the town, and buried them there.

The archers still appeared doubtful whether Jesus was really dead, and the brutality they had shown in breaking the legs of the thieves made the holy women tremble as to what outrage they might next perpetrate on the body of our Lord. But Cassius, the subaltern officer, a young man of about five-and-twenty, whose weak squinting eyes and nervous manner had often excited the derision of his companions, was suddenly illuminated by grace, and being quite overcome at the sight of the cruel conduct of the soldiers, and the deep sorrow of the holy women, determined to relieve their anxiety by proving beyond dispute that Jesus was really dead. The kindness of his heart prompted him, but unconsciously to himself he fulfilled a prophecy. He seized his lance and rode quickly up to the mound on which the Cross was planted, stopped just between the cross of the good thief and that of our Lord, and taking his lance in both hands, thrust it so completely into the right side of Jesus that the point went through the heart, and appeared on the left side. When Cassius drew his lance out of the wound a quantity of blood and water rushed from it, and flowed over his face and body. This species of washing produced effects somewhat similar to the vivifying waters of Baptism : grace and salvation at once entered his soul. He leaped from his horse, threw himself upon his knees, struck his breast, and confessed loudly before all his firm belief in the divinity of Jesus.

The Blessed Virgin and her companions were still standing near, with their eyes fixed upon the Cross, but when Cassius thrust his lance into the side of Jesus they were much startled, and rushed with one accord up to it. Mary looked as if the lance had transfixed her heart instead of that of her Divine Son, and could scarcely support herself. Cassius meantime remained kneeling and thanking God, not only for the graces he had received but likewise for the cure of the complaint in his eyes, which had caused the weakness and the squint. This cure had been effected at the same moment that the darkness with which his soul was previously filled was removed. Every heart was overcome at the sight of the blood of our Lord, which ran into a hollow in the rock at the foot of the Cross. Mary, John, the holy women, and Cassius, gathered up the blood and water in flasks, and wiped up the remainder with pieces of linen.*

Cassius, whose sight was perfectly restored at the same moment that the eyes of his soul were opened, was deeply moved, and continued his humble prayer of thanksgiving. The soldiers were struck with astonishment at the miracle which had taken place, and cast themselves on their knees by his side, at the same time striking their breasts and confessing Jesus. The water and blood continued to flow from the large wound in the side of our Lord ; it ran into the hollow in the rock, and the holy women put it in vases, while Mary and Magdalen mingled their tears. The archers, who had received a message from Pilate, ordering them not to touch the body of Jesus, did not return at all.

All these events took place near the Cross, at a little before four o'clock, during the time that Joseph of Arimathea and Nicodemus were gathering together the articles necessary for the burial of Jesus. But the servants of Joseph having been sent to clean out the tomb, informed the friends of our Lord that their master intended to take the body of Jesus and place it in his new sepulchre. John

---

* Sister Emmerich added : ' Cassius was baptised by the name of Longinus ; and was ordained deacon, and preached the faith. He always kept some of the blood of Christ,—it dried up, but was found in his coffin in Italy. He was buried in a town at no great distance from the locality where St. Clare passed her life. There is a lake with an island upon it near this town, and the body of Longinus must have been taken there.' Sister Emmerich appears to designate Mantua by this description, and there is a tradition preserved in that town to the same effect. I do not know which St. Clare lived in the neighbourhood.

immediately returned to the town with the holy women; in the first place, that Mary might recruit her strength a little, and in the second, to purchase a few things which would be required for the burial. The Blessed Virgin had a small lodging among the buildings near the Cenaculum. They did not reënter the town through the gate which was the nearest to Calvary, because it was closed, and guarded by soldiers placed there by the Pharisees; but they went through that gate which leads to Bethlehem.

CHAPTER XLIX.

A Description of some Parts of ancient Jerusalem.

This chapter will contain some descriptions of places given by Sister Emmerich on various occasions. They will be followed by a description of the tomb and garden of Joseph of Arimathea, that so we may have no need to interrupt the account of the burial of our Lord.

The first gate which stood on the eastern side of Jerusalem, to the south of the south-east angle of the Temple, was the one leading to the suburb of Ophel. The gate of the sheep was to the north of the north-east angle of the Temple. Between these two gates there was a third, leading to some streets situated to the east of the Temple, and inhabited for the most part by stonemasons and other workmen. The houses in these streets were supported by the foundations of the Temple; and almost all belonged to Nicodemus, who had caused them to be built, and who employed nearly all the workmen living there. Nicodemus had not long before built a beautiful gate as an entrance to these streets, called the Gate of Moriah. It was but just finished, and through it Jesus had entered the town on Palm Sunday. Thus he entered by the new gate of Nicodemus, through which no one had yet passed, and was buried in the new monument of Joseph of Arimathea, in which no one had yet been laid. This gate was afterwards walled up, and there was a tradition that the Christians were once again to enter the town through it. Even in the present day, a walled-up gate, called by the Turks the Golden Gate, stands on this spot.

The road leading to the west from the gate of the sheep passed almost exactly between the north-western side of Mount Sion and Calvary. From this gate to Golgotha the distance was about two miles and a quarter; and from Pilate's palace to Golgotha about two miles. The fortress Antonia was situated to the north-west of the mountain of the Temple, on a detached rock. A person going towards the west, on leaving Pilate's palace, would have had this fortress to his left. On one of its walls there was a platform commanding the forum, and from which Pilate was accustomed to make proclamations to the people : he did this, for instance, when he promulgated new laws. When our Divine Lord was carrying his Cross, in the interior of the town, Mount Calvary was frequently on his right hand. This road, which partly ran in a south-westerly direction, led to a gate made in an inner wall of the town, towards Sion. Beyond this wall, to the left, there was a sort of suburb, containing more gardens than houses; and towards the outer wall of the city stood some magnificent sepulchres with stone entrances. On this side was a house belonging to Lazarus, with beautiful gardens, extending towards that part where the outer western wall of Jerusalem turned to the south. I believe that a little private door, made in the city wall, and through which Jesus and his disciples often passed by permission of Lazarus, led to these gardens. The gate standing at the north-western angle of the town led to Bethsur, which was situated more towards the north than Emmaus and Joppa. The western part of Jerusalem was lower than any other : the land on which it was built first sloped in the direction of the surrounding wall, and then rose again when close to it; and on this declivity there stood gardens and vineyards, behind which wound a wide road, with paths leading to the walls and towers. On the other side, without the

wall, the land descended towards the valley, so that the
walls surrounding the lower part of the town looked as
if built on a raised terrace. There are gardens and vineyards even in the present day on the outer hill. When
Jesus arrived at the end of the Way of the Cross, he had
on his left hand that part of the town where there were
so many gardens ; and it was from thence that Simon of
Cyrene was coming when he met the procession. The
gate by which Jesus left the town was not entirely facing
the west, but rather the south-west. The city wall on
the left-hand side, after passing through the gate, ran
somewhat in a southerly direction, then turned towards
the west, and then again to the south, round Mount Sion.
On this side there stood a large tower, like a fortress.
The gate by which Jesus left the town was at no great
distance from another gate more towards the south, leading
down to the valley, and where a road, turning to the
left in the direction of Bethlehem, commenced. The road
turned to the north towards Mount Calvary shortly after
that gate by which Jesus left Jerusalem when bearing his
Cross. Mount Calvary was very steep on its eastern side,
facing the town, and a gradual descent on the western ;
and on this side, from which the road to Emmaus was to
be seen, there was a field, in which I saw Luke gather
several plants when he and Cleophas were going to Emmaus, and met Jesus on the way. Near the walls, to the
east and south of Calvary, there were also gardens, sepulchres, and vineyards. The Cross was buried on the north-
east side, at the foot of Mount Calvary.

The garden of Joseph of Arimathea* was situated near

* We must here remark that, in the four years during which
Sister Emmerich had her visions, she described everything that had
happened to the holy places from the earliest times down to our
own. More than once she beheld them profaned and laid waste,
but always venerated, either publicly or privately. She saw many
stones and pieces of rock, which had been silent witnesses of the
Passion and Resurrection of our Lord, placed by St. Helena in the
Church of the Holy Sepulchre upon occasion of the foundation
of that sacred building. When Sister Emmerich visited it in spirit
she was accustomed to venerate the spots where the Cross had stood
and the Holy Sepulchre been situated. It must be observed, how-

the gate of Bethlehem, at about a seven minutes' walk from Calvary : it was a very fine garden, with tall trees, banks, and thickets in it, which gave much shade, and was situated on a rising ground extending to the walls of the city. A person coming from the northern side of the valley, and entering the garden, had on his left hand a slight ascent extending as far as the city wall ; and on his right, at the end of the garden, a detached rock, where the cave of the sepulchre was situated. The grotto in which it was made looked to the east ; and on the south-western and north-western sides of the same rock were two other smaller sepulchres, which were also new, and with depressed fronts. A pathway, beginning on the western side of this rock, ran all round it. The ground in front of the sepulchre was higher than that of the entrance, and a person wishing to enter the cavern had to descend several steps. The cave was sufficiently large for four men to be able to stand close up to the wall on either side without impeding the movements of the bearers of the body. Opposite the door was a cavity in the rock, in which the tomb was made ; it was about two feet above the level of the ground, and fastened to the rock by one side only, like an altar : two persons could stand, one at the head and one at the foot ; and there was a place also for a third in front, even if the door of the cavity was closed. This door was made of some metal, perhaps of brass, and had two folding doors. These doors could be closed by a stone being rolled against them ; and the stone used for this purpose was kept outside the cavern. Immediately after our Lord was placed in the sepulchre it was rolled in front of the door. It was very large, and could not be removed without the united efforts of several men. Opposite the entrance of the cavern there stood a stone bench, and by mounting on this a person could climb on to the rock,

---

ever, that she used sometimes to see a greater distance between the actual position of the Tomb and the spot where the Cross stood than there is between the chapels which bear their names in the church at Jerusalem.

which was covered with grass, and from whence the city walls, the highest parts of Mount Sion, and some towers could be seen, as well as the gate of Bethlehem and the fountain of Gihon. The rock inside was of a white colour, intersected with red and blue veins.

CHAPTER L.

The Descent from the Cross.

At the time when every one had left the neighbourhood of the Cross, and a few guards alone stood around it, I saw five persons, who I think were disciples, and who had come by the valley from Bethania, draw nigh to Calvary, gaze for a few moments upon the Cross, and then steal away. Three times I met in the vicinity two men who were making examinations and anxiously consulting together. These men were Joseph of Arimathea and Nicodemus. The first time was during the Crucifixion (perhaps when they caused the clothes of Jesus to be brought back from the soldiers), and they were then at no great distance from Calvary. The second was when, after standing to look whether the crowd was dispersing, they went to the tomb to make some preparations. The third was on their return from the tomb to the Cross, when they were looking around in every direction, as if waiting for a favourable moment, and then concerted together as to the manner in which they should take the body of our Lord down from the Cross, after which they returned to the town.

Their next care was to make arrangements for carrying with them the necessary articles for embalming the body, and their servants took some tools with which to detach it from the Cross, as well as two ladders which they found in a barn close to Nicodemus's house. Each of these ladders consisted of a single pole, crossed at regular intervals by pieces of wood, which formed the steps. There were hooks which could be fastened on any part of the pole, and by means of which the ladder could be steadied or on which, perhaps, anything required for the work could also be hung.

The woman from whom they had bought their spices had packed the whole neatly together. Nicodemus had bought a hundred pounds' weight of roots, which quantity is equal to about thirty-seven pounds of our measure, as has been explained to me. They carried these spices in little barrels make of bark, which were hung round their necks, and rested on their breasts. One of these barrels contained some sort of powder. They had also some bundles of herbs in bags made of parchment or leather, and Joseph carried a box of ointment; but I do not know what this box was made of. The servants were to carry vases, leathern bottles, sponges, and tools, on a species of litter, and they likewise took fire with them in a closed lantern. They left the town before their master, and by a differrent gate (perhaps that of Bethania), and then turned their steps towards Mount Calvary. As they walked through the town they passed by the house where the Blessed Virgin, St. John, and the holy women had gone to seek different things required for embalming the body of Jesus, and John and the holy women followed the servants at a certain distance. The women were about five in number, and some of them carried large bundles of linen under their mantles. It was the custom for women, when they went out in the evening, or if intending to perform some work of piety secretly, to wrap their persons carefully in a long sheet at least a yard wide. They began by one arm, and then wound the linen so closely round their body that they could not walk without difficulty. I have seen them wrapped up in this manner, and the sheet not only extended to both arms, but likewise veiled the head. On the present occasion, the appearance of this dress was most striking in my eyes, for it was a real mourning garment. Joseph and Nicodemus were also in mourning attire, and wore black sleeves and wide sashes. Their cloaks, which they had drawn over their heads, were both wide and long, of a common gray colour, and served to conceal everything that they were carrying.

They turned their steps in the direction of the gate leading to Mount Calvary. The streets were deserted and
quiet, for terror kept every one at home. The greatest
number were beginning to repent, and but few were keeping the festival. When Joseph and Nicodemus reached
the gate they found it closed, and the road, streets, and
every corner lined with soldiers. These were the soldiers
whom the Pharisees had asked for at about two o'clock,
and whom they had kept under arms and on guard, as
they still feared a tumult among the people. Joseph
showed an order, signed by Pilate, to let them pass freely,
and the soldiers were most willing that they should do so,
but explained to him that they had endeavoured several
times to open the gate, without being able to move it;
that apparently the gate had received a shock, and been
strained in some part; and that on this account the archers
sent to break the legs of the thieves had been obliged to
return to the city by another gate. But when Joseph
and Nicodemus seized hold of the bolt, the gate opened
as if of itself, to the great astonishment of all the bystanders.

It was still dark and the sky cloudy when they reached
Mount Calvary, where they found the servants who had
been sent on already arrived, and the holy women sitting
weeping in front of the Cross. Cassius and several soldiers who were converted remained at a certain distance,
and their demeanour was respectful and reserved. Joseph
and Nicodemus described to the Blessed Virgin and John
all they had done to save Jesus from an ignominious
death, and learned from them how they had succeeded in
preventing the bones of our Lord from being broken, and
how the prophecy had been fulfilled. They spoke also of
the wound which Cassius had made with his lance. No
sooner was the centurion Abenadar arrived than they began, with the deepest recollection of spirit, their mournful
and sacred labour of taking down from the Cross and embalming the adorable body of our Lord.

The Blessed Virgin and Magdalen were seated at the
foot of the Cross; while, on the right-hand side, between

the cross of Dismas and that of Jesus, the other women were engaged in preparing the linen, spices, water, sponges, and vases. Cassius also came forward, and related to Abenadar the miraculous cure of his eyes. All were deeply affected, and their hearts overflowing with sorrow and love; but, at the same time, they preserved a solemn silence, and their every movement was full of gravity and reverence. Nothing broke the stillness save an occasional smothered word of lamentation, or a stifled groan, which escaped from one or other of these holy personages, in spite of their earnest eagerness and deep attention to their pious labour. Magdalen gave way unrestrainedly to her sorrow, and neither the presence of so many different persons, nor any other consideration, appeared to distract her from it.

Nicodemus and Joseph placed the ladders behind the Cross, and mounted them, holding in their hands a large sheet, to which three long straps were fastened. They tied the body of Jesus, below the arms and knees, to the tree of the Cross, and secured the arms by pieces of linen placed underneath the hands. Then they drew out the nails, by pushing them from behind with strong pins pressed upon the points. The sacred hands of Jesus were thus not much shaken, and the nails fell easily out of the wounds; for the latter had been made wider by the weight of the body, which, being now supported by the cloths, no longer hung on the nails. The lower part of the body, which since our Lord's death had sunk down on the knees, now rested in a natural position, supported by a sheet fastened above to the arms of the Cross. Whilst Joseph was taking out the nail from the left hand, and then allowing the left arm, supported by its cloth, to fall gently down upon the body, Nicodemus was fastening the right arm of Jesus to that of the Cross, as also the sacred crowned head, which had sunk on the right shoulder. Then he took out the right nail, and having surrounded the arm with its supporting sheet, let it fall gently on to the body. At the same time, the centurion Abenadar, with great difficulty, drew out the large nail which transfixed the feet. Cassius devoutly received the nails, and laid them at the feet of the Blessed Virgin.

Then Joseph and Nicodemus, having placed ladders against the front of the Cross, in a very upright position, and close to the body, untied the upper strap, and fastened it to one of the hooks on the ladder; they did the same with the two other straps, and passing them all on from hook to hook, caused the sacred body to descend gently towards the centurion, who having mounted upon a stool received it in his arms, holding it below the knees; while Joseph and Nicodemus, supporting the upper part of the body, came gently down the ladder, stopping at every step, and taking every imaginable precaution, as would be done by men bearing the body of some beloved friend who had been grievously wounded. Thus did the bruised body of our Divine Saviour reach the ground.

It was a most touching sight. They all took the same precautions, the same care, as if they had feared to cause Jesus some suffering. They seemed to have concentrated on the sacred body all the love and veneration which they had felt for their Saviour during his life. The eyes of each were fixed upon the adorable body, and followed all its movements; and they were continually uplifting their hands towards Heaven, shedding tears, and expressing in every possible way the excess of their grief and anguish. Yet they all remained perfectly calm, and even those who were so busily occupied about the sacred body broke silence but seldom, and, when obliged to make some necessary remark, did so in a low voice. During the time that the nails were being forcibly removed by blows of the hammer, the Blessed Virgin, Magdalen, and all those who had been present at the Crucifixion, felt each blow transfix their hearts. The sound recalled to their minds all the sufferings of Jesus, and they could not control their trembling fear, lest they should again hear his piercing cry of suffering; although, at the same time, they grieved at the silence of his blessed lips, which proved, alas too surely, that he was really dead. When the body was taken down it was wrapped in linen from the knees to the waist, and then placed in the arms of the Blessed Virgin, who, over-whelmed with sorrow and love, stretched them forth to receive their precious burden.

CHAPTER LI.

The Embalming of the Body of Jesus.

THE Blessed Virgin seated herself upon a large cloth spread on the ground, with her right knee, which was slightly raised, and her back resting against some mantles, rolled together so as to form a species of cushion. No pre-caution had been neglected which could in any way facili-tate to her—the Mother of Sorrows—in her deep affliction of soul, the mournful but most sacred duty which she was about to fulfil in regard to the body of her beloved Son. The adorable head of Jesus rested upon Mary's knee, and his body was stretched upon a sheet. The Blessed Virgin was overwhelmed with sorrow and love. Once more, and for the last time, did she hold in her arms the body of her most beloved Son, to whom she had been unable to give any testimony of love during the long hours of his martyr-dom. And she gazed upon his wounds and fondly em-braced his blood-stained cheeks, whilst Magdalen pressed her face upon his feet.

The men withdrew into a little cave, situated on the south-west side of Calvary, there to prepare the different things needful for the embalming; but Cassius, with a few other soldiers who had been converted, remained at a re-spectful distance. All ill-disposed persons were gone back to the city, and the soldiers who were present served merely to form a guard to prevent any interruption in the last honours which were being rendered to the body of Jesus. Some of these soldiers even gave assistance when desired. The holy women held the vases, sponges, linen, unction, and spices, according as required; but when not thus employed, they remained at a respectful distance, at-tentively gazing upon the Blessed Virgin as she proceeded in her mournful task.   Magdalen did not leave the body of Jesus; but John gave continual assistance to the Blessed Virgin, and went to and fro from the men to the women, lending aid to both parties.   The women had with them some large leathern bottles and a vase filled with water standing upon a coal fire.   They gave the Blessed Virgin and Magdalen, according as they required, vases filled with clear water, and sponges, which they afterwards squeezed in the leathern bottles.

The courage and firmness of Mary remained unshaken even in the midst of her inexpressible anguish.*   It was absolutely impossible for her to leave the body of her Son in the awful state to which it had been reduced by his sufferings, and therefore she began with indefatigable earnestness to wash and purify it from the traces of the outrages to which it had been exposed.   With the utmost care she drew off the crown of thorns, opening it behind, and then cutting off one by one the thorns which had sunk deep into the head of Jesus, in order that she might not widen the wounds.   The crown was placed by the side of the nails, and then Mary drew out the thorns which had remained in the skin with a species of rounded pincers,† and sorrowfully showed them to her friends.   These

* On Good Friday, March 30th, 1820, as Sister Emmerich was contemplating the descent from the Cross she suddenly fainted, in the presence of the writer of these lines, and appeared to be really dead.   But after a time she recovered her senses and gave the following explanation, although still in a state of great suffering: 'As I was contemplating the body of Jesus lying on the knees of the Blessed Virgin I said to myself : " How great is her strength ! She has not fainted even once !"   My guide reproached me for this thought—in which there was more astonishment than compassion —and said to me, " Suffer then what she has suffered !" And at the same moment a sensation of the sharpest anguish transfixed me like a sword, so that I believed I must have died from it.'   She had to endure this suffering for a long time, and, in consequence of it, had an illness which reduced her almost to the brink of the grave.

† Sister Emmerich said that the shape of these pincers reminded her of the scissors with which Samson's hair was cut off. In her visions of the third year of the public life of Jesus she had seen our Lord keep the Sabbath-day at Misael—a town belonging

thorns were placed with the crown, but still some of them must have been preserved separately.

The divine face of our Saviour was scarcely recognisable, so disfigured was it by the wounds with which it was covered. The beard and hair were matted together with blood. Mary washed the head and face, and passed damp sponges over the hair to remove the congealed blood. As she proceeded in her pious office, the extent of the awful cruelty which had been exercised upon Jesus became more and more apparent, and caused in her soul emotions of compassion and tenderness which increased as she passed from one wound to another. She washed the wounds of the head, the eyes filled with blood, the nostrils, and the ears, with a sponge and a small piece of linen spread over the fingers of her right hand; and then she purified, in the same manner, the half-opened mouth, the tongue, the teeth, and the lips. She divided what remained of our Lord's hair into three parts,* a part falling over each temple, and the third over the back of

---

to the Levites, of the tribe of Aser—and as a portion of the Book of Judges was read in the synagogue, Sister Emmerich beheld upon that occasion the life of Samson.

* Sister Emmerich was accustomed, when speaking of persons of historical importance, to explain how they divided their hair. 'Eve,' she said, 'divided her hair in two parts, but Mary into three.' And she appeared to attach importance to these words. No opportunity presented itself for her to give any explanation upon the subject, which probably would have shown what was done with the hair in sacrifices, funerals, consecrations, or vows, &c. She once said of Samson: 'His fair hair, which was long and thick, was gathered up on his head in seven tresses, like a helmet, and the ends of these tresses were fastened upon his forehead and temples. His hair was not in itself the source of his strength, but only as the witness to the vow which he had made to let it grow in God's honour. The powers which depended upon these seven tresses were the seven gifts of the Holy Ghost. He must have already broken his vows and lost many graces, when he allowed this sign of being a Nazarene to be cut off. I did not see Dalila cut off all his hair, and I think one lock remained on his forehead. He retained the grace to do penance and of that repentance by which he recovered strength sufficient to destroy his enemies. The life of Samson is figurative and prophetic.'

his head; and when she had disentangled the front hair
and smoothed it, she passed it behind his ears. When the
head was thoroughly cleansed and purified, the Blessed
Virgin covered it with a veil, after having kissed the
sacred cheeks of her dear Son. She then turned her attention to the neck, shoulders, chest, back, arms, and
pierced hands. All the bones of the breast and the joints
were dislocated, and could not be bent. There was a
frightful wound on the shoulder which had borne the
weight of the Cross, and all the upper part of the body
was covered with bruises and deeply marked with the
blows of the scourges. On the left breast there was a
small wound where the point of Cassius's lance had come
out, and on the right side was the large wound made by
the same lance, and which had pierced the heart through
and through. Mary washed all these wounds, and Magdalen, on her knees, helped her from time to time; but
without leaving the sacred feet of Jesus, which she bathed
with tears and wiped with her hair.

The head, bosom, and feet of our Lord were now
washed, and the sacred body, which was covered with
brown stains and red marks in those places where the skin
had been torn off, and of a bluish-white colour, like flesh
that has been drained of blood, was resting on the knees
of Mary, who covered the parts which she had washed
with a veil, and then proceeded to embalm all the woun ¹ˢ
The holy women knelt by her side, and in turn presented
to her a box, out of which she took some precious ointment, and with it filled and covered the wounds. She
also anointed the hair, and then, taking the sacred hands
of Jesus in her left hand, respectfully kissed them, and
filled the large wounds made by the nails with this ointment or sweet spice. She likewise filled the ears, nostrils, and wound in the side with the same precious
mixture. Meanwhile Magdalen wiped and embalmed our
Lord's feet, and then again washed them with her tears, and
often pressed her face upon them.

The water which had been used was not thrown away,
but poured into the leathern bottles in which the sponges

had been squeezed. I saw Cassius or some other soldier go several times to fetch fresh water from the fountain of Gihon, which was at no great distance off. When the Blessed Virgin had filled all the wounds with ointment, she wrapped the head up in linen cloths, but she did not as yet cover the face. She closed the half-open eyes of Jesus, and kept her hand upon them for some time. She also closed the mouth, and then embraced the sacred body of her beloved Son, pressing her face fondly and reverently upon his. Joseph and Nicodemus had been waiting for some time, when John drew near to the Blessed Virgin, and besought her to permit the body of her Son to be taken from her, that the embalming might be completed, because the Sabbath was close at hand. Once more did Mary embrace the sacred body of Jesus, and utter her farewells in the most touching language, and then the men lifted it from her arms on the sheet, and carried it to some distance. The deep sorrow of Mary had been for the time assuaged by the feelings of love and reverence with which she had accomplished her sacred task; but now it once more overwhelmed her, and she fell, her head covered with her veil, into the arms of the holy women. Magdalen felt almost as though her Beloved were being forcibly carried away from her, and hastily ran forward a few steps, with her arms stretched forth; but then, after a moment, returned to the Blessed Virgin.

The sacred body was carried to a spot beneath the level of the top of Golgotha, where the smooth surface of a rock afforded a convenient platform on which to embalm the body. I first saw a piece of open-worked linen, looking very much like lace, and which made me think of the large embroidered curtain hung between the choir and nave during Lent.* It was probably worked in that open stitch for the water to run through. I also saw another large sheet unfolded. The body of our Saviour was placed on

---

* This refers to a custom of the Diocese of Munster. During Lent there was hung up in the churches a curtain, embroidered in open work, representing the Five Wounds, the instruments of the Passion, &c.

the open-worked piece of linen, and some of the other men held the other sheet spread above it. Nicodemus and Joseph then knelt down, and underneath this covering took off the linen which they had fastened round the loins of our Saviour, when they took his body down from the Cross. They then passed sponges under this sheet, and washed the lower parts of the body; after which they lifted it up by the help of pieces of linen crossed beneath the loins and knees, and washed the back without turning it over. They continued washing until nothing but clear water came from the sponges when pressed. Next they poured water of myrrh over the whole body, and then, handling it with respect, stretched it out full length, for it was still in the position in which our Divine Lord had died —the loins and knees bent. They then placed beneath his hips a sheet which was a yard in width and three in length, laid upon his lap bundles of sweet-scented herbs, and shook over the whole body a powder which Nicodemus had brought. Next they wrapped up the lower part of the body, and fastened the cloth which they had placed underneath round it strongly. After this they anointed the wounds of the thighs, placed bundles of herbs between the legs, which were stretched out to their full length, and wrapped them up entirely in these sweet spices.

Then John conducted the Blessed Virgin and the other holy women once more to the side of the body. Mary knelt down by the head of Jesus, and placed beneath it a piece of very fine linen which had been given her by Pilate's wife, and which she had worn round her neck under her cloak; next, assisted by the holy women, she placed from the shoulders to the cheeks bundles of herbs, spices, and sweet-scented powder, and then strongly bound this piece of linen round the head and shoulders. Magdalen poured besides a small bottle of balm into the wound of the side, and the holy women placed some more herbs into those of the hands and feet. Then the men put sweet spices around all the remainder of the body, crossed the sacred stiffened arms on the chest, and bound the large white sheet round the body as high as the chest, in the same manner as if they had been swaddling a child. Then, having fastened the end of a large band beneath the armpits, they rolled it round the head and the whole body. Finally, they placed our Divine Lord on the large sheet, six yards in length, which Joseph of Arimathea had bought, and wrapped him in it. He was lying diagonally upon it, and one corner of the sheet was raised from the feet to the chest, the other drawn over the head and shoulders, while the remaining two ends were doubled round the body.

The Blessed Virgin, the holy women, the men—all were kneeling round the body of Jesus to take their farewell of it, when a most touching miracle took place before them. The sacred body of Jesus, with all its wounds, appeared imprinted upon the cloth which covered it, as though he had been pleased to reward their care and their love, and leave them a portrait of himself through all the veils with which he was enwrapped. With tears they embraced the adorable body, and then reverently kissed the wonderful impression which it had left. Their astonishment increased when, on lifting up the sheet, they saw that all the bands which surrounded the body had remained white as before, and that the upper cloth alone had been marked in this wonderful manner. It was not a mark made by the bleeding wounds, since the whole body was wrapped up and covered with sweet spices, but it was a supernatural portrait, bearing testimony to the divine creative power ever abiding in the body of Jesus. I have seen many things relative to the subsequent history of this piece of linen, but I could not describe them coherently. After the resurrection it remained in the possession of the friends of Jesus, but fell twice into the hands of the Jews, and later was honoured in several different places. I have seen it in a city of Asia, in the possession of some Christians who were not Catholics. I have forgotten the name of the town, which is situated in a province near the country of the Three Kings.

CHAPTER LII.

The Body of our Lord placed in the Sepulchre.

THE men placed the sacred body on a species of leathern hand-barrow, which they covered with a brown-coloured cloth, and to which they fastened two long stakes. This forcibly reminded me of the Ark of the Covenant. Nicodemus and Joseph bore on their shoulders the front shafts, while Abenadar and John supported those behind. After them came the Blessed Virgin, Mary of Heli, her eldest sister, Magdalen and Mary of Cleophas, and then the group of women who had been sitting at some distance —Veronica, Johanna Chusa, Mary the mother of Mark, Salome the wife of Zebedee, Mary Salome, Salome of Jerusalem, Susanna, and Anne the niece of St. Joseph. Cassius and the soldiers closed the procession. The other women, such as Marone of Naïm, Dina the Samaritaness, and Mara the Suphanitess, were at Bethania, with Martha and Lazarus. Two soldiers, bearing torches in their hands, walked on first, that there might be some light in the grotto of the sepulchre ; and the procession continued to advance in this order for about seven minutes, the holy men and women singing psalms in sweet but melancholy tones. I saw James the Greater, the brother of John, standing upon a hill the other side of the valley, to look at them as they passed, and he returned immediately afterwards, to tell the other disciples what he had seen.

The procession stopped at the entrance of Joseph's garden, which was opened by the removal of some stakes, afterwards used as levers to roll the stone to the door of the sepulchre. When opposite the rock, they placed the Sacred Body on a long board covered with a sheet. The grotto, which had been newly excavated, had been lately cleaned by the servants of Nicodemus, so that the interior was neat and pleasing to the eye. The holy women sat down in front of the grotto, while the four men carried in the body of our Lord, partially filled the hollow couch destined for its reception with aromatic spices, and spread over them a cloth, upon which they reverently deposited the sacred body. After having once more given expression to their love by tears and fond embraces, they left the grotto. Then the Blessed Virgin entered, seated herself close to the head of her dear Son, and bent over his body with many tears. When she left the grotto, Magdalen hastily and eagerly came forward, and flung on the body some flowers and branches which she had gathered in the garden. Then she clasped her hands together, and with sobs kissed the feet of Jesus ; but the men having informed her that they must close the sepulchre, she returned to the other women. They covered the sacred body with the extremities of the sheet on which it was lying, placed on the top of all the brown coverlet, and closed the folding-doors, which were made of a bronze-coloured metal, and had on their front two sticks, one straight down and the other across, so as to form a perfect cross.

The large stone with which they intended to close the sepulchre, and which was still lying in front of the grotto, was in shape very like a chest* or tomb ; its length was such that a man might have laid himself down upon it, and it was so heavy that it was only by means of levers that the men could roll it before the door of the sepulchre. The entrance of the grotto was closed by a gate made of branches twined together. Everything that was done within the grotto had to be accomplished by torchlight, for daylight never penetrated there.

* Apparently Sister Emmerich here spoke of the ancient cases in which her poor countrymen keep their clothes. The lower part of these cases is smaller than the upper, and this gives them some likeness to a tomb. She had one of these cases, which she called her chest. She often described the stone by this comparison, but her descriptions have not, nevertheless, given us a very clear idea of its shape.

CHAPTER LIII.

The Return from the Sepulchre.—Joseph of Arimathea is put in
Prison.

THE Sabbath was close at hand, and Nicodemus and
Joseph returned to Jerusalem by a small door not far
from the garden, and which Joseph had been allowed by
special favour to have made in the city wall. They told
the Blessed Virgin, Magdalen, John, and some of the
women, who were returning to Calvary to pray there,
that this door, as well as that of the supper-room, would
be opened to them whenever they knocked. The elder
sister of the Blessed Virgin, Mary of Heli, returned to
the town with Mary the mother of Mark, and some
other women. The servants of Nicodemus and Joseph
went to Calvary to fetch several things which had been
left there.

The soldiers joined those who were guarding the city
gate near Calvary; and Cassius went to Pilate with the
lance, related all that he had seen, and promised to give
him an exact account of everything that should happen,
if he would put under his command the guards whom the
Jews would not fail to ask to have put round the tomb.
Pilate listened to his words with secret terror, but only
told him in reply that his superstition amounted to
madness.

Joseph and Nicodemus met Peter and the two Jameses
in the town. They all shed many tears, but Peter was
perfectly overwhelmed by the violence of his grief. He
embraced them, reproached himself for not having been
present at the death of our Saviour, and thanked them
for having bestowed the rites of sepulture upon his sacred
body. It was agreed that the door of the supper-room
should be opened to them whenever they knocked, and
then they went away to seek some other disciples who
were dispersed in various directions. Later I saw the
Blessed Virgin and her companions enter the supper-
room; Abenadar next came and was admitted; and by

degrees the greatest part of the Apostles and disciples assembled there. The holy women retired to that part of the building where the Blessed Virgin was living. They took some food, and spent a few minutes more in tears, and in relating to one another what each had seen. The men changed their dresses, and I saw them standing under the lamp, and keeping the Sabbath. They ate some lambs in the supper-room, but without observing any ceremony, for they had eaten the Paschal lamb the evening before. They were all perturbed in spirit, and filled with grief. The holy women also passed their time in praying with the Blessed Virgin under the lamp. Later, when night had quite fallen, Lazarus, the widow of Naïm, Dina the Samaritan woman, and Mara of Suphan,* came

* According to the visions of Sister Emmerich, the three women named in the text had been living for some time at Bethania, in a sort of community established by Martha for the purpose of providing for the maintenance of the disciples when our Lord was moving about, and for the division and distribution of the alms which were collected. The widow of Naïm, whose son Martial was raised from the dead by Jesus, according to Sister Emmerich, on the 28th Marcheswan (the 18th of November), was named Maroni. She was the daughter of an uncle, on the father's side, of St. Peter. Her first husband was the son of a sister of Elizabeth, who herself was the daughter of a sister of the mother of St. Anne. Maroni's first husband having died without children, she had married Elind, a relation of St. Anne, and had left Chasaluth, near Tabor, to take up her abode at Naïm, which was not far off, and where she soon lost her second husband.

Dina, the Samaritan woman, was the same who conversed with Jesus by Jacob's well. She was born near Damascus, of parents who were half Jewish and half Pagan. They died while she was yet very young, and she being brought up by a woman of bad character, the seeds of the most evil passions were early sown in her heart. She had had several husbands, who supplanted one another in turn, and the last lived at Sichar, whither she had followed him and changed her name from Dina to Salome. She had three grown-up daughters and two sons, who afterwards joined the disciples. Sister Emmerich used to say that the life of this Samaritan woman was prophetic—that Jesus had spoken to the entire sect of Samaritans in her person, and that they were attached to their errors by as many ties as she had committed adulteries.

Mara of Suphan was a Moabitess, came from the neighbourhood of Suphan, and was a descendant of Orpha, the widow of Chélion, Noëmi's son. Orpha had married again in Moab. By from Bethania, and then, once more, descriptions were given of all that had taken place, and many tears shed.

Joseph of Arimathea returned home late from the supper-room, and he was sorrowfully walking along the streets of Sion, accompanied by a few disciples and women, when all on a sudden a band of armed men, who were lying in ambuscade in the neighbourhood of Caiphas's tribunal, fell upon them, and laid hands upon Joseph, whereupon his companions fled, uttering loud cries of terror. He was confined in a tower contiguous to the city wall, not far from the tribunal. These soldiers were pagans, and had not to keep the Sabbath, therefore Caiphas had been able to secure their services on this occasion. The intention was to let Joseph die of hunger, and keep his disappearance a secret.

Here conclude the descriptions of all that occurred on the day of the Passion of our Lord ; but we will add some supplementary matter concerning Holy Saturday, the Descent into Hell, and the Resurrection.

———————

Orpha, the sister-in-law of Ruth, Mara was connected with the family of David, from whom our Lord was descended. Sister Emmerich saw Jesus deliver Mara from four devils and grant her forgiveness of her sins on the 17th Elud (9th September) of the second year of his public life. She was living at Ainon, having been repudiated by her husband, a rich Jew, who had kept the children he had had by her with him. She had with her three others, the offspring of her adulteries.

'I saw,' Sister Emmerich would say,—'I saw how the stray branch of the stock of David was purified within her by the grace of Jesus, and admitted into the bosom of the Church. I cannot express how many of these roots and offshoots I see become entwined with each other, lost to view, and then once more brought to light.'

CHAPTER LIV.

On the Name of Calvary.

WHILST meditating on the name of Golgotha, *Calvary*, the *place of skulls*, borne by the rock upon which Jesus was crucified, I became deeply absorbed in contemplation, and beheld in spirit all ages from the time of Adam to that of Christ, and in this vision the origin of the name was made known to me. I here give all that I remember on this subject.

I saw Adam, after his expulsion from Paradise, weeping in the grotto where Jesus sweated blood and water, on Mount Olivet. I saw how Seth was promised to Eve in the grotto of the manger at Bethlehem, and how she brought him forth in that same grotto. I also saw Eve living in some caverns near Hebron, where the Essenian Monastery of Maspha was afterwards established.

I then beheld the country where Jerusalem was built, as it appeared after the Deluge, and the land was all unsettled, black, stony, and very different from what it had been before. At an immense depth below the rock which constitutes Mount Calvary (which was formed in this spot by the rolling of the waters), I saw the tomb of Adam and Eve. The head and one rib were wanting to one of the skeletons, and the remaining head was placed within the same skeleton, to which it did not belong. The bones of Adam and Eve had not all been left in this grave, for Noah had some of them with him in the ark, and they were transmitted from generation to generation by the Patriarchs. Noah, and also Abraham, were in the habit, when offering sacrifice, of always laying some of Adam's bones upon the altar, to remind the Almighty of his promise. When Jacob gave Joseph his variegated robe, he at the same time gave him some bones of Adam, to be kept as relics. Joseph always wore them on his bosom, and they were placed with his own bones in the first reliquary which the children of Israel brought out of Egypt

I have seen many similar things, but some I have forgotten, and the others time fails me to describe.

As regards the origin of the name of *Calvary*, I here
give all I know. I beheld the mountain which bears this
name as it was in the time of the Prophet Eliseus. It
was not the same then as at the time of our Lord's Crucifixion, but was a hill, with many walls and caverns, resembling tombs, upon it. I saw the Prophet Eliseus descend into these caverns, I cannot say whether in reality
or only in a vision, and I saw him take out a skull from
a stone sepulchre in which bones were resting. Some
one who was by his side—I think an angel—said to him,
'This is the skull of Adam.' The prophet was desirous
to take it away, but his companion forbade him. I saw
upon the skull some few hairs of a fair colour.

I learned also that the prophet having related what
had happened to him, the spot received the name of *Calvary*. Finally, I saw that the Cross of Jesus was placed
vertically over the skull of Adam. I was informed that
this spot was the exact *centre* of the earth; and at the
same time I was shown the numbers and measures proper
to every country, but I have forgotten them, individually
as well as in general. Yet I have seen this centre from
above, and as it were from a bird's-eye view. In that
way a person sees far more clearly than on a map all the
different countries, mountains, deserts, seas, rivers, towns,
and even the smallest places, whether distant or near at
hand.

CHAPTER LV.

The Cross and the Wine-press.

As I was meditating upon these words or thoughts of
Jesus when hanging on the Cross : ' I am pressed like wine
placed here under the press for the first time ; my blood
must continue to flow until water comes, but wine shall
no more be made here,' an explanation was given me by
means of another vision relating to Calvary.

I saw this rocky country at a period anterior to the
Deluge; it was then less wild and less barren than it afterwards became, and was laid out in vineyards and fields.
I saw there the Patriarch Japhet, a majestic dark-complexioned old man, surrounded by immense flocks and
herds and a numerous posterity: his children as well as
himself had dwellings excavated in the ground, and covered
with turf roofs, on which herbs and flowers were growing.
There were vines all around, and a new method of making
wine was being tried on Calvary, in the presence of Japhet.
I saw also the ancient method of preparing wine, but I
can give only the following description of it. At first men
were satisfied with only eating the grapes; then they
pressed them with pestles in hollow stones, and finally in
large wooden trenches. Upon this occasion a new wine-
press, resembling the holy Cross in shape, had been de-
vised; it consisted of the hollow trunk of a tree placed
upright, with a bag of grapes suspended over it. Upon
this bag there was fastened a pestle, surmounted by a
weight; and on both sides of the trunk were arms joined
to the bag, through openings made for the purpose, and
which, when put in motion by lowering the ends, crushed
the grapes. The juice flowed out of the tree by five openings, and fell into a stone vat, from whence it flowed
through a channel made of bark and coated with resin,
into the species of cistern excavated in the rock where
Jesus was confined before his Crucifixion. At the foot of
the wine-press, in the stone vat, there was a sort of sieve
to stop the skins, which were put on one side. When
they had made their wine-press, they filled the bag with
grapes, nailed it to the top of the trunk, placed the pestle,
and put in motion the side arms, in order to make the
wine flow. All this very strongly reminded me of the
Crucifixion, on account of the resemblance between the
wine-press and the Cross. They had a long reed, at the
end of which there were points, so that it looked like an
enormous thistle, and they ran this through the channel
and trunk of the tree when there was any obstruction.
I was reminded of the lance and sponge. There were also

some leathern bottles, and vases made of bark and plastered with resin. I saw several young men, with nothing but a cloth wrapped round their loins like Jesus, working at this wine-press. Japhet was very old; he wore a long beard, and a dress made of the skins of beasts; and he looked at the new wine-press with evident satisfaction. It was a festival day, and they sacrificed on a stone altar some animals which were running loose in the vineyard, young asses, goats, and sheep. It was not in this place that Abraham came to sacrifice Isaac; perhaps it was on Mount Moriah. I have forgotten many of the instructions regarding the wine, vinegar, and skins, and the different ways in which everything was to be distributed to the right and to the left; and I regret it, because the veriest trifles in these matters have a profound symbolical meaning. If it should be the will of God for me to make them known, he will show them to me again.

CHAPTER LVI.

Apparitions on Occasion of the Death of Jesus.

AMONG the dead who rose from their graves, and who were certainly a hundred in number, at Jerusalem, there were no relations of Jesus. I saw in various parts of the Holy Land others of the dead appear and bear testimony to the Divinity of Jesus. Thus I saw Sadoch, a most pious man, who had given all his property to the poor and to the Temple, appear to many persons in the neighbourhood of Hebron. This Sadoch had lived a century before Jesus, and was the founder of a community of Essenians: he had ardently sighed for the coming of the Messias, and had had several revelations upon the subject. I saw some others of the dead appear to the hidden disciples of our Lord, and give them different warnings.

Terror and desolation reigned even in the most distant parts of Palestine, and it was not in Jerusalem only that frightful prodigies took place. At Thirza, the towers of the prison in which the captives delivered by Jesus had been confined fell down. In Galilee, where Jesus had travelled so much, I saw many buildings, and in particular the houses of those Pharisees who had been the foremost in persecuting our Saviour, and who were then all at the festival, shaken to the ground, crushing their wives and children. Numerous accidents happened in the neighbourhood of the Lake of Genazareth. Many buildings fell down at Capharnaum; and the wall of rocks which was in front of the beautiful garden of the centurion Zorobabel cracked across. The lake overflowed into the valley, and its waters descended as far as Capharnaum, which was a mile and a half distant. Peter's house, and the dwelling of the Blessed Virgin in front of the town, remained standing. The lake was strongly convulsed; its shores crumbled in several places, and its shape was very much altered, and became more like what it is at the present day. Great changes took place, particularly at the south-eastern extremity, near Tarichea, because in this part there was a long causeway made of stones, between the lake and a sort of marsh, which gave a constant direction to the course of the Jordan when it left the lake. The whole of this causeway was destroyed by the earthquake. Many accidents happened on the eastern side of the lake, on the spot where the swine belonging to the inhabitants of Gergesa cast themselves in, and also at Gergesa, Gerasa, and in the entire district of Chorazin. The mountain where the second multiplication of the loaves took place was shaken, and the stone upon which the miracle had been worked split in two. In Decapolis, whole towns crumbled to the earth; and in Asia, in several localities, the earthquake was severely felt, particularly to the east and north-east of Paneas. In Upper Galilee, many Pharisees found their houses in ruins when they returned from keeping the feast. A number of them, while yet at Jerusalem, received the news of what had happened, and it was on that account that the enemies of Jesus made such very slight efforts against the Christian community at Pentecost.

A part of the Temple of Garizim crumbled down. An idol stood there above a fountain, in a small temple, the roof of which fell into the fountain with the idol. Half of the synagogue of Nazareth, out of which Jesus had been driven, fell down, as well as that part of the mountain from which his enemies had endeavoured to precipitate him. The bed of the Jordan was much changed by all these shocks, and its course altered in many places. At Macherus, and at the other towns belonging to Herod, everything remained quiet, for that country was out of the sphere of repentance and of threats, like those men who did not fall to the ground in the Garden of Olives, and, consequently, did not rise again.

In many other parts where there were evil spirits, I saw the latter disappear in large bodies amid the falling mountains and buildings. The earthquakes reminded me of the convulsions of the possessed, when the enemy feels that he must take to flight. At Gergesa, a part of the mountain from which the devils had cast themselves with the swine into a marsh, fell into this same marsh; and I then saw a band of evil spirits cast themselves into the abyss, like a dark cloud.

It was at Nice, unless I am mistaken, that I saw a singular occurrence, of which I have only an imperfect remembrance. There was a port there with many vessels in it; and near this port stood a house with a high tower, in which I saw a pagan whose office was to watch these vessels. He had often to ascend this tower, and see what was going on at sea. Having heard a great noise over the vessels in the port, he hurriedly ascended the tower to discover what was taking place, and he saw several dark figures hovering over the port, and who exclaimed to him in plaintive accents: 'If thou desirest to preserve the vessels, cause them to be sailed out of this port, for we must return to the abyss: the great Pan is dead.' They told him several other things; laid injunctions upon him to make known what they were then telling him upon his return from a certain voyage which he was soon to make, and to give a good reception to the messengers who would come to announce the doctrine of him who had just died. The evil spirits were forced in this manner by the power of God to inform this good man of their defeat, and announce it to the world. He had the vessels put in safety, and then an awful storm arose : the devils cast themselves howling into the sea, and half the city fell down. His house remained standing. Soon afterwards he went on a great journey, and announced the death of the great Pan, if that is the name by which our Saviour had been called. Later he came to Rome, where much amazement was caused by what he related. His name was something like Thamus or Thramus.

CHAPTER LVII.

Guards are placed around the Tomb of Jesus.

LATE on Friday night, I saw Caiphas and some of the chief men among the Jews holding a consultation concerning the best course to pursue with regard to the prodigies which had taken place, and the effect they had had upon the people. They continued their deliberations quite into the morning, and then hurried to Pilate's house, to tell him that, as *that seducer said, while he was yet alive,* '*After three days I will rise again,*' it would be right to *command the sepulchre to be guarded until the third day,* as otherwise *his disciples* might *come and steal him away, and say to the people, ' He is risen from the dead,' and the last error* would *be worse than the first.* Pilate was determined to have nothing more to do with the business, and he only answered : ' *You have a guard ; go, guard it as you know.*' However, he appointed Cassius to keep a watch over all that took place, and give him an exact account of every circumstance. I saw these men, twelve in number, leave the town before sunrise, accompanied by some soldiers who did not wear the Roman uniform, being attached to the Temple. They carried lanterns fastened to the end of long poles, in order that they might be able to see every surrounding object, in spite of the darkness of the night, and also that they might have some light in the dark cave of the sepulchre.

No sooner had they reached the sepulchre than, having first seen with their own eyes that the body of Jesus was really there, they fastened one rope across the door of the tomb, and a second across the great stone which was placed in front, sealing the whole with a seal of half-circular shape. They then returned to the city, and the guards stationed themselves opposite the outer door. They were five or six in number, and watched three and three alternately. Cassius never left his post, and usually remained sitting or standing in front of the entrance to the cave, so as to see that side of the tomb where the feet of our Lord rested. He had received many interior graces, and been given to understand many mysteries. Being wholly unaccustomed to this state of spiritual enlightenment, he was perfectly transported out of himself, and remained nearly all the time unconscious of the presence of exterior things. He was entirely changed, had become a new man, and spent the whole day in penance, in making fervent acts of gratitude, and in humbly adoring God.

CHAPTER LVIII.

A Glance at the Disciples of Jesus on Holy Saturday.

THE faithful disciples of our Lord assembled together in the Cenaculum, to keep the eve of the Sabbath. They were about twenty in number, clothed in long white dresses, and with their waists girded. The room was lighted up by a lamp; and after their repast they separated, and for the most part returned home. They again assembled on the following morning, and sat together reading and praying by turns; and if a friend entered the room, they arose and saluted him cordially.

In that part of the house inhabited by the Blessed Virgin there was a large room, divided into small compartments like cells, which were used by the holy women for sleeping in at night. When they returned from the sepulchre, one of their number lighted a lamp which was hanging in the middle of the room, and they all assembled around the Blessed Virgin, and commenced praying in a mournful but recollected manner. A short time afterwards, Martha, Maroni, Dina, and Mara, who were just come with Lazarus from Bethania, where they had passed the Sabbath, entered the room. The Blessed Virgin and her companions gave them a detailed account of the death and burial of our Lord, accompanying each relation with many tears. The evening was advancing, and Joseph of Arimathea came in with a few other disciples, to ask whether any of the women wished to return to their homes, as they were ready to escort them. A few accepted the proposition, and set off immediately ; but before they reached the tribunal of Caiphas, some armed men stopped Joseph of Arimathea, arrested, and shut him up in an old deserted turret.

Those among the holy women who did not leave the Cenaculum retired to take their rest in the cell-like compartments spoken of above : they fastened long veils over their heads, seated themselves sorrowfully on the floor, and leaned upon the couches which were placed against the wall. After a time they stood up, spread out the bed-clothes which were rolled up on the couches, took off their sandals, girdles, and a part of their clothing, and reclined for a time in order to endeavour to get a little sleep. At midnight, they arose, clothed themselves, put up their beds, and reassembled around the lamp to continue their prayer with the Blessed Virgin.

When the Mother of Jesus and her pious companions had finished their nocturnal prayer (that holy duty which has been practised by all faithful children of God and holy souls, who have either felt themselves called to it by a special grace, or who follow a rule given by God and his Church), they heard a knock at the door, which was instantly opened, and John and some of the disciples who had promised to conduct them to the Temple, entered, upon which the women wrapped their cloaks about them, and started instantly. It was then about three in the morning, and they went straight to the Temple, it being customary among many Jews to go there before day dawned, on the day after they had eaten the Paschal lamb; and for this reason the Temple was open from midnight, as the sacrifices commenced very early. They started at about the same hour as that at which the priests had put their seal upon the sepulchre. The aspect of things in the Temple was, however, very different from what was usually the case at such times, for the sacrifices were stopped, and the place was empty and desolate, as every one had left on account of the events on the previous day which had rendered it impure. The Blessed Virgin appeared to me to visit it for the sole purpose of taking leave of the place where she had passed her youth.

The Temple was, however, open; the lamps lighted, and the people at liberty to enter the vestibule of the priests, which was the customary privilege of this day, as well as of that which followed the Paschal supper. The Temple was, as I said before, quite empty, with the exception of a chance priest or server who might be seen wandering about; and every part bore the marks of the confusion into which all was thrown on the previous day by the extraordinary and frightful events that had taken place; besides which it had been defiled by the presence of the dead, and I reflected and wondered in my own mind whether it would be possible ever to purify it again.

The sons of Simeon, and the nephews of Joseph of Arimathea, were much grieved when they heard of the arrest of their uncle, but they welcomed the Blessed Virgin and her companions, and conducted them all over the Temple, which they did without difficulty, as they held the offices of inspectors of the Temple. The holy women stood in silence and contemplated all the terrible and visible marks of the anger of God with feelings of deep awe, and then listened with interest to the many stupendous details recounted by their guides. The effects of the earthquake were still visible, as little had been done towards repairing the numerous rents and cracks in the floor, and in the walls. In that part of the Temple where

the vestibule joined the sanctuary, the wall was so tre-
mendously shaken by the shock of the earthquake, as to
produce a fissure wide enough for a person to walk through,
and the rest of the wall looked unsteady, as if it might
fall down at any moment. The curtain which hung in
the sanctuary was rent in two and hung in shreds at the
sides ; nothing was to be seen around but crumbled walls,
crushed flagstones, and columns either partly or quite
shaken down.

The Blessed Virgin visited all those parts which Jesus
had rendered sacred in her eyes; she prostrated, kissed
them, and with tears in her eyes explained to the others
her reasons for venerating each particular spot, whereupon
they instantly followed her example. The greatest veneration was always shown by the Jews for all places which
had been rendered sacred by manifestations of the Divine
power, and it was customary to place the hands reverently
on such places, to kiss them, and to prostrate to the very
earth before them. I do not think there was anything in
the least surprising in such a custom, for they both knew,
saw, and felt that the God of Abraham, of Isaac, and of
Jacob, was a living God, and that his dwelling among his
people was in the Temple at Jerusalem ; consequently it
would have been infinitely more astonishing if they had
not venerated those holy parts where his power had been
particularly demonstrated, for the Temple and the holy
places were to them what the Blessed Sacrament is to
Christians.

Deeply penetrated with these feelings of respect, the
Blessed Virgin walked through the Temple with her companions, and pointed out to them the spot where she was
presented when still a child, the parts where she passed
her childhood, the place where she was affianced to St.
Joseph, and the spot where she stood when she presented
Jesus and heard the prophecy of Simeon : the remembrance of his words made her weep bitterly, for the
prophecy was indeed fulfilled, and the sword of grief had
indeed transfixed her heart; she again stopped her companions when she reached the part of the Temple where

she found Jesus teaching when she lost him at the age of twelve, and she respectfully kissed the ground on which he then stood. When the holy women had looked at every place sanctified by the presence of Jesus, when they had wept and prayed over them, they returned to Sion.

The Blessed Virgin did not leave the Temple without shedding many tears, as she contemplated the state of desolation to which it was reduced, an aspect of desolation which was rendered still more depressing by the marked contrast it bore to the usual state of the Temple on the festival day. Instead of songs and hymns of jubilee, a mournful silence reigned throughout the vast edifice, and in place of groups of joyful and devout worshippers, the eye wandered over a vast and dreary solitude. Too truly, alas, did this change betoken the fearful crime which had been perpetrated by the people of God, and she remembered how Jesus had wept over the Temple, and said, ' *Destroy this Temple and in three days I will build it up again.*' She thought over the destruction of the Temple of the Body of Jesus which had been brought about by his enemies, and she sighed with a longing desire for the dawning of that third day when the words of eternal truth were to be accomplished.

It was about daybreak when Mary and her companions reached the Cenaculum, and they retired into the building which stood on its right-hand side, while John and some of the disciples reëntered the Cenaculum, where about twenty men, assembled around a lamp, were occupied in prayer. Every now and then new-comers drew nigh to the door, came in timidity, approached the group round the lamp, and addressed them in a few mournful words, which they accompanied with tears. Every one appeared to regard John with feelings of respect; because he had remained with Jesus until he expired; but with these sentiments of respect was mingled a deep feeling of shame and confusion, when they reflected on their own cowardly conduct in abandoning their Lord and Master in the hour of need. John spoke to every one with the greatest charity and kindness; his manner was modest and unassuming as that of a child, and he seemed to fear receiving praise. I saw the assembled group take one meal during that day, but its members were, for the most part, silent; not a sound was to be heard throughout the house, and the doors were tightly closed, although, in fact, there was no likelihood of any one disturbing them, as the house belonged to Nicodemus, and he had let it to them for the time of the festival.

The holy women remained in this room until nightfall; it was lighted up by a single lamp; the doors were closed, and curtains drawn over the windows. Sometimes they gathered round the Blessed Virgin and prayed under the lamp; at other times they retired to the side of the room, covered their heads with black veils, and either sat on ashes (the sign of mourning), or prayed with their faces turned towards the wall; those whose health was delicate took a little food, but the others fasted.

I looked at them again and again, and I saw them ever occupied in the same manner, that is to say, either in prayer or in mourning over the sufferings of their beloved Master. When my thoughts wandered from the contemplation of the Blessed Virgin to that of her Divine Son, I beheld the holy sepulchre with six or seven sentinels at the entrance—Cassius standing against the door of the cave, apparently in deep meditation, the exterior door closed, and the stone rolled close to it. Notwithstanding the thick door which intervened between the body of our Saviour and myself I could see it plainly; it was quite transparent with a divine light, and two angels were adoring at the side. But my thoughts then turned to the contemplation of the blessed soul of my Redeemer, and such an extensive and complicated picture of his descent into hell was shown to me, that I can only remember a small portion of it, which I will describe to the best of my power.

CHAPTER LIX.

A detached Account of the Descent into Hell.

WHEN Jesus, after uttering a loud cry, expired, I saw his heavenly soul under the form of a bright meteor pierce the earth at the foot of the Cross, accompanied by the angel Gabriel and many other angels. His Divine nature continued united to his soul as well as to his body, which still remained hanging upon the Cross, but I cannot explain how this was, although I saw it plainly in my own mind. The place into which the soul of Jesus entered was divided into three parts, which appeared to me like three worlds; and I felt that they were round, and that each division was separated from the other by a hemisphere.

I beheld a bright and beautiful space opposite to Limbo; it was enamelled with flowers, delicious breezes wafted through it; and many souls were placed there before being admitted into Heaven after their deliverance from Purgatory. Limbo, the place where the souls were waiting for the Redemption, was divided into different compartments, and encompassed by a thick foggy atmosphere. Our Lord appeared radiant with light and surrounded by angels, who conducted him triumphantly between two of these compartments; the one on the left containing the patriarchs who lived before the time of Abraham, and that on the right those who lived between the days of Abraham and St. John Baptist. These souls did not at first recognise Jesus, but were filled nevertheless with sensations of joy and hope. There was not a spot in those narrow confines which did not, as it were, dilate with feelings of happiness. The passage of Jesus might be compared to the wafting of a breath of air, to a sudden flash of light, or to a shower of vivifying dew, but it was swift as a whirlwind. After passing through the two compartments, he reached a dark spot in which Adam and Eve were standing; he spoke to them, they prostrated and adored him in a perfect ecstasy of joy, and they immediately joined the band of angels, and accompanied our

Lord to the compartment on the left, which contained the patriarchs who lived before Abraham. This compartment was a species of Purgatory, and a few evil spirits were wandering about among the souls and endeavouring to fill them with anxiety and alarm. The entrance through a species of door was closed, but the angels rapped, and I thought I heard them say, ' Open these doors.' When Jesus entered in triumph the demons dispersed, crying out at the same time, ' What is there between thee and us? What art thou come to do here? Wilt thou crucify us likewise?' The angels hunted them away, having first chained them. The poor souls confined in this place had only a slight presentiment and vague idea of the presence of Jesus; but the moment he told them that it was he himself, they burst out into acclamations of joy, and welcomed him with hymns of rapture and delight. The soul of our Lord then wended its way to the right, towards that part which really constituted Limbo; and there he met the soul of the good thief which angels were carrying to Abraham's bosom, as also that of the bad thief being dragged by demons into Hell. Our Lord addressed a few words to both, and then entered Abraham's bosom, accompanied by numerous angels and holy souls, and also by those demons who had been chained and expelled from the compartment.

This locality appeared to me more elevated than the surrounding parts; and I can only describe my sensations on entering it, by comparing them to those of a person coming suddenly into the interior of a church, after having been for some time in the burial vaults. The demons, who were strongly chained, were extremely loth to enter, and resisted to the utmost of their power, but the angels compelled them to go forward. All the just who had lived before the time of Christ were assembled there; the patriarchs, Moses, the judges, and the kings on the left-hand side; and on the right side, the prophets, and the ancestors of our Lord, as also his near relations, such as Joachim, Anna, Joseph, Zacharias, Elizabeth, and John. There were no demons in this place, and the only discomfort that had been felt by those placed there was a longing desire for the accomplishment of the promise; and when our Lord entered they saluted him with joyful hymns of gratitude and thanksgiving for its fulfilment, they prostrated and adored him, and the evil spirits who had been dragged into Abraham's bosom when our Lord entered were compelled to confess with shame that they were vanquished. Many of these holy souls were ordered by our Lord to return to the earth, reënter their own bodies, and thus render a solemn and impressive testimony to the truth. It was at this moment that so many dead persons left their tombs in Jerusalem; I regarded them less in the light of dead persons risen again than as corpses put in motion by a divine power, and which, after having fulfilled the mission intrusted to them, were laid aside in the same manner as the insignia of office are taken off by a clerk when he has executed the orders of his superiors.

I next saw our Lord, with his triumphant procession, enter into a species of Purgatory which was filled with those good pagans who, having had a faint glimmering of the truth, had longed for its fulfilment: this Purgatory was very deep, and contained a few demons, as also some of the idols of the pagans. I saw the demons compelled to confess the deception they had practised with regard to these idols, and the souls of the poor pagans cast themselves at the feet of Jesus, and adored him with inexpressible joy: here, likewise, the demons were bound with chains and dragged away. I saw our Saviour perform many other actions; but I suffered so intensely at the same time, that I cannot recount them as I should have wished.

Finally, I beheld him approach to the centre of the great abyss, that is to say, to Hell itself; and the expression of his countenance was most severe.

The exterior of Hell was appalling and frightful; it was an immense, heavy-looking building, and the granite of which it was formed, although black, was of metallic brightness; and the dark and ponderous doors were secured with such terrible bolts that no one could behold them without trembling. Deep groans and cries of despair might be plainly distinguished even while the doors were tightly closed; but, O, who can describe the dreadful yells and shrieks which burst upon the ear when the bolts were unfastened and the doors flung open; and, O, who can depict the melancholy appearance of the inhabitants of this wretched place !

The form under which the Heavenly Jerusalem is generally represented in my visions is that of a beautiful and well-regulated city, and the different degrees of glory to which the elect are raised are demonstrated by the magnificence of their palaces, or the wonderful fruit and flowers with which the gardens are embellished. Hell is shown to me under the same form, but all within it is, on the contrary, close, confused, and crowded; every object tends to fill the mind with sensations of pain and grief; the marks of the wrath and vengeance of God are visible everywhere; despair, like a vulture, gnaws every heart, and discord and misery reign around. In the Heavenly Jerusalem all is peace and eternal harmony, the beginning, fulfilment, and end of everything being pure and perfect happiness; the city is filled with splendid buildings, decorated in such a manner as to charm every eye and enrapture every sense; the inhabitants of this delightful abode are overflowing with rapture and exultation, the gardens gay with lovely flowers, and the trees covered with delicious fruits which give eternal life. In the city of Hell nothing is to be seen but dismal dungeons, dark caverns, frightful deserts, fetid swamps filled with every imaginable species of poisonous and disgusting reptile. In Heaven you behold the happiness and peaceful union of the saints; in Hell, perpetual scenes of wretched discord, and every species of sin and corruption, either under the most horrible forms imaginable, or represented by different kinds of dreadful torments. All in this dreary abode tends to fill the mind with horror; not a word of comfort is heard or a consoling idea admitted; the one tremendous thought, that the justice of an all-powerful God inflicts on the damned nothing but what they have fully de-

served is the absorbing tremendous conviction which
weighs down each heart. Vice appears in its own grim
disgusting colours, being stripped of the mask under
which it is hidden in this world, and the infernal viper
is seen devouring those who have cherished or fostered
it here below. In a word, Hell is the temple of anguish and despair, while the kingdom of God is the
temple of peace and happiness. This is easy to understand when seen; but it is almost impossible to describe
clearly.

The tremendous explosion of oaths, curses, cries of
despair, and frightful exclamations which, like a clap of
thunder, burst forth when the gates of Hell were thrown
open by the angels, would be difficult even to imagine;
our Lord spoke first to the soul of Judas, and the angels
then compelled all the demons to acknowledge and adore
Jesus. They would have infinitely preferred the most
frightful torments to such a humiliation; but all were
obliged to submit. Many were chained down in a circle
which was placed round other circles. In the centre of
Hell I saw a dark and horrible-looking abyss, and into
this Lucifer was cast, after being first strongly secured
with chains; thick clouds of sulphureous black smoke
arose from its fearful depths, and enveloped his frightful
form in the dismal folds, thus effectually concealing him
from every beholder. God himself had decreed this; and
I was likewise told, if I remember right, that he will be
unchained for a time fifty or sixty years before the year
of Christ 2000. The dates of many other events were
pointed out to me which I do not now remember; but
a certain number of demons are to be let loose much
earlier than Lucifer, in order to tempt men, and to serve
as instruments of the divine vengeance. I should think
that some must be loosened even in the present day, and
others will be set free in a short time.

It would be utterly impossible for me to describe all
the things which were shown to me; their number was
so great that I could not reduce them sufficiently to
order to define and render them intelligible. Besides

which my sufferings are very great, and when I speak on the subject of my visions I behold them in my mind's eye portrayed in such vivid colours, that the sight is almost sufficient to cause a weak mortal like myself to expire.

I next saw innumerable bands of redeemed souls liberated from Purgatory and from Limbo, who followed our Lord to a delightful spot situated above the celestial Jerusalem, in which place I, a very short time ago, saw the soul of a person who was very dear to me. The soul of the good thief was likewise taken there, and the promise of our Lord, ' *This day thou shalt be with me in Paradise,*' was fulfilled.

It is not in my power to explain the exact time that each of these events occurred, nor can I relate one-half of the things which I saw and heard; for some were incomprehensible even to myself, and others would be misunderstood if I attempted to relate them. I have seen our Lord in many different places. Even in the sea he appeared to me to sanctify and deliver everything in the creation. Evil spirits fled at his approach, and cast themselves into the dark abyss. I likewise beheld his soul in different parts of the earth, first inside the tomb of Adam, under Golgotha; and when he was there the souls of Adam and Eve came up to him, and he spoke to them for some time. He then visited the tombs of the prophets, who were buried at an immense depth below the surface; but he passed through the soil in the twinkling of an eye. Their souls immediately reëntered their bodies, and he spoke to them, and explained the most wonderful mysteries. Next I saw him, accompanied by a chosen band of prophets, among whom I particularly remarked David, visit those parts of the earth which had been sanctified by his miracles and by his sufferings. He pointed out to them, with the greatest love and goodness, the different symbols in the old law expressive of the future; and he showed them how he himself had fulfilled every prophecy. The sight of the soul of our Lord, surrounded by these happy souls, and radiant with light, was inexpressibly grand as he glided triumphantly through the air, sometimes passing, with the velocity of lightning, over rivers, then penetrating through the hardest rocks to the very centre of the earth, or moving noiselessly over its surface.

I can remember nothing beyond the facts which I have just related concerning the descent of Jesus into Limbo, where he went in order to present to the souls there detained the grace of the Redemption which he had merited for them by his death and by his sufferings; and I saw all these things in a very short space of time; in fact, time passed so quickly that it seemed to me but a moment. Our Lord, however, displayed before me, at the same time, another picture, in which I beheld the immense mercies which he bestows in the present day on the poor souls in Purgatory; for on every anniversary of this great day, when his Church is celebrating the glorious mystery of his death, he casts a look of compassion on the souls in Purgatory, and frees some of those who sinned against him before his crucifixion. I this day saw Jesus deliver many souls; some I was acquainted with, and others were strangers to me, but I cannot name any of them.

Our Lord, by descending into Hell, planted (if I may thus express myself), in the spiritual garden of the Church, a mysterious tree, the fruits of which—namely, his merits—are destined for the constant relief of the poor souls in Purgatory. The Church militant must cultivate the tree, and gather its fruits, in order to present them to that suffering portion of the Church which can do nothing for itself. Thus it is with all the merits of Christ; we must labour with him if we wish to obtain our share of them; we must gain our bread by the sweat of our brow. Everything which our Lord has done for us in time must produce fruit for eternity; but we must gather these fruits in time, without which we cannot possess them in eternity. The Church is the most prudent and thoughtful of mothers; the ecclesiastical year is an immense and magnificent garden, in which all those fruits for eternity are gathered together, that we may make use of them in time. Each year contains sufficient to supply the wants of all; but woe be to that careless or dishonest gardener who allows any of the fruit committed to his care to perish; if he fails to turn to a proper account those graces which would restore health to the sick, strength to the weak, or furnish food to the hungry! When the Day of Judgment arrives, the Master of the garden will demand a strict account, not only of every tree, but also of all the fruit produced in the garden.

CHAPTER LX.

The Eve of the Resurrection.

TOWARDS the close of the Sabbath-day, John came to see the holy women. He endeavoured to give some consolation, but could not restrain his own tears, and only remained a short time with them. They had likewise a short visit from Peter and James the Greater, after which they retired to their cells, and gave free vent to grief, sitting upon ashes, and veiling themselves even more closely.

The prayer of the Blessed Virgin was unceasing. She ever kept her eyes fixed interiorly on Jesus, and was perfectly consumed by her ardent desire of once more beholding him whom she loved with such inexpressible love. Suddenly an angel stood by her side, and bade her arise and go to the door of the dwelling of Nicodemus, for that the Lord was very near. The heart of the Blessed Virgin leaped for joy. She hastily wrapped her cloak about her, and left the holy women, without informing them where she was going. I saw her walk quickly to a small entrance which was cut in the town wall, the identical one through which she had entered when returning with her companions from the sepulchre. It was about nine o'clock at night, and the Blessed Virgin had almost reached the entrance, when I saw her stop suddenly in a very solitary spot, and look upwards

in an ecstasy of delight, for on the top of the town wall
she beheld the soul of our Lord, resplendent with light,
without the appearance of a wound, and surrounded by
patriarchs. He descended towards her, turned to his
companions, and presenting her to them, said, 'Behold
Mary, behold my Mother.' He appeared to me to salute her with a kiss, and he then disappeared. The
Blessed Virgin knelt down, and most reverently kissed
the ground on which he had stood, and the impression
of her hands and knees remained imprinted upon the
stones. This sight filled her with inexpressible joy, and
she immediately rejoined the holy women, who were
busily employed in preparing the perfumes and spices.
She did not tell them what she had seen, but her firmness and strength of mind were restored. She was perfectly renovated, and therefore comforted all the rest, and
endeavoured to strengthen their faith.

All the holy women were sitting by a long table, the
cover of which hung down to the floor, when Mary returned; bundles of herbs were heaped around them, and
these they mixed together and arranged; small flasks, containing sweet unctions and water of spikenard, were standing near, as also bunches of natural flowers, among which
I remarked one in particular, which was like a streaked
iris or a lily. Magdalen, Mary the daughter of Cleophas,
Salome, Johanna, and Mary Salome, had bought all these
things in the town during the absence of Mary. Their
intention was to go to the sepulchre before sunrise on
the following day, in order to strew these flowers and
perfumes over the body of their beloved Master.

CHAPTER LXI.

Joseph of Arimathea miraculously set at large.

A SHORT time after the return of the Blessed Virgin to
the holy women, I was shown the interior of the prison in
which the enemies of Joseph of Arimathea had confined

him. He was praying fervently, when suddenly a brilliant light illuminated the whole place, and I heard a voice calling him by name, while at the same moment the roof opened, and a bright form appeared, holding out a sheet resembling that in which he had wrapped the body of Jesus. Joseph grasped it with both hands, and was drawn up to the opening, which closed again as soon as he had passed through; and the apparition disappeared the instant he was in safety at the top of the tower. I know not whether it was our Lord himself or an angel who thus set Joseph free.

He walked on the summit of the wall until he reached the neighbourhood of the Cenaculum, which was near to the south wall of Sion, and then climbed down and knocked at the door of that edifice, as the doors were fastened. The disciples assembled there had been much grieved when they first missed Joseph, who they thought had been thrown into a sink, a report to that effect having become current. Great, therefore, was their joy when they opened the door and found that it was he himself; indeed, they were almost as much delighted as when Peter was miraculously delivered from prison some years after. When Joseph had related what had taken place, they were filled with astonishment and delight; and after thanking God fervently gave him some refreshment, which he greatly needed. He left Jerusalem that same night, and fled to Arimathea, his native place, where he remained until he thought he could return safely to Jerusalem.

I likewise saw Caiphas towards the close of the Sabbath-day, at the house of Nicodemus. He was conversing with him and asking many questions with pretended kindness. Nicodemus answered firmly, and continued to affirm the innocence of Jesus. They did not remain long together.

CHAPTER LXII.

The Night of Resurrection.

I soon after beheld the tomb of our Lord. All was calm and silent around it. There were six soldiers on guard, who were either seated or standing before the door, and Cassius was among them. His appearance was that of a person immersed in meditation and in the expectation of some great event. The sacred body of our Blessed Redeemer was wrapped in the winding-sheet, and surrounded with light, while two angels sat in an attitude of adoration, the one at the head, and the other at the feet. I had seen them in the same posture ever since he was first put into the tomb. These angels were clothed as priests. Their position, and the manner in which they crossed their arms over their breasts, reminded me of the cherubim who surrounded the Ark of the Covenant, only they were without wings; at least I did not see any. The whole of the spulchre reminded me of the Ark of the Covenant at different periods of its history. It is possible that Cassius was sensible of the presence of the angels, and of the bright light which filled the sepulchre, for his attitude was like that of a person in deep contemplation before the Blessed Sacrament.

I next saw the soul of our Lord accompanied by those among the patriarchs whom he had liberated enter into the tomb through the rock. He showed them the wounds with which his sacred body was covered; and it seemed to me that the winding-sheet which previously enveloped it was removed, and that Jesus wished to show the souls the excess of suffering he had endured to redeem them. The body appeared to me to be quite transparent, so that the whole depth of the wounds could be seen; and this sight filled the holy souls with admiration, although deep feelings of compassion likewise drew tears from their eyes.

My next vision was so mysterious that I cannot explain or even relate it in a clear manner. It appeared to me that the soul and body of Jesus were taken together out of the sepulchre, without, however, the former being

completely reunited to the latter, which still remained
inanimate. I thought I saw two angels who were kneeling and adoring at the head and feet of the sacred body,
raise it—keeping it in the exact position in which it was
lying in the tomb—and carry it uncovered and disfigured
with wounds across the rock, which trembled as they
passed. It then appeared to me that Jesus presented his
body, marked with the stigmas of the Passion, to his
Heavenly Father, who, seated on a throne, was surrounded
by innumerable choirs of angels, blissfully occupied in
pouring forth hymns of adoration and jubilee. The case
was probably the same when, at the death of our Lord, so
many holy souls reëntered their bodies, and appeared in
the Temple and in different parts of Jerusalem; for it is
not likely that the bodies which they animated were
really alive, as in that case they would have been obliged
to die a second time, whereas they returned to their
original state without apparent difficulty; but it is to be
supposed that their appearance in human form was similar to that of our Lord, when he (if we may thus express
it) accompanied his body to the throne of his Heavenly
Father.

At this moment the rock was so violently shaken,
from the very summit to the base, that three of the guards
fell down and became almost insensible. The other four
were away at the time, being gone to the town to fetch
something. The guards who were thus thrown prostrate
attributed the sudden shock to an earthquake; but Cassius, who, although uncertain as to what all this might
portend, yet felt an inward presentiment that it was the
prelude to some stupendous event, stood transfixed in
anxious expectation, waiting to see what would follow
next. The soldiers who were gone to Jerusalem soon
returned.

I again beheld the holy women: they had finished
preparing the spices, and were resting in their private
cells; not stretched out on the couches, but leaning against
the bedclothes, which were rolled up. They wished to go
to the sepulchre before the break of day, because they

feared meeting the enemies of Jesus; but the Blessed
Virgin, who was perfectly renovated and filled with fresh
courage since she had seen her Son, consoled and recommended them to sleep for a time, and then go fearlessly
to the tomb, as no harm would come to them; whereupon
they immediately followed her advice, and endeavoured to
sleep.

It was towards eleven o'clock at night when the Blessed
Virgin, incited by irrepressible feelings of love, arose,
wrapped a gray cloak around her, and left the house quite
alone. When I saw her do this, I could not help feeling
anxious, and saying to myself, ' How is it possible for this
holy Mother, who is so exhausted from anguish and
terror, to venture to walk all alone through the streets at
such an hour?' I saw her go first to the house of Caiphas, and then to the palace of Pilate, which was at a
great distance off; I watched her through the whole of
her solitary journey along that part which had been trodden
by her Son, loaded with his heavy Cross; she stopped at
every place where our Saviour had suffered particularly,
or had received any fresh outrage from his barbarous enemies. Her appearance, as she walked slowly along, was
that of a person seeking something; she often bent down
to the ground, touched the stones with her hands, and
then inundated them with kisses, if the precious blood of
her beloved Son was upon them. God granted her at this
time particular lights and graces, and she was able without
the slightest degree of difficulty to distinguish every place
sanctified by his sufferings. I accompanied her through
the whole of her pious pilgrimage, and I endeavoured to
imitate her to the best of my power, as far as my weakness
would permit.

Mary then went to Calvary; but when she had almost
reached it, she stopped suddenly, and I saw the sacred
body and soul of our Saviour standing before her. An
angel walked in front; the two angels whom I had seen
in the tomb were by his side, and the souls whom he had
redeemed followed him by hundreds. The body of Jesus
was brilliant and beautiful, but its appearance was not

that of a living body, although a voice issued from it; and I heard him describe to the Blessed Virgin all he had done in Limbo, and then assure her that he should rise again with his glorified body; that he would then show himself to her, and that she must wait near the rock of Mount Calvary, and that part where she saw him fall down, until he appeared. Our Saviour then went towards Jerusalem, and the Blessed Virgin, having again wrapped her veil about her, prostrated on the spot which he had pointed out. It was then, I think, past midnight, for the pilgrimage of Mary over the Way of the Cross had taken up at least an hour; and I next saw the holy souls who had been redeemed by our Saviour traverse in their turn the sorrowful Way of the Cross, and contemplate the different places where he had endured such fearful sufferings for their sakes. The angels who accompanied them gathered up and preserved the smallest fragments of our Lord's sacred flesh which had been torn off by the frequent blows he received, as also the blood with which the ground was sprinkled on those spots where he had fallen.

I once more saw the sacred body of our Lord stretched out as I first beheld it in the sepulchre; the angels were occupied in replacing the fragments they had gathered up of his flesh, and they received supernatural assistance in doing this. When next I contemplated him it was in his winding-sheet, surrounded with a bright light and with two adoring angels by his side. I cannot explain how all these things came to pass, for they are far beyond our human comprehension; and even if I understand them perfectly myself when I see them, they appear dark and mysterious when I endeavour to explain them to others.

As soon as a faint glimmering of dawn appeared in the east, I saw Magdalen, Mary the daughter of Cleophas, Johanna Chusa, and Salome, leave the Cenaculum, closely wrapped up in their mantles. They carried bundles of spices; and one of their number had a lighted candle in her hand, which she endeavoured to conceal under her cloak. I saw them direct their trembling steps towards the small door at the house of Nicodemus.

CHAPTER LXIII.

The Resurrection of our Lord.

I BEHELD the soul of our Lord between two angels, who were in the attire of warriors : it was bright, luminous, and resplendent as the sun at mid-day; it penetrated the rock, touched the sacred body, passed into it, and the two were instantaneously united, and became as one. I then saw the limbs move, and the body of our Lord, being reunited to his soul and to his divinity, rise and shake off the winding-sheet : the whole of the cave was illuminated and lightsome.

At the same moment I saw a frightful monster burst from the earth underneath the sepulchre. It had the tail of a serpent, and it raised its dragon head proudly as if desirous of attacking Jesus ; and had likewise, if I remember correctly, a human head. But our Lord held in his hand a white staff, to which was appended a large banner ; and he placed his foot on the head of the dragon, and struck its tail three times with his staff, after which the monster disappeared. I had had this same vision many times before the Resurrection, and I saw just such a monster, appearing to endeavour to hide itself, at the time of the conception of our Lord : it greatly resembled the serpent which tempted our first parents in Paradise, only it was more horrible. I thought that this vision had reference to the prophetic words, that ' *by the seed of the woman the head of the serpent should be crushed,*' and that the whole was intended to demonstrate the victory of our Lord over death, for at the same moment that I saw him crush the head of the monster, the tomb likewise vanished from my sight.

I then saw the glorified body of our Lord rise up, and it passed through the hard rock as easily as if the latter had been formed of some ductile substance. The earth shook, and an angel in the garb of a warrior descended from Heaven with the speed of lightning, entered the tomb, lifted the stone, placed it on the right side, and seated himself upon it. At this tremendous sight the soldiers fell to the ground, and remained there apparently lifeless. When Cassius saw the bright light which illuminated the tomb, he approached the place where the sacred body had been placed, looked at and touched the linen clothes in which it had been wrapped, and left the sepulchre, intending to go and inform Pilate of all that had happened. However, he tarried a short time to watch the progress of events; for although he had felt the earthquake, seen the angel move the stone, and looked at the empty tomb, yet he had not seen Jesus.

At the very moment in which the angel entered the sepulchre and the earth quaked, I saw our Lord appear to his holy Mother on Calvary. His body was beautiful and lightsome, and its beauty was that of a celestial being. He was clothed in a large mantle, which at one moment looked dazzlingly white, as it floated through the air, waving to and fro with every breath of wind, and the next reflected a thousand brilliant colours as the sunbeams passed over it. His large open wounds shone brightly, and could be seen from a great distance : the wounds in his hands were so large that a finger might be put into them without difficulty; and rays of light proceeded from them, diverging in the direction of his fingers. The souls of the patriarchs bowed down before the Mother of our Saviour, and Jesus spoke to her concerning his Resurrection, telling her many things which I have forgotten. He showed her his wounds; and Mary prostrated to kiss his sacred feet; but he took her hand, raised her, and disappeared.

When I was at some distance from the sepulchre I saw fresh lights burning there, and I likewise beheld a large luminous spot in the sky immediately over Jerusalem.

CHAPTER LXIV.

The holy Women at the Sepulchre.

THE holy women were very near the door of Nicodemus's house at the moment of our Lord's Resurrection;
but they did not see anything of the prodigies which were
taking place at the sepulchre. They were not aware that
guards had been placed around the tomb, for they had not
visited it on the previous day, on account of its being the
Sabbath. They questioned one another anxiously concerning what would have to be done about the large stone
at the door, as to who would be the best person to ask
about removing it, for they had been so engrossed by grief
that they had not thought about it before. Their intention was to pour precious ointments upon the body of
Jesus, and then to strew over it flowers of the most rare
and aromatic kinds, thus rendering all the honour possible to their Divine Master in his sepulchre. Salome,
who had brought more things than any one else, was a
rich lady, who lived in Jerusalem, a relation of St. Joseph,
but not the mother of John. The holy women came to
the determination of putting down their spices on the
stone which closed the door of the monument, and waiting until some one came to roll it back.

The guards were still lying on the ground, and the
strong convulsions which even then shook them clearly
demonstrated how great had been their terror, and the
large stone was cast on one side, so that the door could
be opened without difficulty. I could see the linen cloth
in which the body of Jesus had been wrapped scattered
about in the tomb, and the large winding-sheet lying in
the same place as when they left it, but doubled together
in such a manner that you saw at once that it no longer
contained anything but the spices which had been placed
round the body, and the bandages were on the outside of
the tomb. The linen cloth in which Mary had enveloped
the sacred head of her Son was still there.

I saw the holy women coming into the garden; but

when they perceived the light given by the lamps of the sentinels, and the prostrate forms of the soldiers round the tomb, they for the most part became much alarmed, and retreated towards Golgotha. Mary Magdalen was, however, more courageous, and, followed by Salome, entered the garden, while the other women remained timidly on the outside.

Magdalen started, and appeared for a moment terrified when she drew near the sentinels. She retreated a few steps and rejoined Salome, but both quickly recovered their presence of mind, and walked on together through the midst of the prostrate guards, and entered into the cave which contained the sepulchre. They immediately perceived that the stone was removed, but the doors were closed, which had been done in all probability by Cassius Magdalen opened them quickly, looked anxiously into the sepulchre, and was much surprised at seeing that the cloths in which they had enveloped our Lord were lying on one side, and that the place where they had deposited the sacred remains was empty. A celestial light filled the cave, and an angel was seated on the right side. Magdalen became almost beside herself from disappointment and alarm. I do not know whether she heard the words which the angel addressed to her, but she left the garden as quickly as possible, and ran to the town to inform the Apostles who were assembled there of what had taken place. I do not know whether the angel spoke to Mary Salome, as she did not enter the sepulchre; but I saw her leaving the garden directly after Magdalen, in order to relate all that had happened to the rest of the holy women, who were both frightened and delighted at the news, but could not make up their minds as to whether they would go to the garden or not.

In the mean time Cassius had remained near the sepulchre in hopes of seeing Jesus, as he thought he would be certain to appear to the holy women; but seeing nothing, he directed his steps towards Pilate's palace to relate to him all that had happened, stopping, however, first at the place where the rest of the holy women were assembled, to tell them what he had seen, and to exhort them to go immediately to the garden. They followed his advice, and went there at once. No sooner had they reached the door of the sepulchre than they beheld two angels clothed in sacerdotal vestments of the most dazzling white. The women were very much alarmed, covered their faces with their hands, and prostrated almost to the ground; but one of the angels addressed them, bade them not fear, and told them that they must not seek for their crucified Lord there, for that he was alive, had risen, and was no longer an inhabitant of the tomb. He pointed out to them at the same moment the empty sepulchre, and ordered them to go and relate to the disciples all that they had seen and heard. He likewise told them that Jesus would go before them into Galilee, and recalled to their minds the words which our Saviour had addressed to them on a former occasion : '*The Son of Man will be delivered into the hands of sinners, he will be crucified, and the third day rise again.*' The angels then disappeared, and left the holy women filled with joy, although of course greatly agitated ; they wept, looked at the empty tomb and linen clothes, and immediately started to return to the town. But they were so much overcome by the many astounding events which had taken place, that they walked very slowly, and stopped and looked back often, in hopes of seeing our Lord, or at least Magdalen.

In the mean time Magdalen reached the Cenaculum. She was so excited as to appear like a person beside herself, and knocked hastily at the door. Some of the disciples were still sleeping, and those who were risen were conversing together. Peter and John opened the door, but she only exclaimed, without entering the house, '*They have taken away the body of my Lord, and I know not where they have laid him,*' and immediately returned to the garden. Peter and John went back into the house, and after saying a few words to the other disciples followed her as speedily as possible, but John far outstripped Peter. I then saw Magdalen reënter the garden, and direct her steps towards the sepulchre ; she appeared greatly agitated, partly from grief, and partly from having walked so fast. Her garments were quite moist with dew, and her veil hanging on one side, while the luxuriant hair in which she had formerly taken so much pride fell in dishevelled masses over her shoulders, forming a species of mantle. Being alone, she was afraid of entering the cave, but stopped for a moment on the outside, and knelt down in order to see better into the tomb. She was endeavouring to push back her long hair, which fell over her face and obscured her vision, when she perceived the two angels who were seated in the tomb, and I heard one of them address her thus: ' *Woman, why weepest thou?*' She replied, in a voice choked with tears (for she was perfectly overwhelmed with grief at finding that the body of Jesus was really gone), ' *Because they have taken away my Lord, and I know not where they have laid him.*' She said no more, but seeing the empty winding-sheet, went out of the sepulchre and began to look about in other parts. She felt a secret presentiment that not only should she find Jesus, but that he was even then near to her ; and the presence of the angels seemed not to disturb her in the least ; she did not appear even to be aware that they were angels, every faculty was engrossed with the one thought, ' Jesus is not there ! where is Jesus?' I watched her wandering about like an insane person, with her hair floating loosely in the wind : her hair appeared to annoy her much, for she again endeavoured to push it from off her face, and having divided it into two parts, threw it over her shoulders.

She then raised her head, looked around, and perceived a tall figure, clothed in white, standing at about ten paces from the sepulchre on the east side of the garden, where there was a slight rise in the direction of the town ; the figure was partly hidden from her sight by a palm-tree, but she was somewhat startled when it addressed her in these words : ' *Woman, why weepest thou? Whom seekest thou?*' She thought it was the gardener ; and, in fact, he had a spade in his hand, and a large hat (apparently made of the bark of trees) on his head. His dress was similar to that worn by the gardener described in the parable which Jesus

had related to the holy women at Bethania a short time
before his Passion.   His body was not luminous, his whole
appearance was rather that of a man dressed in white and
seen by twilight.   At the words, ' *Whom seekest thou?*' she
looked at him, and answered quickly, ' *Sir, if thou hast
taken him hence, tell me where thou hast laid him; and I
will take him away.*'   And she looked anxiously around.
Jesus said to her, ' *Mary.*'   She then instantly recognised
his beloved voice, and turning quickly, replied, ' *Rabboni
(Master)!*'   She threw herself on her knees before him,
and stretched out her hands to touch his feet; but he
motioned her to be still, and said, ' *Do not touch me,
for I am not yet ascended to my Father; but go to my
brethren and say to them: I ascend to my Father and to
your Father, to my God and your God.*'   He then disappeared.

The reason of the words of Jesus, ' *Do not touch me,*'
was afterwards explained to me, but I have only an indistinct remembrance of that explanation.   I think he made
use of those words because of the impetuosity of Magdalen's
feelings, which made her in a certain degree forget the
stupendous mystery which had been accomplished, and
feel as if what she then beheld was still mortal instead of
a glorified body.   As for the words of Jesus, ' *I am not
yet ascended to my Father,*' I was told that their meaning
was that he had not presented himself to his Father since
his Resurrection, to return him thanks for his victory
over death, and for the work of the redemption which he
had accomplished.   He wished her to infer from these
words, that the first-fruits of joy belong to God, and that
she ought to reflect and return thanks to him for the accomplishment of the glorious mystery of the redemption, and
for the victory which he had gained over death; and if she
had kissed his feet as she used before the Passion, she
would have thought of nothing but her Divine Master, and
in her raptures of love have totally forgotten the wonderful
events which were causing such astonishment and joy in
Heaven.   I saw Magdalen arise quickly, as soon as our
Lord disappeared, and run to look again in the sepulchre.

as if she believed herself under the influence of a dream.
She saw the two angels still seated there, and they spoke
to her concerning the resurrection of our Lord in the same
words as they had addressed the two other women.   She
likewise saw the empty winding-sheet, and then, feeling
certain that she was not in a state of delusion, but that the
apparition of our Lord was real, she walked quickly back
towards Golgotha to seek her companions, who were wandering about to and fro, anxiously looking out for her return, and indulging a kind of vague hope that they should
see or hear something of Jesus.

The whole of this scene occupied a little more than two
or three minutes.   It was about half-past three when our
Lord appeared to Magdalen, and John and Peter entered
the garden just as she was leaving it.   John, who was a
little in advance of Peter, stopped at the entrance of the
cave and looked in.   He saw the linen clothes lying on
one side, and waited until Peter came up, when they entered the sepulchre together, and saw the winding-sheet
empty as has been before described.   John instantly believed in the Resurrection, and they both understood
clearly the words addressed to them by Jesus before his
Passion, as well as the different passages in Scripture relating to that event, which had until then been incomprehensible to them.   Peter put the linen clothes under his
cloak, and they returned hastily into the town through the
small entrance belonging to Nicodemus.

The appearance of the holy sepulchre was the same
when the two apostles entered as when Magdalen first
saw it.   The two adoring angels were seated, one at the
head, and the other at the extremity of the tomb, in precisely the same attitude as when his adorable body was
lying there.   I do not think Peter was conscious of their
presence.   I afterwards heard John tell the disciples of
Emmaus, that when he looked into the sepulchre he saw
an angel.   Perhaps he was startled by this sight, and
therefore drew back and let Peter enter the sepulchre first ;
but it is likewise very possible that the reason of his not
mentioning the circumstance in his gospel was because

humility made him anxious to conceal the fact of his having been more highly favoured than Peter.

The guards at this moment began to revive, and rising,
gathered up their lances, and took down the lamps, which
were on the door, from whence they cast a glimmering
weak light on surrounding objects. I then saw them walk
hastily out of the garden in evident fear and trepidation,
in the direction of the town.

In the mean time Magdalen had rejoined the holy women, and given them the account of her seeing the Lord
in the garden, and of the words of the angels afterwards,
whereupon they immediately related what had been seen
by themselves, and Magdalen wended her way quickly to
Jerusalem, while the women returned to that side of the
garden where they expected to find the two apostles. Just
before they reached it, Jesus appeared to them. He was
clothed in a long white robe, which concealed even his
hands, and said to them, '*All hail.*' They started with
astonishment, and cast themselves at his feet; he spoke a
few words, held forth his hand as if to point out something to them, and disappeared. The holy women went
instantly to the Cenaculum, and told the disciples who
were assembled there that they had seen the Lord; the
disciples were incredulous, and would not give credence
either to their account or to that of Magdalen. They
treated both the one and the other as the effects of their excited imaginations; but when Peter and John entered the
room and related what they likewise had seen, they knew
not what to answer, and were filled with astonishment.

Peter and John soon left the Cenaculum, as the wonderful events which had taken place rendered them extremely silent and thoughtful, and before long they met
James the Less and Thaddeus, who had wished to accompany them to the sepulchre. Both James and Thaddeus
were greatly overcome, for the Lord had appeared to them
a short time before they met Peter and John. I also saw
Jesus pass quite close to Peter and John. I think the
former recognised him, for he started suddenly, but I do
not think the latter saw him.

CHAPTER LXV.

The Relation which was given by the Sentinels who were placed around the Sepulchre.

CASSIUS hastened to the house of Pilate about an hour after the Resurrection, in order to give him an account of the stupendous events which had taken place. He was not yet risen, but Cassius was allowed to enter his bedroom. He related all that had happened, and expressed his feelings in the most forcible language. He described how the rock had been rent, and how an angel had descended from Heaven and pushed aside the stone; he also spoke of the empty winding-sheet, and added that most certainly Jesus was the Messiah, the Son of God, and that he was truly risen. Pilate listened to this account; he trembled and quivered with terror, but concealed his agitation to the best of his power, and answered Cassius in these words : 'Thou art exceedingly superstitious; it was very foolish to go to the Galilæan's tomb; his gods took advantage of thy weakness, and displayed all these ridiculous visions to alarm thee. I recommend thee to keep silence, and not recount such silly tales to the priests, for thou wouldst get the worst of it from them.' He pretended to believe that the body of Jesus had been carried away by his disciples, and that the sentinels, who had been bribed, and had fallen asleep, or perhaps been deceived by witchcraft, had fabricated these accounts in order to justify their conduct. When Pilate had said all he could on the subject, Cassius left him, and he went to offer sacrifice to his gods.

The four soldiers who had guarded the tomb arrived shortly after at Pilate's palace, and began to tell him all that he had already heard from Cassius; but he would listen to nothing more, and sent them to Caiphas. The rest of the guards were assembled in a large court near the Temple which was filled with aged Jews, who, after

some previous consultation, took the soldiers on one side,
and by dint of bribes and threats endeavoured to persuade
them to say that they fell asleep, and that while they were
asleep the disciples came and carried away the body of our
Lord. The soldiers, however, demurred, because the statement which their comrades were gone to make to Pilate
would contradict any account which they could now fabri-
cate, but the Pharisees promised to arrange everything
with the governor. Whilst they were still disputing, the
four guards returned from their interview with Pilate, and
the Pharisees endeavoured to persuade them to conceal
the truth; but this they refused to do, and declared firmly
that they would not vary their first statement in the
smallest degree. The miraculous deliverance of Joseph of
Arimathea from prison was become public, and when the
Pharisees accused the soldiers of having allowed the
Apostles to carry off the body of Jesus, and threatened
them with the infliction of the most severe punishment if
they did not produce the body, they replied, that it would
be as utterly impossible for them to produce the body of
Jesus, as it was for the soldiers who had charge of Joseph
of Arimathea to bring him back into his prison again.
They spoke with the greatest firmness and courage;
promises and menaces were equally ineffectual. They declared that they would speak the truth and nothing but
the truth; that the sentence of death which had been
passed upon Jesus was both unjust and iniquitous; and
that the crime which was perpetrated in putting him to
death was the sole cause of the interruption in the Paschal
solemnity. The Pharisees, being perfectly furious, caused
the four soldiers to be arrested and thrown into prison,
and the others, who had accepted the bribes they offered,
then affirmed that the body of Jesus had been carried off
by the disciples while they slept; and the Pharisees, Sadducees, and Herodians endeavoured to disseminate this lie
to the utmost of their power, not only in the synagogue
but also among the people; and they accompanied this
false statement by the most slanderous lies concerning
Jesus.

All these precautions, however, availed but little, for, after the Resurrection, many persons who had been long dead arose from their graves, and appeared to those among their descendants who were not sufficiently hardened to be impervious to grace, and exhorted them to be converted. These dead persons were likewise seen by many of the disciples, who, overcome with terror, and shaken in faith, had fled into the country. They both exhorted and encouraged them to return, and restored their drooping courage. The resurrection of these dead persons did not in the slightest degree resemble the Resurrection of Jesus. He arose with a glorified body, which was no longer susceptible of either corruption or death, and ascended into heaven with this glorified body in the sight of all his disciples; but the dead bodies of which we spoke above were motionless corpses, and the souls which once inhabited them were only allowed to enter and reanimate them for a time, and after performing the mission given them, the souls again quitted these bodies, which returned to their original state in the bowels of the earth, where they will remain until the resurrection at the day of judgment. Neither could their return to life be compared to the raising of Lazarus from the dead; for he really returned to a new life, and died a second time.

CHAPTER LXVI.

The End of the Lenten Meditations.

On the following Sunday,* if I remember right, I saw the Jews washing and purifying the Temple. They offered up expiatory sacrifices, cleared away the rubbish, and endeavoured to conceal the effects of the earthquake

---

* The above relation was given later, and it is impossible to say whether it relates to the day of the Resurrection or to the following Sunday.

by placing planks and carpets over the chasms and fissures made by it in the walls and on the pavement; and they recommenced the Paschal solemnities, which had been interrupted in the midst, declared that the disturbance had been caused by the presence of impure persons, and endeavoured to explain away the apparition of the dead. They referred to a vision of Ezechiel, but how I can no longer remember. They threatened all who dared to say a syllable concerning the events which had taken place, or who presumed to murmur, with excommunication and other severe punishments. They succeeded in silencing some few hardened persons who, conscious of their own guilt, wished to banish the subject from their minds, but they made no impression on those whose hearts still retained some remains of virtue; they remained silent for a time, concealing their inward belief, but later, regaining courage, proclaimed their faith in Jesus loudly to the world. The High Priests were much disconcerted, when they perceived how rapidly the doctrines of Christ spread over the country. When Stephen was deacon, the whole of Ophel and the eastern side of Sion was too small to contain the numerous Christian communities, and a portion were obliged to take up their residence in the country between Jerusalem and Bethania.

I saw Annas in such a state of frenzy as to act like one possessed; he was at last obliged to be confined, and never again to make his appearance in public. Caiphas was outwardly less demonstrative, but he was inwardly devoured with such rage and extreme jealousy that his reason was affected.

I saw Pilate on Easter Thursday; he was instituting a search for his wife in every part of the city, but his efforts for her recovery were fruitless; she was concealed in the house of Lazarus, in Jerusalem. No one thought of looking there, as the house contained no other female; but Stephen carried food to her there, and let her know all that was going on in the city. Stephen was first-cousin to St. Paul. They were the sons of two brothers. On the day after the Sabbath, Simon of Cyrene went to the Apostles and begged to be instructed and to receive baptism.

The visions of Sister Emmerich, which had continued from the 18th of February to the 6th of April 1823, here came to a conclusion.

APPENDIX.

Detached Account of Longinus.

On the 15th of March 1821, Sister Emmerich gave the following detached account of parts of a vision which she had had the previous night concerning St. Longinus, whose festival happened to fall upon that very day, although she did not know it.

'Longinus, who had, I think, another name, held an office, partly civil and partly military, in the household of Pilate, who intrusted him with the duty of superintending all that passed, and making a report of it to him. He was trustworthy and ready to do a service, but previous to his conversion was greatly wanting in firmness and strength of character. He was excessively impetuous in all that he did, and anxious to be thought a person of great importance, and as he squinted and had weak eyes, he was often jeered at and made the laughing-stock of his companions. I have seen him frequently during the course of this night, and in connection with him I have at the same time seen all the Passion, I do not know in what manner; I only remember that it was in connection with him.

'Longinus was only in a subordinate position, and had to give an account to Pilate of all that he saw. On the night that Jesus was led before the tribunal of Caiphas he was in the outer court among the soldiers, and unceasingly going backwards and forwards. When Peter was alarmed at the words of the maid-servant

standing near the fire, it was he who said once : *"Art
thou not also one of this man's disciples ?"*

'When Jesus was being led to Calvary, Longinus, by
Pilate's orders, followed him closely, and our Divine Lord
gave him a look which touched his heart. Afterwards I
saw him on Golgotha with the soldiers. He was on
horseback, and carried a lance ; I saw him at Pilate's
house, after the death of our Lord, saying that the legs of
Jesus ought not to be broken. He returned at once to
Calvary. His lance was made of several pieces which
fitted one into the other, so that by drawing them out,
the lance could be made three times its original length.
He had just done this when he came to the sudden determination of piercing the side of our Saviour. He was
converted upon Mount Calvary, and a short time afterwards expressed to Pilate his conviction that Jesus was
the Son of God. Nicodemus prevailed upon Pilate to let
him have Longinus's lance, and I have seen many things
concerning the subsequent history of this lance. Longinus,
after his conversion, left the army, and joined the disciples. He and two other soldiers, who were converted
at the foot of the Cross, were among the first baptised
after Pentecost.

'I saw Longinus and these two men, clothed in long
white garments, return to their native land. They lived
there in the country, in a barren and marshy locality.
Here it was that the forty martyrs died. Longinus was
not a priest, but a deacon, and travelled here and there in
that capacity, preaching the name of Christ, and giving,
as an eye-witness, a history of his Passion and Resurrection. He converted a large number of persons, and cured
many of the sick, by allowing them to touch a piece of
the sacred lance which he carried with him. The Jews
were much enraged at him and his two companions because they made known in all parts the truth of the Resurrection of Jesus, and the cruelty and deceits of his
enemies. At their instigation, some Roman soldiers were
dispatched to Longinus's country to take and judge him
on the plea of his having left the army without leave, and

being a disturber of public peace. He was engaged in cultivating his field when they arrived, and he took them to his house, and offered them hospitality. They did not know him, and when they had acquainted him with the object of their journey, he quietly called his two companions who were living in a sort of hermitage at no great distance off, and told the soldiers that they and himself were the men for whom they were seeking. The same thing happened to the holy gardener, Phocas. The soldiers were really distressed, for they had conceived a great friendship for him. I saw him led with his two companions to a small neighbouring town, where they were questioned. They were not put in prison, but permitted to go whither they pleased, as prisoners on their word, and only made to wear a distinctive mark on the shoulder. Later, they were all three beheaded on a hill, situated between the little town and Longinus's house, and there buried. The soldiers put the head of Longinus at the end of a spear, and carried it to Jerusalem, as a proof that they had fulfilled their commission. I think I remember that this took place a very few years after the death of our Lord.

'Afterwards I had a vision of things happening at a later period. A blind countrywoman of St. Longinus went with her son on a pilgrimage to Jerusalem, in hopes of recovering her sight in the holy city where the eyes of Longinus had been cured. She was guided by her child, but he died, and she was left alone and disconsolate. Then St. Longinus appeared to her, and told her that she would recover her sight when she had drawn his head out of a sink into which the Jews had thrown it. This sink was a deep well, with the sides bricked, and all the filth and refuse of the town flowed into it through several drains. I saw some persons lead the poor woman to the spot ; she descended into the well up to her neck, and drew out the sacred head, whereupon she recovered her sight. She returned to her native land, and her companions preserved the head. I remember no more upon this subject.'

Detached Account of Abenadar.

ON the 1st of April 1823, Sister Emmerich said that that day was the Feast of St. Ctésiphon, the centurion who had assisted at the Crucifixion, and that she had seen during the night various particulars concerning his life. But she had also suffered greatly, which, combined with exterior distractions, had caused her to forget the greatest part of what she had seen. She related what follows :

' Abenadar, afterwards called Ctésiphon, was born in a country situated between Babylon and Egypt in Arabia Felix, to the right of the spot where Job dwelt during the latter half of his life. A certain number of square houses, with flat roofs, were built there on a slight ascent. There were many small trees growing on this spot, and incense and balm were gathered there. I have been in Abenadar's house, which was large and spacious, as might be expected of a rich man's house, but it was also very low. All these houses were built in this manner, perhaps on account of the wind, because they were much exposed. Abenadar had joined the garrison of the fortress Antonia, at Jerusalem, as a volunteer. He had entered the Roman service for the purpose of enjoying more facilities in his study of the fine arts, for he was a learned man. His character was firm, his figure short and thick-set, and his complexion dark.

' Abenadar was early convinced, by the doctrine which he heard Jesus preach, and by a miracle which he saw him work, that salvation was to be found among the Jews, and he had submitted to the law of Moses. Although not yet a disciple of our Lord, he bore him no ill-will, and held his person in secret veneration. He was naturally grave and composed, and when he came to Golgotha to relieve guard, he kept order on all sides, and forced everybody to behave at least with common decency, down to the moment when truth triumphed over him, and he rendered public testimony to the Divinity of Jesus. Being a rich man, and a volunteer, he had no difficulty in resigning his post at once. He assisted at the descent from the Cross and the burial of our Lord, which put him into familiar connection with the friends of Jesus, and after the day of Pentecost he was one of the first to receive baptism in the Pool of Bethsaida, when he took the name of Ctésiphon. He had a brother living in Arabia, to whom he related the miracles he had beheld, and who was thus called to the path of salvation, came to Jerusalem, was baptised by the name of Cæcilius, and was charged, together with Ctésiphon, to assist the deacons in the newly-formed Christian community.

'Ctésiphon accompanied the Apostle St. James the Greater into Spain, and also returned with him. After a time, he was again sent into Spain by the Apostles, and carried there the body of St. James, who had been martyred at Jerusalem. He was made a bishop, and resided chiefly in a sort of island or peninsula at no great distance from France, which he also visited, and where he made some disciples. The name of the place where he lived was rather like Vergui, and it was afterwards laid waste by an inundation. I do not remember that Ctésiphon was ever martyred. He wrote several books containing details concerning the Passion of Christ; but there have been some books falsely attributed to him, and others, which were really from his pen, ascribed to different writers. Rome has since rejected these books, the greatest part of which were apocryphal, but which nevertheless did contain some few things really from his pen. One of the guards of our Lord's sepulchre, who would not let himself be bribed by the Jews, was his fellow countryman and friend. His name was something like Sulei or Suleii. After being detained some time in prison, he retired into a cavern of Mount Sinai, where he lived seven years. God bestowed many special graces upon this man, and he wrote some very learned books in the style of Denis the Areopagite. Another writer made use of his works, and in this manner some extracts from them have come down to us. Everything concerning these facts was made known to me, as well as the name of the book, but I have forgotten it. This countryman of Ctésiphon afterwards followed him into Spain. Among the companions of Ctésiphon in that country were his brother Cæcilius, and some other men, whose names were Intalecius, Hesicius, and Euphrasius. Another Arab, called Sulima, was converted in the very early days of the Church, and a fellow countryman of Ctésiphon, with a name like Sulensis, became a Christian later, in the time of the deacons.'

THE END.